THE WILEY BICENTENNIAL—KNOWLEDGE FOR GENERATIONS

*E*ach generation has its unique needs and aspirations. When Charles Wiley first opened his small printing shop in lower Manhattan in 1807, it was a generation of boundless potential searching for an identity. And we were there, helping to define a new American literary tradition. Over half a century later, in the midst of the Second Industrial Revolution, it was a generation focused on building the future. Once again, we were there, supplying the critical scientific, technical, and engineering knowledge that helped frame the world. Throughout the 20th Century, and into the new millennium, nations began to reach out beyond their own borders and a new international community was born. Wiley was there, expanding its operations around the world to enable a global exchange of ideas, opinions, and know-how.

For 200 years, Wiley has been an integral part of each generation's journey, enabling the flow of information and understanding necessary to meet their needs and fulfill their aspirations. Today, bold new technologies are changing the way we live and learn. Wiley will be there, providing you the must-have knowledge you need to imagine new worlds, new possibilities, and new opportunities.

Generations come and go, but you can always count on Wiley to provide you the knowledge you need, when and where you need it!

WILLIAM J. PESCE
PRESIDENT AND CHIEF EXECUTIVE OFFICER

PETER BOOTH WILEY
CHAIRMAN OF THE BOARD

Business Math

Steve Slavin
with
Tere Stouffer

BICENTENNIAL
1807
WILEY
2007
BICENTENNIAL

Credits

Publisher
Anne Smith

Project Editor
Betn Tripmacher

Marketing Manager
Jennifer Slomack

Senior Editorial Assistant
Tiara Kelly

Production Manager
Kelly Tavares

Production Assistant
Courtney Leshko

Creative Director
Harry Nolan

Cover Designer
Hope Miller

Cover Photo
GlowImages/Getty Images, Inc.

This book was set in Times New Roman

This book is printed on acid free paper.

To order books or for customer service please, call 1-800-CALL WILEY (225-5945).

ISBN-13 978-0-470-00719-8

ISBN-10 0-470-00719-2

10 9 8 7 6 5 4 3 2 1

PREFACE

College classrooms bring together learners from many backgrounds with a variety of aspirations. Although the students are in the same course, they are not necessarily on the same path. This diversity, coupled with the reality that these learners often have jobs, families, and other commitments, requires a flexibility that our nation's higher education system is addressing. Distance learning, shorter course terms, new disciplines, evening courses, and certification programs are some of the approaches that colleges employ to reach as many students as possible and help them clarify and achieve their goals.

Wiley Pathways books, a new line of texts from John Wiley & Sons, Inc., are designed to help you address this diversity and the need for flexibility. These books focus on the fundamentals, identify core competencies and skills, and promote independent learning. The focus on the fundamentals helps students grasp the subject, bringing them all to the same basic understanding. These books use clear, everyday language, presented in an uncluttered format, making the reading experience more pleasurable. The core competencies and skills help students succeed in the classroom and beyond, whether in another course or in a professional setting. A variety of built-in learning resources promote independent learning and help instructors and students gauge students' understanding of the content. These resources enable students to think critically about their new knowledge, and apply their skills in any situation.

Our goal with *Wiley Pathways* books—with its brief, inviting format, clear language, and core competencies and skills focus—is to celebrate the many students in your courses, respect their needs, and help you guide them on their way.

CASE Learning System

To meet the needs of working college students, *Business Math* uses a four-step process: The CASE Learning System. Based on Bloom's Taxonomy of Learning, CASE presents key math topics in easy-to-follow chapters. The text then prompts analysis, synthesis, and evaluation with a variety of learning aids and assessment tools. Students move efficiently from reviewing what they have learned, to acquiring new information and skills, to applying their new knowledge and skills to real-life scenarios:

▲ Content
▲ Analysis
▲ Synthesis
▲ Evaluation

Using the CASE Learning System, students not only achieve academic mastery of business math *topics,* but they master real-world math *skills.* The CASE Learning System also helps students become independent learners, giving them a distinct advantage whether they are starting out or seek to advance in their careers.

Organization, Depth and Breadth of the Text

Business Math offers the following features:

▲ **Modular format.** Research on college students shows that they access information from textbooks in a non-linear way. Instructors also often wish to reorder textbook content to suit the needs of a particular class. Therefore, although *Business Math* proceeds logically from the basics to increasingly more challenging material, chapters are further organized into sections (4 to 6 per chapter) that are self-contained for maximum teaching and learning flexibility.

▲ **Numeric system of headings.** *Business Math* uses a numeric system for headings (for example, 2.3.4 identifies the fourth subsection of section 3 of chapter 2). With this system, students and teachers can quickly and easily pinpoint topics in the table of contents and the text, keeping class time and study sessions focused.

▲ **Core content.** This volume is designed to teach students the basic math skills that are essential in the business world. Written in clear language and illustrated with examples and step-by-step equations, the book is designed to take away the fear of math. Anyone who needs to prepare balance sheets or be able to interpret a profit and loss statement will benefit from mastering the skills presented in this text.

The American economy has changed dramatically in the past century. As a nation, we have gone from the Industrial Revolution to the Information Revolution. Along the way, there have been many success stories in American business and many casualties. One thing that does not change, however, is the mathematical principles that every business is based on. While corporate scandals have shown us that CEOs may lie, the numbers will always tell the truth.

A grasp of the fundamental math skills is essential to success in the business world. Every decision a business makes is made based on numbers. Hiring more employees, laying employees off, launching a new product, and moving to a different office building are all decisions based on the economic health of a company. Numbers also drive personal decisions. Contributing to a 401k, taking out a loan, and buying life insurance are decisions driven by the economic health of the individual. All of these decisions, both business and personal, are made easier when one understands the math behind the decisions and how the decisions will affect the future.

The book is divided into three distinct sections. The first section is, "Math Principles," and it provides a firm foundation of basic math skills as a jumping off point for complicated equations. The second section, "Retailing Applications," examines how math is used in a retail environment, both in terms of inventory and in terms of discounting. The third section, which is also the bulk of the book, "General Business Applications," takes the basic math skills that the students have mastered and applies them to a wide range of real-world business scenarios. For example, property taxes, calculating interest, and promissory notes are all covered in this section. Taken together, this book takes the student from the basic definition of what a whole number is through more complicated equations all the way to business statistics. Along the way there are examples of how to apply the math skills to real-world business problems.

Part I: Math Principles

This text begins with an introductory chapter entitled, Whole Numbers, Decimals, and Negative Numbers. This chapter provides an introduction and overview to whole numbers, counting numbers, natural numbers, and integers.

Chapter 2, Fractions, defines fractions and how to add, subtract, multiply, and divide them.

Chapter 3, Calculating Percents, defines how to convert decimals and fractions to percents, examines the relationship between percentage, rate, and base, and outlines the business uses of percent calculations.

Chapter 4, Using Algebraic Equations to Solve Business Problems, examines how to solve for x and y in different equations.

Part II: Retailing Applications

Chapter 5, Markup, Markdown, and Inventory Management, discusses the retail environment and why stores markup and markdown their inventory. The chapter also examines inventory management and how inventory management is the key to high profits in retail establishments.

Chapter 6, Discounts, assesses different types of discounts and how they are calculated.

Part III: General Business Applications

Chapter 7, Banking and Insurance, examines different banking options and how checking and savings accounts differ. The chapter also discusses insurance and how it is used as protection against a catastrophic financial loss.

Chapter 8, Taxes, compares personal, sales, and property taxes and the implications of taxing income, property, and retail sales.

Chapter 9, Calculating Interest, discusses simple and compound interest and how each affects the future value of money.

Chapter 10, Loans and Consumer Credit, examines the use of promissory notes, mortgages, and credit cards and how to calculate the cost of each.

Chapter 11, Depreciation, assesses different ways to determine the loss of value of business property and equipment and the effect of depreciation on taxes.

Chapter 12, Financial Statements, examines two fundamental accounting tools; the income statement and the balance sheet. This chapter describes the key ratios derived from financial statements and how to determine relative profitability.

Chapter 13, Business Statistics, discusses how to calculate the mean, median, mode, and range of data. Constructing a bar graph, line graph, and pie chart are also discussed.

Learning Aids

Each chapter of *Business Math* features the following learning and study aids to activate students' prior knowledge of the topics and orient them to the material.

▲ **Pre-test.** This pre-reading assessment tool in multiple-choice format not only introduces chapter material, but it also helps students anticipate the chapter's learning outcomes. By focusing students' attention on what they do not know, the self-test provides students with a benchmark against which they can measure their own progress. The pre-test is available online at www.wiley.com/college/slavin.

▲ **What You'll Learn in This Chapter and After Studying This Chapter.** These bulleted lists tell students what they will be learning in the chapter and why it is significant for their careers. They also explain why the chapter is important and how it relates to other chapters in the text. "What You'll Learn..." lists focus on the *subject matter* that will be taught (e.g. what a fraction is). "After Studying This Chapter..." lists emphasize *capabilities and skills* students will learn (e.g. how to multiply fractions).

▲ **Goals and Outcomes.** These lists identify specific student capabilities that will result from reading the chapter. They set students up to synthesize and evaluate the chapter material, and relate it to the real world.

▲ **Figures and tables.** Line art and photos have been carefully chosen to be truly instructional rather than filler. Tables distill and present information in a way that is easy to identify, access, and understand, enhancing the focus of the text on essential ideas.

Within-text Learning Aids

The following learning aids are designed to encourage analysis and synthesis of the material, and to support the learning process and ensure success during the evaluation phase:

▲ **Introduction.** This section orients the student by introducing the chapter and explaining its practical value and relevance to the book as a whole. Short summaries of chapter sections preview the topics to follow.

▲ **"For Example" Boxes.** Found within each section, these boxes tie section content to real-world organizations, scenarios, and applications.

▲ **Self-Check.** Related to the "What You'll Learn" bullets and found at the end of each section, this battery of short answer questions emphasizes student understanding of concepts and mastery of section content. Though the questions may either be discussed in class or studied by students outside of class, students should not go on before they can answer all questions correctly. Each *Self-Check* question set includes a link to a section of the pre-test for further review and practice.

▲ **Summary.** Each chapter concludes with a summary paragraph that reviews the major concepts in the chapter and links back to the "What You'll Learn" list.

▲ **Key Terms and Glossary.** To help students develop a professional vocabulary, key terms are bolded in the introduction, summary and when they first appear in the chapter. A complete list of key terms with brief definitions appears at the end of each chapter and again in a glossary at the end of the book. Knowledge of key terms is assessed by all assessment tools (see below).

Evaluation and Assessment Tools

The evaluation phase of the CASE Learning System consists of a variety of within-chapter and end-of-chapter assessment tools that test how well students have learned the material. These tools also encourage students to extend their learning into different scenarios and higher levels of understanding and thinking. The following assessment tools appear in every chapter of *Business Math:*

▲ **Summary Questions** help students summarize the chapter's main points by asking a series of multiple choice and true/false questions that emphasize student understanding of concepts and mastery of chapter content. Students should be able to answer all of the Summary Questions correctly before moving on.

▲ **Review Questions** in short answer format review the major points in each chapter, prompting analysis while reinforcing and confirming student understanding of concepts, and encouraging mastery of chapter content. They are somewhat more difficult than the *Self-Check* and *Summary Questions,* and students should be able to answer most of them correctly before moving on.

▲ **Applying This Chapter Questions** drive home key ideas by asking students to synthesize and apply chapter concepts to new, real-life situations and scenarios.

▲ **You Try It Questions** are designed to extend students' thinking, and so are ideal for discussion or writing assignments. Using an open-ended format and sometimes based on Web sources, they encourage students to draw conclusions using chapter material applied to real-world situations, which fosters both mastery and independent learning.

▲ **Post-Test** should be taken after students have completed the chapter. It includes all of the questions in the pre-test, so that students can see how their learning has progressed and improved.

Instructor and Student Package

Business Math is available with the following teaching and learning supplements. All supplements are available online at the text's Book Companion Website, located at www.wiley.com/college/ Slavin.

▲ **Instructor's Resource Guide.** Provides the following aids and supplements for teaching:

  ▲ *Diagnostic Evaluation of Grammar, Mechanics, and Spelling.* A useful tool that instructors may administer to the class at the beginning of the course to determine each student's basic writing skills. The Evaluation is accompanied by an Answer Key and a Marking Key. Instructors are encouraged to use the Marking key when grading students' Evaluations, and to duplicate and distribute it to students with their graded evaluations.

  ▲ *Sample syllabus.* A convenient template that instructors may use for creating their own course syllabi.

  ▲ *Teaching suggestions.* For each chapter, these include a chapter summary, learning objectives, definitions of key terms, lecture notes, answers to select text question sets, and at least 3 suggestions for classroom activities, such as ideas for speakers to invite, videos to show, and other projects.

▲ **Test Bank.** One test per chapter, as well as a mid-term and two finals. Each includes true/false, multiple choice, and open-ended questions. Answers and page references are provided for the true/false and multiple choice questions, and page references for the open-ended questions. Available in Microsoft Word and computerized formats.

▲ **PowerPoints.** Key information is summarized in 10 to 15 PowerPoints per chapter. Instructors may use these in class or choose to share them with students for class presentations or to provide additional study support.

ACKNOWLEDGMENTS

No book is solely the product of its authors. Books tend to be culminations of accumulated experience that grow from many influences. We would like to thank all of the reviewers for their feedback and suggestions during the text's development. Their advice on how to shape *Business Math* into a solid learning tool that meets both their needs and those of their busy students is deeply appreciated. We would like to thank:

Desmond Chun, Chabot College
Norris Dorsey, California State University-Northridge
David Hollomon, Victor Valley College
Jim Monroe, Indiana Business College
Frank Paiano, Southwestern College-Chula Vista
Emanuel Stein, Queensborough Community College
Albert Taccone, Cuyamaca College
Robin Turner, Rowan Cabarrus Community College
Joseph Turner, College of the Albemarle
Scott Wallace, Blue Mountain Community College

The editors would also like to gratefully acknowledge the Robert Bennett, Delaware County Community College, for his extensive contributions to the book.

BRIEF CONTENTS

CONTENTS

Part II: Retailing Applications

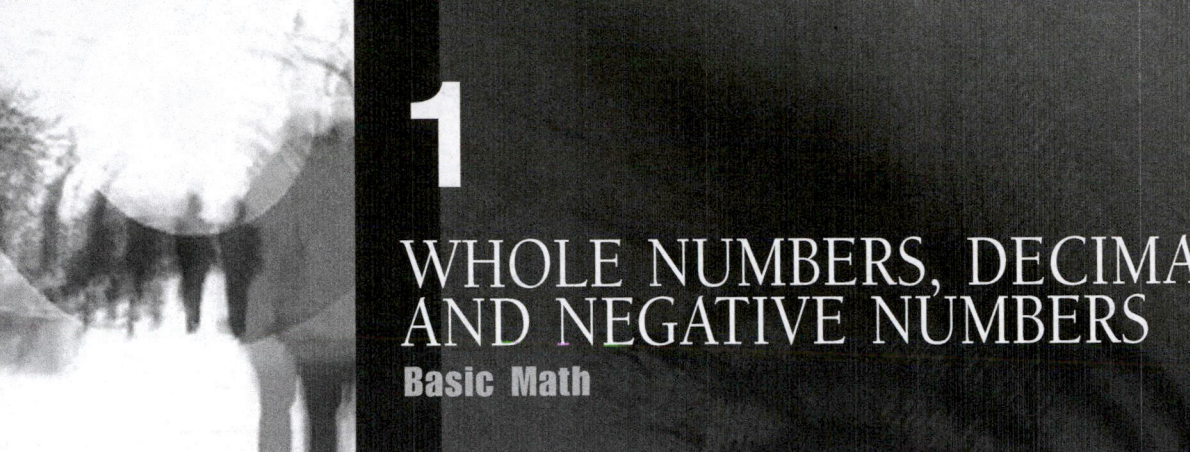

1

WHOLE NUMBERS, DECIMALS, AND NEGATIVE NUMBERS

Basic Math

Starting Point

Go to www.wiley.com/college/slavin to assess your knowledge of the basics of positive integers (whole numbers), decimals, and negative integers. *Determine where you need to concentrate your effort.*

What You'll Learn in This Chapter

▲ How to describe whole numbers, counting numbers, and natural numbers
▲ How to identify decimal numbers
▲ How to relate the concepts of negative numbers and integers

After Studying This Chapter, You'll Be Able To

▲ Discuss relationship between whole numbers and counting numbers
▲ Describe how to add, subtract, multiply, and divide decimals
▲ Identify the rules of addition, subtraction, multiplication, and division of negative numbers
▲ Calculate problems involving negative numbers

Goals and Outcomes

▲ Identify whole numbers, counting numbers, natural numbers, and integers
▲ Evaluate the methods for solving decimal problems
▲ Understand the differences between calculations involving negative and positive numbers

INTRODUCTION

Before you rush headlong into business math applications, you need to first make sure you understand the foundations of basic math: whole numbers, decimals, and negative numbers.

1.1 Whole Numbers

Whole numbers are the numbers you use every day: 0, 1, 2, 3, and so on. They are also called **natural numbers** and **counting numbers.** (Note, however, that 0 is not considered a counting number because we start counting objects with the number 1.) All these terms just mean plain old numbers, such as 5 and 6,782,346,601. We assume, in this book, that you know how to add, subtract, multiply, and divide whole numbers.

Whole numbers do not include portions of whole numbers. Portions of whole numbers are expressed as decimals and fractions. For example, 20 is a whole number, but 20.25 is a decimal, and $20\frac{1}{4}$ is a fraction. Each contains the

---

FOR EXAMPLE

Zero, Zilch, Zip, Nil, Nada!

Zero means nothing: the absence of value. If you have zero money, you're broke. If you have two sisters, five cousins, and zero brothers, you don't have any brothers. For this reason, zero is not included in counting numbers: If you have enough of something (dollars or brothers) to be counting them, you must have at least one, so the counting starts there.

Not so with time, however. On December 31, 1999, people debated whether the next day would begin a new millennium or whether the new millennium would begin on January 1, 2001. The controversy was whether time began at zero (the ways humans celebrate age) or at 1 (the way items are counted).

Time, unlike counting, always begins at zero. For example, your birth is considered zero. A year later, you celebrate your first birthday, meaning that you have completed one year of life. Likewise, a stopwatch begins timing a race at zero, not a one second or one minute. Given that time begins at zero, when the first year ended, the first "birthday" was celebrated, and Year 1 began. A year later, Year 2 began. A decade was complete when Year 10 began (not when it ended); likewise, a millennium was complete when Year 1,000 began.

whole number 20, but the decimal or fraction (0.25 or $\frac{1}{4}$) is also a portion of a number. Decimals are discussed in the Section 1.2, and see Chapter 2 for information on fractions.

Numbers can also be negative, in which case they have values less than zero. (Section 1.3 discusses negative numbers.) When all the whole numbers are combined with all the negative whole numbers, they are called **integers**.

SELF-CHECK

- Define **whole number** and similar terms.
- Describe how fractions and decimals differ from whole numbers.
- Explain how integers differ from whole numbers.

1.2 Decimals

A decimal is a portion of a number, expressed as one or more digits to the right of a decimal point. Examples of decimals include 10.2 (1 digit to the right of the decimal point), 0.3768 (4 digits to the right of the decimal point), 1,368.58 (2 digits to the right of the decimal point), and 3.14159265358979323846 (20 digits to the right of the decimal point).

In this section, you'll discover the simplicity of adding, subtracting, multiplying, and dividing decimal numbers. Check out Chapter 2 for information on converting decimals into fractions.

1.2.1 Adding and Subtracting Decimals

You add and subtract decimals exactly the same way you add and subtract whole numbers: Line up the numbers vertically, aligned on the decimal points, and add or subtract. (Note that with whole numbers, even though you don't see a decimal point, it's implied as being to the right of the right-most number.)

A concept to remember when adding and subtracting decimals is that you can add any number of zeros *after* the decimal point without altering the value of the number. Therefore, 2 is the same as 2.0, which is the same as 2.00000.

For example, say you want to add 4.7 + 3.84 + 10. Here's how you set it up:

$$
\begin{array}{r}
4.70 \\
3.84 \\
+\ 10.00 \\
\hline
18.54
\end{array}
$$

Now say you want to find the answer to 8.255 + 1 + 1.5 + 30. You do the following:

$$
\begin{array}{r}
8.255 \\
1.000 \\
1.500 \\
+\ 30.000 \\
\hline
40.755
\end{array}
$$

Next, say you want to try the decimal subtraction problem 10 − 8.5. Here's what you do:

$$
\begin{array}{r}
10.0 \\
-\ 8.5 \\
\hline
1.5
\end{array}
$$

Finally, you want to try a subtraction problem that involves several decimal places: 2.18 − 1.5468. Here's how you figure it out:

$$
\begin{array}{r}
2.1800 \\
-\ 1.5468 \\
\hline
0.6332
\end{array}
$$

Practice with the following decimal addition and subtraction problems:

1. 24.11 + 5.10 + 9.41
2. 64.20 + 11.90 + 4.01
3. 98.60 − 9.70
4. 204.90 − 193.80
5. 494.78 − 82.89
6. 64.25 + 9.75

1.2.2 Multiplying Decimals

Multiplying decimals is similar to multiplying whole numbers, except that you have to figure out what to do with the decimals. To solve multiplication problems with decimals, you follow these steps:

Step 1: Multiply the numbers as if the decimals weren't there. For example, $1.36 \times 2.4 = 136 \times 24 = 3{,}264$.

Step 2: Looking at the numbers you're multiplying, count how many numbers are to the right of the decimal. For example, if you're multiplying 1.36×2.4, you have three numbers (.36 and .4) that are to the right of the decimal point.

Step 3: Starting at the right of the product, count over that many numbers to the left, and add the decimal point: 3.264.

For example, to find the answer to 1.903 × 2.231, you do the following:

$$
\begin{array}{r}
1.903 \\
\times\ 2.231 \\
\hline
4.245593
\end{array}
$$

Say you now want to solve 4.7845 × 1.2. Here's how you do it:

$$
\begin{array}{r}
4.7845 \\
\times\ 1.2 \\
\hline
5.74140
\end{array}
$$

Here's how you figure out 1.5 × 2:

$$
\begin{array}{r}
1.5 \\
\times\ 2 \\
\hline
3.0
\end{array}
$$

Now say you want to multiply two numbers that have several decimal places, such as 3.876 × 22.49. Here's what you do:

$$
\begin{array}{r}
3.876 \\
\times\ 22.49 \\
\hline
87.17124
\end{array}
$$

Practice with the following decimal multiplication problems:

1. 124.9 × 10
2. 83.6 × 11.4
3. 12.6 × 9.1
4. 2.75 × 0.03
5. 1.99 × 0.06
6. 23.95 × 0.18

1.2.3 Dividing Decimals

Like adding and subtracting decimals, dividing decimals also requires that you align the decimal points. The most important rule to remember if dividing decimals by hand is that you cannot divide if there is a decimal in the divisor. If the denominator does not have a decimal but the numerator does, the problem is very simple.

For example, say you want to find the answer to 18.00 ÷ 9. You simply line up the decimals and solve, like this:

$$
9\overline{)18.00}^{\ 2.00}
$$

You know that 9 goes into 18 twice, and you let the extra decimals and zeros remain where they are.

Now consider a division problem in which you have to add zeros beyond the decimal point: $30 \div 4$. You can solve this by using remainders, as you did in general math class, or you can add a zero beyond the decimal and continue to solve:

$$
\begin{array}{r}
7.5 \\
4\overline{)30} \\
28 \\
\hline
2.0 \\
2.0 \\
\hline
0
\end{array}
$$

You know that 4 goes into 30 seven times, with a remainder of 2. Because 2 is smaller than 4, you add a zero beyond the decimal and also put a decimal at the same point in the answer. Now you solve as if the decimal weren't there: How many times does 4 go into 20? Five times. The answer is 7.5.

If the denominator has a decimal, you get rid of the decimal by moving it to the right until the denominator is a whole number. You then move the decimal point in the numerator the same number of places. Next, you put a decimal at the same place in your answer. So, for example,

$$
25 \div 1.25 = 1.25\overline{)25}
$$
$$
= 125.\overline{)2500.}
$$

FOR EXAMPLE

Significant Digits

The concept of **significant digits** is used extensively in math, chemistry, physics, and engineering. Although most business applications ignore the rules of significant digits, knowing the concept can help you understand why some answers may appear to have been truncated.

Here are the basic rules of significant digits: Nonzero digits are *always* significant; zeros placed before the decimal are *not* significant, and zeros placed after the decimal or between other numbers *are* significant. So, for example, the number 102 has three significant digits, 102.3 has four significant digits, and 0.21 has two significant digits.

In multiplication, division, and so on, the number of significant digits in the answer should equal the *least* number of significant digits in the numbers being multiplied or divided. Therefore, 2.3457×2.68 is not 6.286476; rather, it is rounded to 6.29. The numbers being multiplied have five and three significant digits, respectively; therefore, the answer has three significant digits.

You can then solve the problem as if the decimals weren't there:

$$\begin{array}{r} 20. \\ 125.\overline{)2500.} \end{array}$$

Here are some decimal division problems to try on your own:

1. $9.1 \div 0.52$
2. $6 \div 1.33$
3. $12 \div 10.5$
4. $1.6 \div 0.357$

SELF-CHECK

- Understand the difference between decimals and whole numbers.
- Describe how to add and subtract decimals.
- Explain how to multiply and divide decimals.

1.3 Negative Numbers

A **positive number** is any number greater than zero. Positive numbers can be whole numbers, fractions, or decimals. A **negative number** is a number that is less than zero, and a negative sign goes in front of the number to indicate that it is negative (e.g., -5). Negative numbers can be added, subtracted, multiplied, and divided, just like positive numbers.

1.3.1 Adding and Subtracting Integers

To add integers, you follow these guidelines:

▲ **If both numbers are positive:** Add the numbers and keep the positive sign.
▲ **If both numbers are negative:** Add the numbers and keep the negative sign.
▲ **If one number is positive and one is negative:** Subtract the smaller (disregarding the sign) from the larger and keep the sign of the larger.

To subtract integers, you change the minus sign to a plus sign and change the sign of the second number. Then you use the addition rules just described.

For example, say you want to figure out $5 - (-2)$. Here's what you do:

$$5 - (-2) = 5 + 2 = 7$$

To figure out $18 + (-8)$, you do this:

$$18 + (-8) = 18 - 8 = 10$$

You find the answer to $25 - (-10) + (-20)$ as follows:

$$25 - (-10) + (-40) = 25 + 10 - 40 = -5$$

Finally, if you want to find the answer to $8.2 - (-4.95)$, you do the following:

$$8.2 - (-4.95) = 8.20 + 4.95 = 13.15$$

Try these examples of adding and subtracting integers, which are set up as word problems:

1. Suppose you arrive at your office with $15 in your pocket. You spend $10 on your coffee break. How much do you have in your pocket?
2. If the temperature is -2 and it drops another 9 degrees, what's the temperature?
3. If you weighed 157 pounds and you lost 13 pounds, how much do you weigh now?
4. If the stock market is at 11,458 on Monday morning and drops 60 points both Monday and Tuesday, what is its opening number on Wednesday morning?

1.3.2 Multiplying Integers

You multiply two negative numbers exactly as you do positive numbers, using the following rules to determine whether the product will be positive or negative (remember, these rules only apply when multiplying *two* numbers):

▲ **If the signs are the same:** The answer is positive.
▲ **If the signs are different:** The answer is negative.

Remember from your experience multiplying positive numbers that any number multiplied by 0 is always 0. This also holds true if you're multiplying a negative number by 0.

Test these rules by trying a few examples:

1. 14×-2
2. -1.26×-2.3
3. 148×-1
4. -32×2.4578

> ### For Example
>
> **Negative Numbers in Everyday Life**
>
> Unless you live in a warm part of the country, the most common negative numbers you see as you go about your day occur when the temperature falls below 0 (e.g., −10 degrees). Here are a couple other examples:
>
> ▲ In personal finance, if you're in debt (that is, you owe more than you own), your net worth is a negative number (e.g., −$12,000).
> ▲ In football, when the quarterback is sacked behind the line of scrimmage, he has a yardage loss (e.g., −4 yards).

1.3.3 Dividing Integers

The rules for division of integers are the same as those for multiplication. Remember from your experience dividing positive numbers that you cannot divide a number by zero. ~~This, of course, holds true for negative numbers, too.~~

Try a few sample problems:

1. $25 \div -5$
2. $-7.29 \div -3$
3. $28 \div -1$
4. $-125 \div 5$

SELF-CHECK

- Define **negative number.**
- Describe the rules for adding and subtracting negative numbers.
- Discuss how to determine the positive or negative sign of a product.

SUMMARY

Need to brush up on some basic math concepts? This chapter provides the basics on whole numbers, natural numbers, counting numbers, decimal numbers, negative numbers, and integers. They all follow similar rules and patterns, and this chapter lays them out for you.

KEY TERMS

Counting number	A whole number other than zero.
Integer	A positive or negative whole number.
Natural number	A positive integer or zero. Also known as a *whole number*.
Negative number	A number less than zero.
Positive number	A number greater than zero.
Whole number	A positive integer or zero. Also known as a *natural number*.

Study

all positive and negative whole numbers

ASSESS YOUR UNDERSTANDING

Go to www.wiley.com/college/slavin to evaluate your knowledge of the basics of whole numbers, decimals, and negative numbers.
Measure your learning by comparing pre-test and post-test results

Summary Questions

1. 5.25 is a whole number. True or False?
2. A negative multiplied by a negative equals a negative. True or False?
3. To add decimal numbers, you line up the decimal points. True or False?
4. You cannot divide a number by a negative number. True or False?
5. A negative multiplied by a positive equals a positive. True or False?

Review Questions

1. Explain the difference between whole numbers and counting numbers.
2. How do whole numbers and integers relate to one another?
3. Explain the difference between whole numbers and decimals.
4. Can negative numbers be decimals?

Applying This Chapter

1. Solve the following problems:
   (a) $2 + 1.375$
   (b) $102.3 - 14.5690$
   (c) 12.3×12.3
   (d) $45.75 \div 2.75$
2. Solve the following problems:
   (a) $-57 + (-21.3)$
   (b) -18×2.5
   (c) $-2.3 \times (-2.3)$
   (d) $37 \div (-2.5)$
3. Solve the following problems:
   (a) $3 + 4.56$
   (b) $497.5 - 11.5$
   (c) 7.12×10
   (d) $52 \div 6.35$

4. Solve the following problems:
   (a) $-5 + (-9)$
   (b) $12.5 + (-11)$
   (c) $7.6 - 3$
   (d) $-42.6 + (-11)$

5. Solve the following problems:
   (a) 3×4.81
   (b) $4.9 \div 2.4$
   (c) $98.6 - 22.8$
   (d) $212 - 17.4$

6. Solve the following problems:
   (a) $104.5 + 5.7 + 92$
   (b) $0.27 + 209 + 30 + 275$
   (c) $233.4287 - 92.476$
   (d) 0.335×0.44
   (e) 0.0001×872.6
   (f) $302.88 \div 6.7$
   (g) $165.27 \div 0.01$

7. Solve the following addition problems:
   (a) $-4 + (-3)$
   (b) $12 + (-4)$
   (c) $-6 + (-6)$
   (d) $-4 + (-18)$
   (e) $-14 + 5$
   (f) $14 + (-8)$
   (g) $2 + (-8)$
   (h) $-8 + 3$

8. Solve the following subtraction problems:
   (a) $-5 - 9$
   (b) $-5 - (-7)$
   (c) $2 - 9$
   (d) $4 - 5$
   (e) $-2 - (-3)$
   (f) $-6 - 10$
   (g) $9 - (-10)$
   (h) $-40 - 8$
   (i) $0 - 12$
   (j) $-6 - 6$

9. Solve the following multiplication and division problems:
   (a) $-5 \times (-4)$
   (b) $30 \times (-2)$
   (c) $0 \times (-5)$
   (d) $-35 \div (-7)$
   (e) $7 \div (-1)$
   (f) -10×10
   (g) $72 \div (-8)$
   (h) -10×3
   (i) 9×6
   (j) $-6 \div (-3)$
   (k) $14.7 \div (-2.1)$
   (l) $0.2 \times (-0.3)$
   (m) $-12 \div 5 \times 20 \div 3$

Freezing Temperatures

The lowest recorded temperatures in northern Europe is −47 degrees, and the lowest in Siberia is −72 degrees. How much higher is the lowest temperature in Northern Europe than the lowest temperature in Siberia?

Water Levels

The water level of a reservoir fluctuates with the amount of rainfall. Recently, during a 6-month period, the water went down 2 feet, then up 3 feet, down 5 feet, down another 1 foot, up 5 feet, and down 3 feet. How much has the water level changed over the past 6 months? (**Hint:** Add all numbers, using the sign rules.)

Sungard, Inc., Stock

One day in April, Sungard, Inc., stock started at a price of $15.23 on the New York Stock Exchange. During that day, the price rose $3.13, then dropped $6.25, and then rose $8.22. What was the value of the stock at day's end?

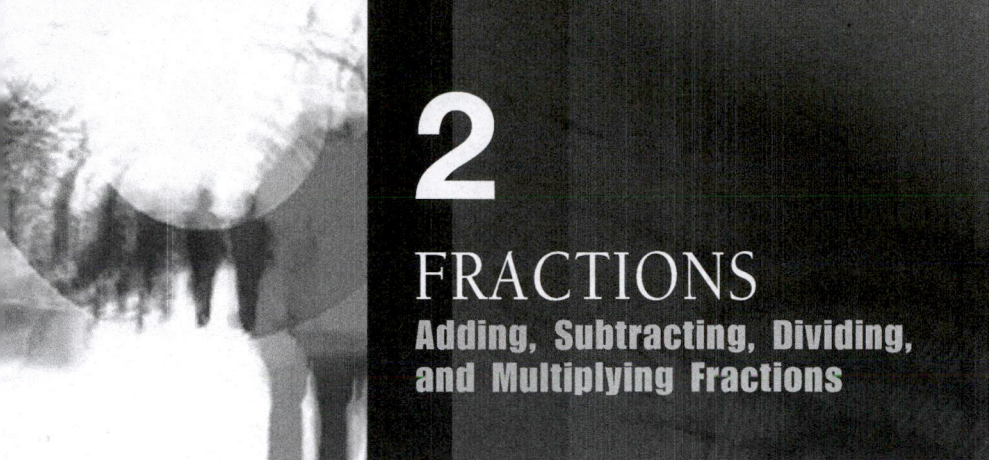

2

FRACTIONS
Adding, Subtracting, Dividing, and Multiplying Fractions

Starting Point

Go to www.wiley.com/college/slavin to test your knowledge of fractions.
Determine where you need to concentrate your effort.

What You'll Learn in This Chapter

▲ The basic characteristics of fractions
▲ How to add and subtract fractions
▲ How to multiply and divide fractions
▲ How to convert decimals into fractions and fractions into decimals

After Studying This Chapter, You'll Be Able To

▲ Discuss the relationship between improper fractions and mixed numbers
▲ Practice simplifying fractions
▲ Identify the critical factors that influence whether you can add, subtract, multiply, or divide fractions
▲ Practice the simple steps for converting a decimal to a fraction and converting a fraction to a decimal

Goals and Outcomes

▲ Master the terminology, understand the procedures, and recognize the tools of working with fractions
▲ Identify whether a fraction needs to be further simplified
▲ Use tools and techniques to add, subtract, multiply, and divide fractions
▲ Apply the ideas and techniques described in this chapter to sample problems

INTRODUCTION

Fractions are portions of whole numbers, and they can be proper, improper, or mixed. By following simple rules, you can convert them into decimals, add them, subtract them, multiply them, and divide them. The following sections spell out those rules and give you examples to work. Section 2.5 describes how to convert a decimal to a fraction.

2.1 Basics of Fractions

A **fraction**, also called a **proper fraction**, is a portion of a whole number, expressed as one number over the other, such as:

$$\frac{2}{3}$$

The number can also be written with a slash between the numbers (e.g., $\frac{2}{3}$). The top number is called the **numerator**; the bottom number is the **denominator**. To convert a fraction into a decimal, you simply divide the numerator by the denominator, either on a calculator or using longhand (e.g., $2 \div 3 = 0.67$).

An **improper fraction** has a numerator that's larger than the denominator, such as $\frac{9}{2}$. Improper fractions can be converted to decimals in the same way as a proper fraction: You simply divide the numerator by the denominator (e.g., $9 \div 2 = 4.5$). An improper fraction is considered bad form; instead, you should always convert an improper fraction to a decimal or to a mixed fraction.

A **mixed fraction** is a fraction that, as the name suggests, mixes a whole number and a fraction (e.g., $3\frac{5}{8}$). To convert an improper fraction to a mixed fraction, you figure out how many times the denominator can go into the numerator, like this:

$$\frac{\cancel{9}^{\,4(+1)}}{\cancel{2}_{1}} = 4\frac{1}{2}$$

The denominator, 2, goes into the numerator, 9, four times, with one remaining. As you can see, the one remaining becomes the numerator in the fractional part of the number.

To convert a mixed fraction into a decimal, you again divide the numerator by the denominator, and then you add that decimal to the whole number, like so:

$$3\frac{5}{8} = 3 + \left(\frac{5}{8}\right) = 3 + 0.625 = 3.625$$

Just as you want to convert an improper fraction to a mixed fraction, you also need to simplify all fractions. A **simplified fraction** is one that cannot be

FOR EXAMPLE

Mixed Numbers Make More Sense

You convert improper fractions to mixed fractions or decimals because the latter are more meaningful to people reading or seeing those numbers. "Eleven-thirds," for example, is not a meaningful number to most people, but "three and two-thirds" is a number that's easier to envision. Suppose your boss orders pizza for the office one Friday afternoon. She asks you to count how much pizza is left over, so that she has a better idea of how many pizzas to order in the future. No whole pies are left, but several slices are in each box. You count the number of slices and tell your boss that 43 slices are left. But she wants to know what that means in terms of pizzas. You know that each pizza had 10 slices, so you say, "forty-three tenths of a pizza." Now she's getting frustrated. So, you tell her the mixed number: "Four and three-tenths pizzas were left." Your grateful boss now knows to order four fewer pizzas for the next office pizza day.

reduced any further and still remain a fraction. So, for example, $\frac{1}{2}$ is a simplified fraction, but $\frac{2}{4}$ is not because 2 can go into the numerator one time, and 2 can go into the denominator two times, further reducing the fraction:

$$\frac{2^1}{4_2} = \frac{1}{2}$$

Is $\frac{6}{9}$ simplified? No, because the 3 can go into the numerator two times, and 3 goes into the denominator three times:

$$\frac{9^2}{9_3} = \frac{2}{3}$$

SELF-CHECK

- List and define the key terms used in relationship to fractions.
- Describe how to convert fractions to decimals.
- Discuss how to convert improper fractions to mixed fractions.
- Explain how to simplify fractions.

2.2 Addition and Subtraction of Fractions

You can add or subtract fractions only when they have the same denominator. So, for example, you can do the following addition:

$$\frac{2}{5} + \frac{1}{5}$$

but you cannot do this subtraction:

$$\frac{11}{15} - \frac{5}{6}$$

To add or subtract fractions that don't have the same denominator, you must find the **lowest common denominator**, or, the smallest possible number divisible by both the denominators you're trying to add or subtract. For example, to do the following subtraction, you must find a common denominator:

$$\frac{11}{15} - \frac{5}{6}$$

Often, you can simply multiply the denominators. But sometimes, that results in a huge, unwieldy number. Instead, you can use this trick: Count off by the larger of the two denominators until you find one that both have in common. So, for this example, start with the number 15. Does 6 go into that? No. Multiply 15 by 2 to get 30. Does 6 go into that? Yes, five times. So, you're going to use a common denominator of 30, and you multiply the numerators to keep the values of the fractions the same, as follows:

$$\frac{11 \times 2}{15 \times 2} - \frac{5 \times 5}{6 \times 5}$$

$$= \frac{22}{30} - \frac{25}{30}$$

This is now a problem you can solve.

2.2.1 Adding Fractions

After finding a common denominator and multiplying the numerators to keep the values of the fractions the same, adding fractions becomes simple arithmetic. Here's an example:

$$\frac{2}{5} + \frac{1}{5} = \frac{3}{5}$$

Solve the following after first finding the common denominator:

1. $\frac{2}{3} + \frac{4}{8}$
2. $\frac{1}{9} + \frac{14}{20} + \frac{7}{12}$
3. $\frac{1}{6} + \frac{1}{5} + \frac{1}{4} + \frac{1}{3} + \frac{1}{2}$

> ### FOR EXAMPLE
>
> #### Adding Fractions in the Retail World
>
> Can you imagine when you might have to add fractions in the business world? Imagine this: You own a small bead shop, and as you're about to place an order, you do a quick count of how many 4mm pearl beads you have. They come in 100-count boxes. You see 6 boxes in the storeroom and note that 1 of those boxes appears to be about half full. In the display rack, you see another four boxes, one of which is about one-quarter full. You quickly do the math: $5\frac{1}{2} + 3\frac{1}{4}$. You find that you have about $8\frac{3}{4}$ boxes. You don't like to have fewer than 10 full boxes, so you know you need to order 2 more.

2.2.2 Subtracting Fractions

As with addition, after you find a common denominator and multiply the numerators, subtracting is simple. An example follows:

$$\frac{22}{30} - \frac{25}{30}$$
$$= -\frac{3}{30}$$
$$= -\frac{1}{10}$$

Now practice solving the following:

1. $\frac{14}{5} - \frac{2}{7}$
2. $2\frac{3}{8} - 11\frac{1}{3}$
3. $\frac{1}{2} - \frac{1}{3} - \frac{1}{4} - \frac{1}{5} - \frac{1}{6}$

SELF-CHECK

- Discuss how to find the common denominator.
- Explain how to solve addition and subtraction problems with fractions.
- Describe how to simplify answers.

2.3 Multiplication and Division of Fractions

Multiplying and dividing fractions is actually simpler than adding and subtracting them because you don't have to find a common denominator.

2.3.1 Multiplying Fractions

To multiply fractions, you multiply the numerators, multiply the denominators, and simplify the answer, if needed. Here's an example:

$$\frac{3}{4} \times \frac{2}{5}$$

$$= \left(\frac{3 \times 2}{4 \times 5} \right)$$

$$= \frac{6}{20}$$

$$= \frac{3}{10}$$

Some multiplication problems are more complicated, such as the following:

$$\frac{3}{42} \times \frac{6}{15}$$

$$= \left(\frac{3 \times 6}{42 \times 15} \right)$$

$$= \frac{18}{630}$$

$$= \frac{1}{35}$$

To avoid working with large numerators and denominators, you can first check whether you can simplify the fraction involved in the original equation before you begin solving the problem, like this:

$$\frac{\cancel{3}^{1}}{\cancel{42}_{7}} \times \frac{\cancel{6}^{1}}{\cancel{15}_{5}}$$

$$= \left(\frac{1 \times 1}{7 \times 5} \right)$$

$$= \frac{1}{35}$$

Try these problems to test your skills:

1. $\frac{1}{5} \times \frac{10}{15}$
2. $3 \times \frac{7}{8}$
3. $\frac{24}{13} \times \frac{11}{8}$

FOR EXAMPLE

Rules of Division and Inverse Multiplication

Why do you invert the second fraction in a division problem? Think of it in terms of whole numbers, and you'll see why it works: $10 \div 2$ is a pretty straightforward division problem. But if, for some reason, you wanted to multiply instead of divide, you could change the problem to this, $10 \times [\frac{1}{2}]$, and you'd get the same answer, 5. That's *always* true for any division problem, not just for fractions: You can always invert the second term (the term by which you're dividing) and multiply the two terms instead.

2.3.2 Dividing Fractions

Dividing fractions is just as simple as multiplying, but first, you have to **invert** (i.e., flip) the fraction you're dividing by, and then you multiply the two fractions. Here's an example:

$$\frac{6}{7} \div \frac{3}{11}$$

$$= \frac{6}{7} \times \frac{11}{3}$$

$$= \left(\frac{6^2 \times 11}{7 \times 3^1}\right)$$

$$= \left(\frac{2 \times 11}{7 \times 1}\right)$$

$$= \frac{22}{7}$$

Now try a few division problems on your own:

1. $\frac{8}{20} \div \frac{9}{21}$

2. $\frac{6}{9} \div \frac{8}{12}$

3. $2\frac{1}{2} \div 4\frac{3}{8}$

SELF-CHECK

- Describe the procedures for multiplying and dividing fractions.
- Discuss how to invert a fraction to solve division problems.
- Simplify terms to make problems easier to solve.

2.4 Converting Fractions to Decimals

Converting a fraction into a decimal is a simple problem of division. For instance, try converting $\frac{1}{4}$ into a decimal. Were you able to do it? Did you get .25? Here's how it works:

$$\frac{1}{4} = 4\overline{)1.00}^{\,.25} = .25$$

Why do you divide the 4 into the 1? The rule is, whenever you have a fraction, it can be read as follows: Divide the top number by the bottom number (i.e., the numerator by the denominator).

You may raise the objection that you can't divide 4 into 1. It doesn't fit. Although it's true that 4 doesn't go into 1 completely, it does go in one-quarter of the way. For example, if a 400-foot train went through a 100-foot tunnel, only one-quarter of the train would be in the tunnel. So we could say that 400 goes into 100 one-quarter (or $\frac{100}{400}$, or $\frac{1}{4}$) of the way. When you divide a large number into a smaller one, your quotient, or answer, is less than 1.

Try another one. Convert $\frac{3}{5}$ into a decimal. Here's what you do:

$$\frac{3}{5} = 5\overline{)3.0}^{\,.6} = .6$$

Try converting these fractions into decimals:

1. $\frac{5}{8}$
2. $\frac{3}{4}$
3. $\frac{5}{12}$

Do you always have to divide the denominator into the numerator to convert a fraction into a decimal? The answer is yes. But sometimes you can take a shortcut. For example, you can take that shortcut to convert the fraction $\frac{3}{10}$ into a decimal. When you divide a number by 10, you move the decimal point one place to the left. For example, you get .5 when you divide 5 by 10. What you really did was move the decimal point one place to the left. The fraction $\frac{3}{10}$ can be read as 3 divided by 10. If you took the number 3, or 3.0, and divided it by 10, you'd end up with .3, or .30.

Now change the fraction $\frac{7}{10}$ into a decimal. You should get .7.

Working with hundredths is similar to working with tenths. The fraction $\frac{19}{100}$ is read as "nineteen hundredths." Can you change it into a decimal? Here's how you do it:

$$\frac{19}{100} = .19$$

> ## For Example
>
> ### Converting Decimals to Fractions and Vice Versa
>
> In the business world, you generally convert decimals to fractions (or fractions to decimals) so that you can add them to other fractions (or to other decimals). If, for example, you know that one-third of your customers prefer diet soft drinks, one-fifth opt for sugar-free iced tea, and 0.20 like black coffee best, how many of your customers drink sugar-free beverages? The only way to find out is to either convert the fractions to decimals or the decimal to a fraction. Either way, you discover that nearly three-quarters (0.73) prefer sugar-free beverages.

What you do is take the 19 and move the decimal two places to the left: .19. When you divide a number by 100, you just move the decimal two places to the left.

Try converting each of the following fractions into decimals:

1. $\frac{4}{10}$
2. $\frac{9}{10}$
3. $\frac{23}{100}$
4. $\frac{47}{100}$

SELF-CHECK

- Describe how to convert fractions to decimals.
- Practice converting decimals to fractions.

2.5 Converting Decimals to Fractions

To convert fractions to decimals, you have to do some division. Changing decimals into fractions is even simpler. You can read 0.7 as "seven-tenths." And seven-tenths, in fraction form, is $\frac{7}{10}$. When you change a number from a decimal to a fraction, it's still the same number, with the same numeric value; just its form changes.

Here's how you convert 0.7 to a fraction:

Step 1: Move the decimal to the right as many places as necessary. In this case, you move the decimal *one* place to the right, like this: 07. By moving the decimal one place to the right, you have multiplied the number by 10. You know from Chapter 1 that any zero to the *left* of a number can be eliminated, so this number is simply 7, and it will be your numerator.

Step 2: To find the denominator, use the following table:

If You Moved the Decimal This Many Places	Use This Number as Your Denominator
1	10
2	100
3	1,000
4	10,000

Because you moved the decimal one place in this example, you use 10 as your denominator, which makes the fraction $\frac{7}{10}$.

Another way to think of this is to make the decimal your numerator and to make 1 the denominator. (Dividing any number by 1 is always the same as the number by itself.) Then you multiply both the top and bottom by 10 to get rid of the decimal point, like this:

$$0.7 = \frac{0.7}{1} = \frac{0.7 \times 10}{1 \times 10} = \frac{7}{10}$$

If the number you're trying to convert has two numbers past the decimal, you multiply by 100; for three numbers past the decimal, you multiply by 1,000.

Try your hand at converting 0.33 to a fraction. If you use the first method, you move the decimal *two places*, to get 33 (your numerator) and use 100 (from the table) as your denominator. Using the second method, you do the following:

$$0.33 = \frac{0.33}{1} = \frac{0.33 \times 100}{1 \times 100} = \frac{33}{100}$$

Try one more example: 0.489. With the first method, you move the decimal *three places*, to get 489 (the numerator) and use 1,000 (from the table) as the denominator. Or, you can use the second method, as follows:

$$0.489 = \frac{0.489}{1} = \frac{0.489 \times 1,000}{1 \times 1,000} = \frac{489}{1,000}$$

Finally, keep in mind that you might still need to simplify after converting a decimal to the fraction. For example, if you convert 0.5 to a fraction, you get $\frac{5}{10}$, which you can simplify to $\frac{1}{2}$.

Try converting the following decimals to fractions:

1. .9
2. .61
3. .807
4. .92
5. .763
6. .5

SELF-CHECK

- Describe both methods for converting decimals to fractions.
- Practice converting decimals to fractions.

SUMMARY

This chapter describes the simple rules for converting fractions into decimals, simplifying fractions, adding and subtracting fractions, multiplying and dividing fractions, and even converting decimals into fractions.

KEY TERMS

Common denominator	A number divisible by both denominators in a multiplication problem.
Denominator	The bottom number in a fraction.
Fraction	A portion of a whole number, expressed as one number over the other. Also known as a *proper fraction*.
Improper fraction	A fraction with a numerator that's larger than the denominator.
Invert	To flip a fraction so that the denominator is the numerator and the numerator is the denominator.
Lowest common denominator	The smallest possible number divisible by both the denominators in an addition or subtraction problem.
Mixed fraction	A fraction that mixes a whole number and a fraction.
Numerator	The top number in a fraction.
Proper fraction	A portion of a whole number, expressed as one number over another. Also known as a *fraction*.
Simplified fraction	A fraction that cannot be reduced any further.

ASSESS YOUR UNDERSTANDING

Go to www.wiley.com/college/slavin to evaluate your knowledge of fractions.
Measure your learning by comparing pre-test and post-test results.

Summary Questions

1. A **fraction** is:
   (a) a portion of a mixed number.
   (b) a portion of a whole number.
   (c) a portion of a decimal.
   (d) all of above.
2. An improper fraction is a fraction that is made up of a whole number and a fraction. True or False?
3. $\frac{84}{189}$ is simplified. True or False?

Review Questions

1. Describe the process of converting a fraction to a decimal.
2. What is the first step in adding or subtracting fractions?
3. How do you solve a problem that involves division of fractions?

Applying This Chapter

1. Convert the following fractions into decimals:
   (a) $\frac{3}{4}$
   (b) $3\frac{1}{2}$
   (c) $\frac{15}{8}$
2. Simplify the following fractions:
   (a) $\frac{8}{32}$
   (b) $\frac{28}{3}$
   (c) $\frac{92}{161}$
3. Convert the following decimals into fractions:
   (a) .807
   (b) .92
   (c) .2

4. Add the following fractions and simplify the result, if necessary:

   (a) $\frac{4}{6} + \frac{3}{6}$

   (b) $\frac{7}{9} + \frac{5}{9}$

   (c) $\frac{5}{8} + \frac{4}{12}$

   (d) $\frac{24}{76} + \frac{45}{152}$

   (e) $\frac{76}{150} + \frac{35}{300}$

   (f) $\frac{7}{9} + \frac{8}{27}$

   (g) $\frac{5}{20} + \frac{5}{80}$

   ~~(h) $\frac{24}{75} + \frac{6}{150}$~~

   (i) $\frac{3}{4} + \frac{1}{2}$

   (j) $\frac{1}{16} + \frac{1}{32}$

5. Subtract the following fractions and simplify the result, if necessary:

   (a) $\frac{5}{16} - \frac{11}{4}$

   (b) $\frac{3}{4} - \frac{11}{16}$

   (c) $\frac{1}{2} - \frac{2}{32}$

   (d) $\frac{5}{6} - \frac{2}{3}$

   (e) $\frac{6}{75} - \frac{11}{150}$

   (f) $\frac{7}{8} - \frac{4}{4}$

   (g) $\frac{8}{10} - \frac{9}{20}$

   (h) $\frac{24}{12} - \frac{9}{18}$

   (i) $\frac{31}{8} - \frac{1}{4}$

   (j) $\frac{25}{100} - \frac{59}{300}$

6. Multiply the following fractions and simplify the result, if necessary:

   (a) $\frac{11}{16} \times \frac{12}{31}$

   (b) $\frac{5}{8} \times \frac{1}{4}$

   (c) $\frac{7}{8} \times \frac{1}{2}$

   (d) $2\frac{1}{2} \times 4\frac{3}{4}$

   (e) $4\frac{1}{4} \times 7\frac{1}{2}$

   (f) $7\frac{1}{8} \times \frac{1}{2}$

   (g) $6\frac{1}{8} \times 4$

   (h) $\frac{1}{7} \times \frac{5}{32}$

   (i) $\frac{50}{100} \times \frac{5}{20}$

   (j) $\frac{3}{8} \times 1\frac{1}{4}$

7. Divide the following fractions and simplify the quotient, if necessary:

   (a) $\frac{24}{11} \div \frac{38}{11}$

   (b) $\frac{1}{4} \div \frac{1}{6}$

   (c) $\frac{150}{800} \div \frac{120}{300}$

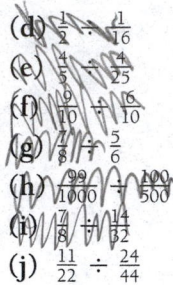

(d) $\frac{1}{2} \div \frac{1}{16}$

(e) $\frac{4}{5} \div \frac{4}{25}$

(f) $\frac{9}{10} \div \frac{6}{10}$

(g) $\frac{7}{8} \div \frac{5}{6}$

(h) $\frac{99}{1000} \div \frac{100}{500}$

(i) $\frac{7}{8} \div \frac{14}{32}$

(j) $\frac{11}{22} \div \frac{24}{44}$

8. Solve the following problem:

$$\left(2\frac{3}{6} + \frac{1}{3}\right) \times \left(\frac{3}{5} - 1\right) \div 0.2$$

YOU TRY IT

Day Care Dilemma

Rosie runs a day-care center and wants to serve the children Cheerios for breakfast. A box of Cheerios contains 18 cups of cereal. If each child will eat a $1\frac{1}{2}$-cup serving, how many children can receive Cheerios that morning?

Long Drive Home

Jose drove home from his job at the Best Buy electronics store at 40 miles per hour. If the trip took $1\frac{3}{4}$ hours, how far does Jose live from the store?

Fondue Night

Lizzie owns a restaurant and wants to serve a fondue appetizer one evening. However, she has only $\frac{1}{4}$ pound of American cheese and $\frac{2}{3}$ pound of cheddar on hand. How much cheese does she have in all?

Office Space

Bob had $8\frac{1}{4}$ gallons of paint. He painted his new office space and had $6\frac{2}{5}$ gallons left. How much paint did Bob use to paint the office?

Space for Books

Mr. Jones's shelf in his headquarters office is 64 inches long. He wants to put his college business books on the shelf. Each book is $2\frac{3}{4}$ inches wide. How many books can he place on the shelf?

3

CALCULATING PERCENTAGES
Converting Decimals and Fractions

Starting Point

Go to www.wiley.com/college/slavin to assess your knowledge of calculating percentages.
Determine where you need to concentrate your effort.

What You'll Learn in This Chapter

▲ How to convert decimals and fractions to percentages
▲ The definition of **percentage**, **rate**, and **base**
▲ How to calculate percentage increase and percentage decrease
▲ How to find a percentage distribution

After Studying This Chapter, You'll Be Able To

▲ Apply the methods for converting decimals and fractions to percentages
▲ Examine the relationship between percentage, rate, and base
▲ Calculate percentage increase and percentage decrease
▲ Compare the uses of percentage distribution

Goals and Outcomes

▲ Master the terminology, understand the procedures/perspectives, and recognize the tools used in calculating percentages
▲ Understand the business uses of percentage calculations
▲ Use tools and technique to analyze percentage changes and distributions

INTRODUCTION

Much of the business world requires a thorough understanding of percentages. Percentages are really decimals and fractions (see Chapters 1 and 2) dressed up to look a little different. When you learn how to convert percentages into decimals or fractions and vice versa, solving percentage problems is a snap, including those tricky "30% off" and "50% increase" problems.

3.1 Writing Decimals and Fractions as Percentages

The first step in solving any percentage problem is to understand the connection between percentages and decimals (or fractions). Any percentage can be expressed as a fraction or as a decimal, and any decimal or fraction can be expressed as a percentage.

3.1.1 Converting Decimals to Percentages

To convert a decimal to a percentage, you move the decimal place two places to the right and add a **percent** sign (%). For example, to convert the decimal 0.255, you move the **decimal point** two places to the right and add a percent sign, to get 25.5%. (Keep in mind that with a whole number such as 25, you don't need the decimal point at the end [i.e., 25.] because a decimal point at the end of any whole number is implied.)

Try converting these decimals to percentages:

1. 0.32
2. 0.835
3. 1.29
4. 0.03
5. 0.41

How do you convert the decimal 1.2? In this case, you simply add a 0 to the end of the number so that you can move the decimal point two places: 1.20 = 120%. You can add a zero if doing so doesn't change the value of the number. So, you can't add a zero to 30, because the new value would be 300. But you can add a zero to 1.2, because 1.2 and 1.20 are the same number.

How would you convert the decimal 5? To figure this one out, you place the implied decimal point at the end of the number (i.e., 5.) and add two zeros (i.e., 5.00). Then you move the decimal two places, and you get 500%.

You would follow the same procedure for 82 or 306. You simply add the implied decimal point and any zeros, as needed, and move the decimal two places: 82.00 = 8200% and 306.00 = 30600%.

3.1.2 Converting Percentages to Decimals

To change a percentage to a decimal, you simply reverse the process: Move the decimal point two places to the *left*. For example, 78% = 78.0% = 0.78.

Try converting the following percentages to their decimal equivalents:

1. 25%
2. 33%
3. 45.2%
4. 82.25%
5. 600%
6. 42%
7. 326.9%
8. 7.125%
9. 82%
10. 500%

3.1.3 Converting Fractions to Percentages

To convert a fraction to a percentage, you must first convert the fraction to a decimal (i.e., divide the numerator by the denominator) and then use the procedure described in Section 3.1.1. See Chapter 2 for information on converting fractions to decimals.

Let's take a closer look at the relationship among decimals, fractions, and percentages. We'll begin with the fraction $\frac{1}{100}$. How much is $\frac{1}{100}$ as a percentage? It's 1%. How much is the decimal? It's 0.01. So,

$$\frac{1}{100} = 0.01 = 1\%$$

In fact, any time you have a fraction with 100 in the denominator, the percentage will be the numerator. For this reason, if you can get 100 in the denominator (e.g., by multiplying), you can easily find the percentage.

For example, suppose you are given $\frac{1}{50}$ and asked to find the percentage. You want to get 100 in the denominator, so you multiply both the numerator and denominator by 2, as follows:

$$\frac{1}{50} \times \frac{2}{2} = \frac{2}{100} = 2\%$$

If you have $\frac{2}{20}$, you multiply both the numerator and the denominator by 5, as follows:

$$\frac{2}{20} \times \frac{5}{5} = \frac{10}{100} = 10\%$$

This is a simple shortcut that prevents you from having to divide the numerator by the denominator, as you are instructed to do in Chapter 2. Hint: This works only if the denominator is a factor of 100, such as 2, 4, 5, 10, 20, 40, or 50.

Try converting the following fractions to percentages:

1. $\frac{1}{25}$
2. $\frac{7}{25}$
3. $\frac{40}{80}$
4. $3\frac{1}{2}$
5. $\frac{4}{50}$
6. $\frac{2}{30}$
7. $4\frac{1}{5}$
8. $\frac{9}{10}$
9. $\frac{45}{90}$
10. $\frac{16}{32}$

FOR EXAMPLE

Why Do We Need to Know Percentages?

In the business world, the use of percentages, decimals, and fractions is intertwined. Business leaders and others—and even advertisements—talk in terms of percentages when those numbers sound impressive: "300% increase in profits," "200% reduction in defects," "20% more for your money," and "50% off sale." When fractions sound better, those terms are used instead: "One-quarter of our staff," "Three-quarters of those surveyed," and so on. But in order to put a fraction into an equation and make quick calculations, you need to know its decimal equivalent. If you can easily calculate that 300% is 3.0, 20% is 0.20, and three-quarters is 0.75, you can fiddle with—and even question—the numbers you see in corporate reports and in company advertisements.

It is useful to memorize the common percentages and their decimal and fractional equivalents. The following chart lists some of the most common:

Percentage	Decimal	Fraction
25%	.25	$\frac{1}{4}$
$33\frac{1}{3}$%	.3333	$\frac{1}{3}$
50%	.50	$\frac{1}{2}$
$12\frac{1}{2}$%	.125	$\frac{1}{8}$
75%	.75	$\frac{3}{4}$
$66\frac{2}{3}$%	.67	$\frac{2}{3}$
20%	.2	$\frac{1}{5}$
80%	.8	$\frac{4}{5}$

SELF-CHECK

- Describe how to convert decimals to percentages and vice versa.
- Review how to convert fractions to decimals.
- Draw basic conclusions about the relationship between decimals and percentages.

3.2 Finding the Percentage, Base, and Rate

Percentage (amount), base, and rate are three components involved in calculating percentages. The **rate**, which is the number of hundredths parts taken, is commonly followed by a percent sign or a decimal; it is a fraction representing a relationship between the percentage and the base. The **base** is the number on which the rate operates, the starting amount. The **percentage** is the part of the base determined by the rate. Confused? It's really quite simple if you look at the following equation:

$$P = B \times R$$

So, for example, in the equation $9 = 90 \times 10\%$

- ▲ 10% is the rate.
- ▲ 90 is the base.
- ▲ 9 is the percentage.

3.2.1 Finding the Percentage When the Base and Rate Are Known

As mentioned in the preceding section, if you know the base and rate, you can calculate the percentage, by using this formula:

$$P = B \times R$$

For example, what number is 8% of 65? In this case, the base is 65, and the rate is 8%. To find the percentage, you say "8% of 65 is what?" (Note that of always means "multiply," and is always means "equals.") In this case, you can set up the following equation:

$$P = B \times R$$
$$8\% \times 65 = ?$$
$$0.08 \times 65 = 5.2$$

Therefore, 8% of 65 is 3.

Try finding the percentages for the following:

1. 25% of 100
2. 10% of 300
3. 5% of 25
4. 6% of 9.95
5. 11% of 10
6. $\frac{1}{2}$% of 100
7. 400% of 50
8. 2% of 90
9. 1% of 9
10. 20% of 16.95

3.2.2 Finding the Rate When the Base and Percentage Are Known

If you know the base and percentage, you can find the rate, by using this formula:

$$R = [P/B]$$

For example, 18 is what percentage of 72? Here, the base is 72, and the percentage is 18. You can make this into a simple equation:

$$18 = ?\% \times 72$$

To find the answer, you divide each side of the equation (that is, each set of numbers on either side of the equals sign) by 72, as follows:

$$R = [P/B]$$
$$18 = [?\%/72]$$
$$\frac{18}{72} = \frac{?\%}{72}$$
$$0.25 = ?\%$$
$$= 25\%$$

Chapter 4 discusses this process in more depth.

Try finding the following rates:

1. 60 is what percentage of 600?
2. 15 is what percentage of 150?
3. 700 is what percentage of 70,000?
4. 45 is what percentage of 180?
5. 200 is what percentage of 25?
6. 27 is what percentage of 200?
7. $4 is what percentage of $100?
8. 9 is what percentage of 10?

9. 1,000 is what percentage of 1,200?

10. $82\frac{1}{2}$ is what percentage of 141?

3.2.3 Finding the Base When the Percentage and Rate Are Known

If you know the percentage and rate, you can find the base by again using this formula:

$$P = R \times B$$

For example, 10 is 25% of what number? In this case, the rate is 25%, and the percentage is 10. To solve this, you make it into a simple equation:

$$10 = 25\% \times ?$$

Then you convert the rate to a decimal, 0.25, and plug that in to the equation:

$$10 = 0.25 \times ?$$

To find the answer, you divide each side of the equation by 0.25, like this:

$$10 = 0.25 \times ?$$

$$\frac{10}{0.25} = \frac{0.25}{0.25} \times ?$$

$$40 = ?$$

Try finding the following bases:

1. 10 is 40% of what?

2. 15 is 30% of what?

3. 25 is 4% of what?

4. 40 is 10% of what?

5. 60 is 300% of what?

FOR EXAMPLE

Base, Rate, and Percentage in the Real World

Base, rate, and percentage are used extensively in business and personal finance. Suppose you're planning to buy a house that costs $130,000. The mortgage company wants you to put down 20%. In this case, you know the rate (20%) and the base ($130,000). You need to find the percentage to know how much money you need to put down. In words, you say this as "20% of $130,000 is what?" This equates to the simple equation 20% × $130,000 = ? or 0.20 × $130,000 = $26,000. So you need to come up with a $26,000 down payment.

SELF-CHECK

- Define **base, rate,** and **percentage.**
- Describe how these three terms interrelate.
- Set up simple equations.
- Calculate one quantity when you know the other two.

3.3 Percentage Increases and Decreases

Suppose you were earning $500 per week and got a $20 raise. By what percentage did your salary go up? You use the following equation to find out:

$$\text{Percentage change} = \frac{\text{Change}}{\text{Original number}}$$

Your salary is the original number, and your raise is the change:

$$\text{Percentage change} = \frac{\$20}{\$500} = \frac{2}{50} = \frac{4}{100} = 4\%$$

Therefore, the percentage change is an increase of 4%.

Here's an example of a percentage decrease problem: On New Year's Eve, you made a resolution to lose 30 pounds by the end of July. After eating less and exercising five days per week for seven months, your weight dropped from 140 pounds to 110 pounds. By what percentage did your weight decrease? Here's how you figure it out:

$$\text{Percentage change} = \frac{\text{Change}}{\text{Original number}}$$

$$\text{Percentage change} = \frac{30}{140} = \frac{3}{14} = 0.2143 = 21.43\%$$

If you know the original number and the percentage change and want to calculate the amount of the change, you use the following formula:

$$\text{Change} = \text{Original number} \times \text{Percentage change}$$

For example, say your corporation is giving you a 5% bonus for your excellent work on the Alpha Project. If the bonus is based on your current salary of $42, 000, how much is your bonus? Here's how you figure it out:

$$? = 42{,}000 \times .05 = \$2{,}100.00$$

If you want to know not just the change but also the new number, you have to add in the original number:

New number = Change + Original number

Here's an example: Your restaurant bill is $40.00, and you would like to leave the service staff a 20% tip. How much cash must you leave? Here's how you figure it out:

New number = (Original number × Percentage change) + Original number

New number = (40 × 20%) + 40

New number = (40 × 0.20) + 40

New number = $8 + $40 = $48

If you're calculating a percentage change that results in a *decrease* from the original number, you subtract the change from the original number, as follows:

New number = Original number − (Original number × Percentage change)

Try figuring out the following percentage changes:

1. You expect an increase in sales this summer at your water and ice stand, from 150 cups per day to 175. What is the rate of increase?

2. As a result of spending $6 million in additional advertising this year, your local cable provider forecasts new installations to be at a 20% rate of increase over the prior year. If the company installed 30 new cable customers per week in the prior year, how many can be expected per week this year?

For Example

Percentage Change Applications

Not sure where you'll use percentage change in the real world? In business, percentage change comes up all the time. Suppose you manage human resources for a small company. Because the company's profits grew 30% last year, you've been allocated an additional 30% in your annual budget to hire new employees. If last year's budget was $720,000, how much do you have to spend this year? Here's how you figure it out:

New number = (Original number × Percentage change) + Original number

New number = ($720,000 × 30%) + $720,000

New number = ($720,000 × 0.20) + 40

New number = $216,000 + $720,000 = $936,000

3. Say that sales increase by 210 units. What is the rate increase if original sales were 1,415 units?

4. Your salary increases from \$435 per week to \$497. What is the rate of increase?

SELF-CHECK

- Calculate **percentage increase, percentage decrease,** and **percentage change.**
- Discuss the amount you have left when you experience a 100% decrease.

3.4 Percentage Distribution

A corporate in-service training session is composed of half men and half women. What percentage of the session is men and what percentage is women? The answers are pretty obvious: 50% and 50%. In a nutshell, that's all there is to percentage distribution. Sure, the problems get a little more complex than this, but the totals always add up to 100%.

Suppose one-quarter of the management team is in sales, one-quarter is from the accounting department, and the rest are support staff. What is the team's percentage distribution of sales, accounting, and support staff? Here's how you figure it out:

▲ Sales are $\frac{1}{4}$, or 25%.

▲ Accountants are also $\frac{1}{4}$, or 25%.

▲ Support staff must be the remaining 50%.

Here's a more challenging example: If, over the course of a week, sales team A sold 250 MP-3 players, sales team B sold 150, sales team C sold 100, and sales team D sold 50, what percentage of the total sales was each team responsible for? A total of 550 MP-3 players (250 + 150 + 100 + 50) were sold, and the sales for each team are determined as follows:

$$\text{Sales team A}: [250/550] = 45.5\%$$

$$\text{Sales team B}: [150/550] = 27.3\%$$

$$\text{Sales team C}: [100/550] = 18.2\%$$

$$\text{Sales team D}: [50/550] = 9.1\%$$

For Example

Percentage Distribution

Percentage distribution is a major component of financial statements and business statistics. You analyze income statements by determining the percentage of sales, inventory, purchases, expenses, and so on, as compared to net sales. Likewise, when completing a balance sheet, you compare each individual component of assets and liabilities as a percentage distribution of total assets and total liabilities. You cannot create a pie chart without being able to figure percentage distribution. In fact, if you created a pie chart for the sales example in this section, the chart would look like the one shown in Figure 3-1.

To check whether you're correct, you add up all four percentages, and you get 100.1%. (The 0.1 is due to rounding; if you end up with 100.1 or 99.9, that's close enough to 100%.)

Try figuring out the following percentage distribution:

1. A manufacturer for the upcoming fiscal year projects sales of power drills of 42,500. The marketing department believes the sales mix will be as following:
   (a) 40% Construction-grade drills
   (b) 35% Handyman-grade drills
   (c) 25% Craft-making–grade drills

Figure 3-1

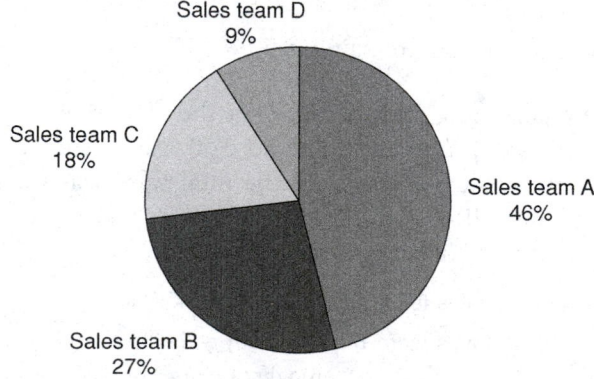

Pie Chart.

- Given raw data, calculate percentage distribution.
- Check that the totals add up to 100%.
- Consider the uses of percentage distribution in the business world.

SUMMARY

The ability to calculate percentages is a key business tool. In the business world, you may need to convert fractions and percentages to decimals and vice versa; find the rate, base, or percentage when two of those numbers are known; calculate percentage changes (increases and decreases); and find the percentage distribution for given data.

KEY TERMS

Base	The beginning whole amount on which the rate operates.
Decimal point	A period located between units and tenths.
Fraction	An expression of a part of a whole amount.
Percentage	The part of the base that is determined by the rate.
Percentage change	The amount by which a percentage (an amount) increases or decreases.
Percentage distribution	The percentage (part) of the total in each class or category.
Rate	A number that is followed by a percent sign, which expresses how the base and percentage are related to each other.

ASSESS YOUR UNDERSTANDING

Go to www.wiley.com/college/slavin to evaluate your knowledge of the basics of calculating percentages.

Measure your learning by comparing pre-test and post-test results.

Summary Questions

1. Changing a decimal to a percentage involves moving the decimal point two places to the left and adding a percent sign. True or False?
2. By definition, **base** is:
   (a) a number followed by a percent sign.
   (b) the number on which the rate operates.
   (c) the part of the base determined by the rate.
   (d) all of the above.
3. Given the original number and the amount of change, you find the percentage change by:
   (a) dividing the change by the original number.
   (b) dividing the original number by the change.
   (c) multiplying the change by the original number.
   (d) adding the original number to the change.
4. The percentage distribution always adds up to:
   (a) the amount of the base.
   (b) the total number of units.
   (c) 100, give or take 0.1%.
   (d) 100.00.

Review Questions

1. Convert the following to percentages:
   (a) 0.32
   (b) 17.3
   (c) 1
   (d) 200.1
   (e) 10
2. Given $\left[\frac{2.3}{10}\right]$, what is the percentage?
3. What is the percentage change if you go from 150 to 180?

4. The $50 utility bill at your apartment falls by 30%. What is the new utility bill?

5. What number is 120% of 1,500?

6. The time for processing an order fell from 11 minutes to 8 minutes. By what percentage did the time fall?

7. If a company's business taxes were $12,200 and rose by 18%, how much would the company now be paying?

Applying This Chapter

1. Mr. Potts, the college pastry chef, baked three apple pies, two blueberry pies, five cherry pies, and six key lime pies for the student fundraiser. What percentage of the pies were apple, blueberry, cherry, and key lime?

2. An alumni association has 45,000 members. Women younger than 40 total 4,500; 12,800 are men younger than 40; 7,900 are women older than 40; and the remainder are men older than 40. Find the percentage distribution of all four membership categories.

3. A bottling company can fill 100 bottles in 5 minutes. A quality assurance survey indicates that 2% of the bottles do not reach the fill standards and are therefore rejected. How many bottles are rejected each hour?

4. Mr. Ness, a retired professor, placed $5,000 in a CD (certificate of deposit) over 10 years ago. The CD is now worth 125% of its original value. How much is the CD worth?

5. A shipping company has seen an increase in gasoline from about $2.30 per gallon to $3.40. What is the percentage increase?

6. Steve earns $3,250 per month. He pays federal and state income taxes of 26%. What is the dollar amount of his taxes per month?

7. As a water quality assurance employee for your local Aqua America, Inc., branch, you record a drop in water levels from 28 feet to 7 feet at your reservoir. What is the percentage decrease?

8. This year's capital budget for the purchase of any equipment valued at over $1,500 will be increased from a total of $450,000 to $638,000 due to an increase in state funding. What is the percentage increase for your college?

9. At your online sportswear company, backorders resulting from a poorly designed webpage are 28 per day. With a change in the webpage design, this number drops to an average of 7.25 per day. What is the rate of decrease?

10. The motel night audit performed at the end of a motel's business day (3 A.M.) required the downloading of management reports, which took

9 minutes. Thanks to a new property management system, this download time was reduced to 3.25 minutes. What is the rate of reduction?

11. A marketing specialist earned $12.75 per hour and worked 38 hours per week. If her total deductions were 35%, what was the amount deducted from her pay?

12. The "win" at the newest casino increased by 125% over the past three years, and the original win was $43 million. What is the current win?

13. A team project group that formed in a college leadership course designed, fabricated, and sold dolls. About 6.5% of them were male dolls. During one semester, the team sold 150 dolls. How many were male (rounded)?

14. Tools returned to a hardware store as damaged are re-sold as damaged, at a reduced price 32% of the original price of $164.95. What is the new price?

15. Best Font Printing Company was attempting to reduce its holiday card inventory by offering a 40% discount on orders over $10,000. It placed this information on its customer emailer, and a local card retailer placed an order of $16,000. (Hint: The discount applies to the entire order.) What was the dollar discount on this order?

16. The price of a share of stock in a hotel company rose on Tuesday to a new 52-week high of $38.50. Last month the price was $21.30. What was the percentage increase?

17. The Big Men retailer reduces the price of its $350 sport coats by 30%. What is the new price?

18. A 230-employee collective bargaining association (union) agreed to a 2% reduction in their health benefit package. If the original package was valued at $9,450 for the average employee, how much money did the company save with the reduction?

19. There are 251,500 potential customers for your company's services. If you plan to achieve a 16% market share after your new promotional campaign, how many new customers are you expecting?

20. The Rosa Pasta sauce brand manager visits a local supermarket to obtain additional shelf space. Originally, Rosa had 60 square feet of space. If the manager was able to obtain a 14% increase, what is the total new space?

21. If the CPI (consumer price index) of 141 increased 8.3% this year, what would the CPI be at the end of the year?

22. The American Red Cross reached its annual goal of increasing contributions by 18% over the prior year total of $1,200,650. What was the increase?

23. During the World Series, the host city's citywide hotel occupancy rose 21% over the previous busiest night. If the busiest night had been 76%, what was the new record?

24. An incentive clause in Barry Bonds's contract allows for a 3.4% bonus if he hits more than 719 home runs this season. His contract is currently valued at $14.5 million. What would the bonus be worth?

25. Last week, 145 new customers were registered through your company's website. This week, 267 new customers were registered. What is the rate of increase?

Terry's Videos

Last year during Thanksgiving weekend, Terry's Videos rented 937 movies. This year, the total reached 1,150 movies. Of those, 300 were comedies, 450 were dramas, 100 were musicals, 250 were children's movies, and the rest were martial arts films. Next year, Terry wants to increase movie rentals by another 25%.

1. What is the percentage change from last year to this year?
2. What is the percentage distribution for each movie category?
3. If Terry meets her goal next year, how many movies will be rented?

Coffee Hour

A local coffee shop has announced new hours of operation. Previously, the hours were 7 A.M. to 4 P.M. Monday through Friday and 7 A.M. to noon Saturday and Sunday. The new hours will be 7 A.M. to 7 P.M. Monday through Friday and 7 A.M. to 4 P.M. Saturday and Sunday.

1. What is the increase in total hours open?
2. Assuming that the hourly wage will stay the same (weekly original payroll $385), what will be the total weekly pay under the new hours?
3. What is the percentage increase in total pay?

4

USING ALGEBRAIC EQUATIONS TO SOLVE BUSINESS PROBLEMS
Algebra Basics

Starting Point

Go to www.wiley.com/college/slavin to test your knowledge of the basics of algebra.

Determine where you need to concentrate your effort.

What You'll Learn in This Chapter

▲ The key objective in algebra
▲ How to arrange an equation so that x is alone on one side
▲ How to identify when you've found the answer to an algebra problem

After Studying This Chapter, You'll Be Able To

▲ Isolate x through a variety of means
▲ Solve for x to obtain an answer
▲ Identify the information you're trying to find in a story problem
▲ Set up an equation based on data in a story problem

Goals and Outcomes

▲ Use addition, subtraction, multiplication, and division to isolate x
▲ Understand the procedures for solving for x
▲ Read a story problem and set up an equation that allows you to solve it
▲ Solve problems in which x is a fraction or a decimal.

INTRODUCTION

You need to know only a few basic concepts of algebra to solve business problems, and they're covered in this chapter. This brief study and review of algebra involves one objective: Finding the value of x, which stands for some number you're trying to find. In business math, x can stand for nearly anything, from a company's profits to the interest rate charged on a loan to the percentage of women who occupy positions in upper management at a corporation. If you can isolate x in an equation or a story problem, you can find the number you're looking for.

4.1 Isolating x Using Basic Math

This section describes how to isolate x in the four simplest ways: by using addition, subtraction, division, and multiplication.

4.1.1 Isolating x by Using Addition and Subtraction

One of the universal rules of math is that when you do something to one side of an equation, you must do the same thing to the other side of the equation. If x is on one side of an equation (e.g., $x - 5 = 3$), you can isolate x by adding or subtracting the same number to both sides of the equation. For example,

$$x - 5 = 3$$
$$x - 5 + 5 = 3 + 5$$
$$x = 3 + 5$$
$$x = 8$$

In order to determine whether this is the correct answer, you go back to the original equation and **check** the answer—that is, you substitute the answer, 8, for x, as follows:

$$x - 5 = 3$$
$$8 - 5 = 3$$
$$3 = 3$$

So, it checks.

Let's try another example: If $x - 7 = 9$, how much is x? Here's the solution:

$$x - 7 = 9$$
$$x - 7 + 7 = 9 + 7$$
$$x = 9 + 7$$
$$x = 16$$

Here, we added 7 to both sides. Why are we allowed to do that? The rule is that what we do to one side of the equation, we must to do the other side as well. If it served our purposes in another problem, we could subtract the same number from both sides of an equation.

We found in the last problem that x is 16. Here's how we check that work:

$$x - 7 = 9$$
$$16 - 7 = 9$$
$$9 = 9$$

Here's another problem: If $x - 6 = 11$, how much is x? We find the answer like this:

$$x - 6 = 11$$
$$x - 6 + 6 = 11 + 6$$
$$x = 17$$

If you're not sure whether to add or subtract, keep in mind that you want to isolate x, which means you have to get rid of whatever number is on the same side of the equation as x. If a positive number is on the same side of the equation as x, you subtract that number to get rid of it. Likewise, if a negative number is on the same side of the equation as x, you add that number to get rid of it.

Try these problems:

1. $x - 5 = 16$
2. $x + 8 = 14$
3. $x + 5 = 12$
4. $x - 12 = 21$

Now, try $x + 4 = 2$. Here's how you figure it out:

$$x + 4 = 2$$
$$x + 4 - 4 = 2 - 4$$
$$x = -2$$

Here you do exactly what you did in every preceding problem to isolate x and then find its value. But its value happens to be negative. Sometimes, when you add or subtract, you get a negative value for x. That's perfectly okay because there are plenty of real-world business examples in which x can be negative.

Try solving $x + 9 = -8$ for x. Here's how you figure it out:

$$x + 9 - 9 = -8 - 9$$
$$x = -17$$

FOR EXAMPLE

Negative x

Suppose we are trying to figure out whether Company ABC made a profit or had a loss last year. The total sales for the year were $3 million. Expenses included materials ($1.4 million), payroll ($400,000), advertising and sponsorship ($350,000), legal costs due to a lawsuit ($900,000). We know that a company's profit (or loss) equals sales minus expenses. Because we want to know the profit (or loss), we let x = profit (or loss). Then we set up an equation like this:

$$x = 3,000,000 - (1,400,000 + 400,000 + 350,000 + 900,000)$$
$$x = 3,000,000 - 3,050,000$$
$$x = -50,000$$

The profit (or loss) equals $-$$50,000. In this case, a negative number means a loss because expenses were higher than sales. If the number were positive, the company would have made a profit.

Now let's try a few more problems. First, solve $x - 5 = 16$. Here's how you solve it:

$$x - 5 = 16$$
$$x - 5 + 5 = 16 + 5$$
$$x = 16 + 5$$
$$x = 21$$

Here's how you check it:

$$x - 5 = 16$$
$$21 - 5 = 16$$
$$16 = 16$$

Now try $x + 8 = 14$. Here's the solution:

$$x + 8 = 14$$
$$x + 8 - 8 = 14 - 8$$
$$x = 14 - 8$$
$$x = 6$$

Here's the check:

$$x + 8 = 14$$
$$6 + 8 = 14$$
$$14 = 14$$

Here's another example: $x + 7 = 5$. Here's how you solve it:

$$x + 7 = 5$$
$$x + 7 - 7 = 5 - 7$$
$$x = 5 - 7$$
$$x = -2$$

Here's how you check it:

$$x + 7 = 5$$
$$-2 + 7 = 5$$
$$5 = 5$$

Now try $5 + x = 12$. Here's how you solve it:

$$5 + x = 12$$
$$5 - 5 + x = 12 - 5$$
$$x = 12 - 5$$
$$x = 7$$

Here's how you check it:

$$5 + x = 12$$
$$5 + 7 = 12$$
$$12 = 12$$

Here's another example: $x + 7 = 0$. Here's the solution:

$$x + 7 = 0$$
$$x + 7 - 7 = 0 - 7$$
$$x = 0 - 7$$
$$x = -7$$

And here's the check:

$$x + 7 = 0$$
$$-7 + 7 = 0$$
$$0 = 0$$

Finally, solve $x - 120 = 210$. Here's how you do it:

$$x - 120 = 210$$
$$x - 120 + 120 = 210 + 120$$
$$x = 210 + 120$$
$$x = 330$$

Here's how you check it:

$$x - 120 = 210$$
$$330 - 120 = 210$$
$$210 = 210$$

Try these problems:

1. $x + 7 = 5$
2. $x + 6 = -16$
3. $x + 7 = 0$
4. $x + 4 = -3$

4.1.2 Isolating x by Using Multiplication

Keep in mind the basic algebra principle that what you do to one side of an equation, you must do to the other. In this section, we're going to multiply both sides of an equation by the same number. Take this equation as an example:

$$\frac{x}{2} = 9$$

To isolate x on the left side of the equation, you multiply both sides by 2, as follows:

$$\frac{x}{2} \times 2 = 9 \times 2$$

$$\frac{x}{2^1} \times 2^1 = 9 \times 2$$

$$x = 9 \times 2$$

$$x = 18$$

In order to determine whether this is the correct answer, you go back to the original equation and substitute the answer, 18, for x, as follows:

$$\frac{x}{2} = 9$$

$$\frac{18}{2} = 9$$

$$9 = 9$$

As you can see, it checks.

As with addition and subtraction, with multiplication, you can get negative answers for x. The following problem shows how you isolate x by using multiplication:

$$\frac{x}{4} = -2$$

Here's how you solve it:

$$\frac{x}{4} \times 4 = -2 \times 4$$

$$\frac{x}{4^1} \times 4^1 = -2 \times 4$$

$$x = -2 \times 4$$
$$x = -8$$

Here's how you check your work on this problem:

$$\frac{x}{4} = -2$$

$$\frac{-8}{4} = -2$$

$$-2 = -2$$

Here's another problem:

$$\frac{x}{9} = 435$$

Here's how you solve it:

$$\frac{x}{9} = 435$$

$$\frac{x}{9} \times 9 = 435 \times 9$$

$$\frac{x}{9^1} \times 9^1 = 435 \times 9$$

$$x = 435 \times 9$$

$$x = 3{,}915$$

And here's how you check it:

$$\frac{x}{9} = 435$$

$$\frac{3{,}915}{9} = 435$$

$$435 = 435$$

Try these problems:

1. Find x if $\dfrac{x}{4} = 2$

2. Find x if $\dfrac{x}{3} = 5$

3. Find x if $\dfrac{5x}{4} = 5$

4. Find x if $\dfrac{2x}{5} = 8$

4.1.3 Isolating x by Using Division

Recall that whatever you do to one side of an algebra equation, you must do to the other. You can isolate x in an equation by dividing both sides of an equation such as $2x = 10$ by the same number. Here's how it works:

$$2x = 10$$

$$\frac{2x}{2} = \frac{10}{2}$$

$$x = \frac{10}{2}$$

$$x = 5$$

In order to determine whether this is the correct answer, you go back to the original equation and substitute the answer, 5, for x, as follows:

$$2x = 10$$

$$2(5) = 10$$

$$10 = 10$$

So, it checks.

As another example, solve the problem $5x = 100$. Here's how you do it:

$$\frac{5x}{5} = \frac{100}{5}$$

$$x = \frac{100}{5}$$

$$x = 20$$

And here's how you check it:

$$5x = 100$$

$$5(20) = 100$$

$$100 = 100$$

As with addition, subtraction, and multiplication, with division, you can get a negative value for x. For example, try to solve $6x = -24$. Here's how you do it:

$$\frac{6x}{6} = \frac{-24}{6}$$

$$x = \frac{-24}{6}$$

$$x = -4$$

And here's how you check it:

$$6x = -24$$

$$6(-4) = -24$$

$$-24 = -24$$

Now try some more examples of using division to isolate x. For example, try $800x = 4,000$. Here's how you solve it:

$$\frac{800x}{800} = \frac{4,000}{800}$$

$$x = \frac{4,000}{800}$$

$$x = 5$$

Here's how you check it:

$$800x = 4,000$$

$$500(5) = 4,000$$

$$4,000 = 4,000$$

Finally, try the following:

$$-70x = 560$$

Here's how you solve it:

$$-70x = 560$$

$$\frac{-70x}{-70} = \frac{560}{-70}$$

$$x = \frac{560}{-70}$$

$$x = -8$$

Here's how you check it:

$$-70x = 560$$

$$-70(-8) = 560$$

$$560 = 560$$

4.1.4 Isolating *x* by Combining Addition, Subtraction, Multiplication, and Division

Many algebra problems are more complex than those you've seen so far in this chapter. Here's an example:

$$\frac{3x}{4} + 2 = 11$$

To find x in this case, you need to combine the skills learned in Sections 4.1.1 through 4.1.3. First, you multiply each side by 4:

$$\frac{3x}{4} + 2 = 11$$

$$4 \times \frac{3x}{4} + (4 \times 2) = 11 \times 4$$

$$\cancel{4}^1 \times \frac{3x}{\cancel{4}^1} + 8 = 44$$
$$3x + 8 = 44$$

Then, you subtract 8 from each side:

$$3x + 2 = 44$$
$$3x + 8 - 8 = 44 - 8$$
$$3x = 36$$

Finally, you divide each side by 3:

$$3x = 36$$
$$\frac{3x}{3} = \frac{36}{3}$$
$$x = 12$$

Try another problem:

$$\frac{2x}{5} - 6 = 10$$

To solve it, you first multiply each side by 5:

$$\frac{2x}{5} - 6 = 10$$

$$5 \times \frac{2x}{5} - (5 \times 6) = 10 \times 5$$

$$\cancel{5}^1 \times \frac{2x}{\cancel{5}^1} - 30 = 50$$

$$2x - 30 = 50$$

Then, you add 30 to each side:

$$2x - 30 = 50$$
$$2x - 30 + 30 = 50 + 30$$
$$2x = 80$$

Finally, you divide each side by 2:

$$2x = 80$$
$$\frac{2x}{2} = \frac{80}{2}$$
$$x = 40$$

Now try this problem:

$$\frac{3x}{4} + 3 = 0$$

To solve it, first, you multiply each side by 4:

$$\frac{3x}{4} + 3 = 0$$

$$4 \times \frac{3x}{4} + (4 \times 3) = 0 \times 4$$

$$\cancel{4}^{1} \times \frac{3x}{\cancel{4}^{1}} + 12 = 0$$

$$3x + 12 = 0$$

Then, you subtract 12 from each side:

$$3x + 12 = 0$$
$$3x + 12 - 12 = 0 - 12$$
$$3x = -12$$

Finally, you divide each side by 3:

$$3x = -12$$
$$\frac{3x}{3} = \frac{-12}{3}$$
$$x = -4$$

Try these problems:

1. $\dfrac{2x}{3} - 6 = 8$

2. $\dfrac{9x}{2} + 3 = 39$

3. $\dfrac{2x}{5} - 6 = 4$

4. $\dfrac{7x}{3} + 7 = 0$

4.1.5 Isolating *x* When *x* Is a Fraction or Decimal

Not everything in the business world can be measured solely using whole numbers. That's why we have fractions and decimals. But even when x is a fraction or decimal, you isolate x using addition, subtractions, multiplication, and division, as described in Sections 4.1.1 through 4.1.4. The only difference is that the "answer" (x) is a fraction or decimal.

Here's an example in which x is part of a fraction:

$$\frac{9x}{4} + 7 = -12$$

To solve it, you first multiply each side by 4:

$$\frac{9x}{4} + 7 = -12$$

$$4 \times \frac{9x}{4} + (4 \times 7) = -12 \times 4$$

$$\cancel{4}^1 \times \frac{9x}{\cancel{4}^1} + 28 = -48$$

$$9x + 28 = -48$$

Then, you subtract 28 from each side:

$$9x + 28 = -48$$
$$9x + 28 - 28 = 48 - 28$$
$$9x = -76$$

Finally, you divide each side by 9:

$$9x = -76$$
$$\frac{9x}{9} = \frac{-76}{9}$$
$$x = -8\frac{4}{9}$$

The following example shows how to handle a decimal x:

$$3.5x = 19$$

To solve this problem you divide each side by 3.5:

$$3.5x = 19$$
$$\frac{3.5x}{3.5} = \frac{19}{3.5}$$
$$x = 5.4$$

Try these problems:

1. $\dfrac{7x}{2} - 6 = 3$

2. $\dfrac{2x}{3} + 1 = 4$

3. $\dfrac{7x}{9} - 4 = 12$

4. $\dfrac{4x}{5} + 2 = 0$

5. $4.2x = 15$

6. $0.3x = 7$

7. $14.5x = 29$

SELF-CHECK

- Understand the basic principles of algebra.
- Isolate x in any equation.
- Solve for x by using addition, subtraction, multiplication, or division.
- Find x when it's a fraction or decimal.

4.2 Story Problems: Setting Up Equations to Solve for x

If you know what information you're trying to find, and you call it x, you can set up an equation, substitute numbers into that equation, and then solve for x by using simple arithmetic. For example, say that Kelly is 5 years older than Jason, and the sum of their ages is 21. How old is Kelly, and how old is Jason? To solve this problem, you let Jason's age $= x$ and you let Kelly's age $= x + 5$. Then you set up the following equation:

$$x + x + 5 = 21$$

You solve the equation like this:

$$2x + 5 = 21$$
$$2x + 5 - 5 = 21 - 5$$
$$2x = 16$$
$$x = 8$$
$$x + 5 = 13$$

You find that Jason is 8, and Kelly is 13.

There is another way to set up this equation and get the same answer. First, you can let Kelly's age $= x$ and let Jason's age $= x - 5$. Then you set up the following equation:

$$x + x - 5 = 21$$

You then solve the equation like this:

$$2x - 5 = 21$$
$$2x - 5 + 5 = 21 + 5$$
$$2x = 26$$
$$x = 13$$
$$x - 5 = 8$$

You find that Kelly is 13, and Jason is 8.

Now say that Emma pays twice as much in taxes as Michelle. Michelle pays twice as much in taxes as Ellen. The three of them pay a total of $70,000 in taxes. How much tax does each pay? To solve this problem, you let Ellen's taxes = x, you let Michelle's taxes = $2x$, and you let Emma's taxes = $4x$. So you have the following equation:

$$x + 2x + 4x = \$70,000$$

You solve it like this:

$$7x = \$70,000$$
$$x = \$10,000$$
$$2x = \$20,000$$
$$4x = \$40,000$$

You find that Ellen pays $10,000, Michelle pays $20,000, and Emma pays $40,000.

Now let's work through some more complicated problems. If you use the same process you've been using to set up the equation, isolate x, and then solve for x, these problems will be a breeze.

FOR EXAMPLE

Story-Problem Advice

Some story problems give you word clues that help you set up the equation. Here are some examples:

- *Is* and *are* indicate = .
- *Than* indicates + when preceded by words that imply *bigger*, such as *greater*, *more*, *older*, *larger*, and so on. Sometimes, these words also appear on their own, without *than*.
- *Than* indicates − when preceded by words that imply *smaller*, such as *less*, *younger*, and so on.
- *Of* and *times* (such as "three times") indicate ×.
- *Per* indicates ÷.

Here are some examples:

- Ben is three inches taller than Sherry: Ben = 3 + Sherry
- Bob's mortgage is $200 less than Monica's: Bob's mortgage = Monica's mortgage − $200
- Michael is twice as old as Sheila: Michael = 2 × Sheila
- Ten of the items are defective: Defective = 10 × Items

Say that the James Madison High School orchestra has 40 members. If one-eighth of them are in the percussion section, one-quarter are in the woodwind section, one-quarter are in the string section, and the rest are in the brass section, how many orchestra members play brass instruments? To solve this problem, you let x = the number of brass players. Then you set up the following equation and solve it:

$$x + \frac{1}{8} \times 40 + \frac{1}{4} \times 40 + \frac{1}{4} \times 40 = 40$$

$$x + \frac{40}{8} + \frac{40}{4} + \frac{40}{4} = 40$$

$$x + 5 + 10 + 10 = 40$$

$$x + 25 = 40$$

$$x + 25 - 25 = 40 - 25$$

$$x = 15$$

Now say that the First National Bank of Phoenix has twice as many loans in commercial real estate as in residential real estate. It has half as many business loans as residential real estate loans. If its loans total $700 million, how much of that total is in each category? To solve this problem, you let x = residential real estate loans, you let $2x$ = commercial real estate loans, and you let $[\frac{x}{2}]$ = business loans. Then you set up the following equation and solve it:

$$x + 2x + \frac{x}{2} = \$700{,}000{,}000$$

$$3x + \frac{x}{2} = \$700{,}000{,}000$$

$$\frac{2}{1} \times \frac{3x}{1} + \frac{2^1}{1} \times \frac{x}{2^1} = 2 \times \$700{,}000{,}000$$

$$6x + x = \$14{,}000{,}000{,}000$$

$$7x = \$14{,}000{,}000{,}000$$

$$x = \$200{,}000{,}000$$

$$2x = \$400{,}000{,}000$$

$$\frac{x}{2} = \$100{,}000{,}000$$

If you want to avoid dealing with fractions, you solve the First National Bank problem by letting x = business loans. $2x$ = residential real estate loans, and $4x$ = commercial real estate loans. Then you set up the following equation and solve it:

$$x + 2x + 4x = \$700{,}000{,}000$$

$$7x = \$700{,}000{,}000$$

$$x = \$100,000,000$$
$$2x = \$200,000,000$$
$$4x = \$400,000,000$$

Try several more problems:

1. Sales for the year were $245,000. In the first quarter, sales totaled $74,000; in the second, sales were $82,000; in the third, sales were $53,000. How much were sales in the fourth quarter?
2. Michael is twice as old as Diane and four times as old as Kyra. The sum of their ages is 56. How old is each?
3. Roger earns $50 a week more than Marsha. Eileen earns $40 more than Roger. And Beth earns $30 more than Eileen. The three of them earn a total of $1,060 a week. How much does each of them earn?
4. Max is two times as old as Wendy. Wendy is twice as old as Sue. If the sum of their ages is 140, how old is each?

SELF-CHECK

- Understand that story problems can be solved by using algebraic equations.
- Set up equations using the information given in story problems.
- Solve for x and plug it back into the story problem to get the answer.

SUMMARY

Algebra is a lot easier than it first appears. The trick is to identity what information you're looking for, call it x, and then use basic math to solve for x. This chapter shows you how to isolate x in a variety of ways, even when x is a fraction or decimal, and it even lets you in on the secrets of solving story problems.

KEY TERMS

Check	To substitute the solution into a problem to confirm that the correct answer has been determined.

ASSESS YOUR UNDERSTANDING

Go to www.wiley.com/college/slavin to evaluate your knowledge of the basics of algebra.

Measure your learning by comparing pre-test and post-test results.

Summary Questions

1. To isolate x, you:
   (a) use any means to get x by itself on one side of the equation.
   (b) add or subtract to get x by itself on one side of the equation.
   (c) multiply or divide to get x by itself on one side of the equation.
   (d) all of the above.
2. When x is a fraction, you isolate x by using the same technique as when x is a whole number. True or False?
3. In a story problem, the word *that* indicates an $=$ sign. True or False?
4. The first step in solving a story problem is to:
   (a) set up an equation.
   (b) solve for x.
   (c) identify the information you're trying to find.
   (d) none of the above.

Review Questions

1. Solve for x in each of these problems:
   (a) $4x = 20$
   (b) $8x = 56$
2. Solve for x in each of the following:
   (a) $\dfrac{x}{2} = 10$
   (b) $\dfrac{5x}{9} + 4 = 2$
   (c) $\dfrac{2x}{3} + 1 = 4$
   (d) $\dfrac{3x}{7} + 5 = 6$

Applying This Chapter

1. Solve for x for each of the following:

    (a) $\dfrac{3x}{7} + 5 = -6$

    (b) $\dfrac{7x}{9} - 4 = 12$

2. Solve for x in each of the following:

    (a) $0.8x = 14$

    (b) $.7x = 12$

    (c) $11.8x = 18$

3. Mr. Wong earns twice as much as Ms. Kerenski and five times as much as Mr. Mostelli. If their combined incomes total $340,000, how much does each person earn?

4. Bob is three years older than Harvey. Harvey is twice George's age. Mel is four years younger than George. The sum of their ages is 29. How old is each?

5. North Carolina has three times the population of Utah and twice the population of Oregon. Arkansas has 1 million people fewer than Oregon. If the total population of these four states is 27 million, how many people live in each state?

6. The XYZ Corporation is owned by four people, who hold a total of 3,500 shares. Mike holds 100 more shares than Sue and 200 fewer than Joe. Stu holds twice as many shares as Joe. How many shares does each person hold?

7. In September, Sally earned twice as much in commission as Alice. Alice earned $100 more than Joan. Joan earned $300 less than Robin. These four people earned a total of $4,600 in commissions. How much did each person earn?

YOU TRY IT

Figuring Acres

Three brothers and a sister together own a total of 1,800 acres for farming. Alan owns three times as much land as Bob, who lives next door. Bob owns twice as much as Calvin. Denise owns 100 acres more than Alan. How many acres does each sibling own?

GGG Corporation

One out of 20 employees at employee-owned GGG Corporation has an advanced degree. In addition, 1 out of 10 is a college graduate, 2 in 10 have had some college, and 3 out of 10 are high school graduates. There are 175 other employees without high school diplomas.

1. How many employees does the company have?
2. How many employees have advanced degrees?
3. How many employees have college degrees?
4. How many employees have had some college?
5. How many employees are high school graduates?

Trading Corporation

Rico owns 10% of the Bangor Trading Corporation, Astrid owns 15%, Pei owns 35%, and Nils owns the rest. If each shares the profits in proportion to his or her percentage of the ownership, how would they split $400,000 in profits?

First National Bank of Akron

The First National Bank of Akron had deposits of $100 million greater than those of the First National Bank of Toledo. The First National Bank of Toledo had deposits of $200 million greater than those of the First National Bank of Canton. The deposits of these four banks totaled $1 billion (i.e., one thousand million). What were the deposits of each bank?

5

MARKUP, MARKDOWN, AND INVENTORY MANAGEMENT
The Key to High Profits

Starting Point

Go to www.wiley.com/college/slavin to assess your knowledge of the basics of markup, markdown, and inventory management.
Determine where you need to concentrate your effort.

What You'll Learn in This Chapter

▲ How and why retail stores mark up their inventory
▲ Why stores sometimes need to mark down merchandise
▲ How to determine the value of inventory
▲ How inventory turnover affects profitability

After Studying This Chapter, You'll Be Able To

▲ Practice setting retail prices through markups
▲ Compute multiple markdowns correctly
▲ Demonstrate various methods for valuing inventory
▲ Calculate inventory turns

Goals and Outcomes

▲ Master the terminology and recognize the tools of inventory management
▲ Understand the implications of markups and markdowns
▲ Identify why inventory management is critical to the success of retail businesses
▲ Use inventory evaluation tools and techniques

INTRODUCTION

Retail selling is all about managing inventory. Buy too much inventory or too much of the wrong inventory, and you have tied up money that could be spent on other business expenses and will likely lose money. Buy too little inventory or too little of hot-selling merchandise, and you lose opportunities to make money. Tracking inventory is critical to the success of a retail business. This chapter shows how inventory is marked up, marked down, and evaluated. Retail stores buy up merchandise to sell, try to sell it for a profit, and sometimes sell it at a loss in order to make way for more merchandise. The key is to manage inventory, buying neither too much nor too little and marking up and marking down prices in a way that leads to high profits.

5.1 Markup

When a store buys merchandise at one price and sells it at a higher price, the store has marked up the price of those goods. The **markup** on merchandise may be 50%, 100%, 200%, or even more, which can make consumers feel as though they're being ripped off. But stores have many other costs besides paying for the merchandise they sell or the service they provide, including rent or mortgage payments, utilities, salaries, advertising, insurance, and taxes. In general, retailing is extremely competitive, so few stores can make huge profits by overpricing.

There are two main ways to mark up merchandise: based on cost and based on selling price.

5.1.1 Markup Based on Cost

A store owner must charge a price high enough not only to cover cost but also to make a profit. A store owner needs to mark up what he or she sells well above cost in order to cover operating costs. For instance, if a store owner purchased inventory for $100,000, he or she might need to sell it for $150,000 just to cover the $50,000 it costs to run the store for a few months, considering rent, salaries, utilities, and other operating costs.

Marking up products based on cost is the most commonly used form of markup. (Markup can also be based on selling price, as discussed in Section 5.1.2.) **Cost** is the amount paid for goods, and **selling price** is the amount the seller sells it for (i.e., the cost of the item or service plus a profit margin). The two are related in this way:

$$\text{Cost} + \text{Dollar markup} = \text{Selling price}$$

You can think of cost as being 100%; markup as being, say, 50%; and selling price as being 150%. Or, if markup were 40%, then selling price would be 140%.

If selling price were 140%, then it would be 140% of cost. And if selling price happened to be 150%, then it would be 150% of cost.

Here's an example: Marcus sells MP3 players. He received a shipment in which each unit cost him $120 each. If he marks them up by 50%, what is the selling price? You figure it out like this:

$$\text{Cost} + \text{Dollar markup} = \text{Selling price}$$
$$\$120 + (\$120 \times 0.5) = \text{Selling price}$$
$$\$120 + \$60 = \text{Selling price}$$
$$\$180 = \text{Selling price}$$

Many retailers get to decide what the selling prices for their items will be. For some items and some retailers, however, the selling price is marked on the item (e.g., books), which means retailers have little choice in how to price their items. If a bookseller buys a paperback book for $4 and the book is labeled with a selling price of $6.99, how much is the dollar markup? Here's how you figure it out:

$$\text{Cost} + \text{Dollar markup} = \text{Selling price}$$
$$\$4 + \text{Dollar markup} = \$6.99$$
$$\text{Dollar markup} = \$6.99 - \$4$$
$$\text{Dollar markup} = \$2.99$$

Therefore, the markup percentage is as follows:

$$\text{Cost} + \text{Markup} = \text{Selling price}$$
$$100\% + \text{Markup} = 250\%$$
$$\text{Markup} = 150\%$$

You've learned how to find selling price and how to find dollar markup. You can also use the markup equation to find cost. For example, Tyra is a florist who marks up her tulips 50% and sells them for $20 per dozen. How much do they cost her? Here's how you figure it out:

$$\text{Cost} + \text{Dollar markup} = \text{Selling price}$$
$$\text{Cost} + 50\% \text{ (of cost)} = \$20$$
$$100\% \text{ (of cost)} + 50\% \text{ (of cost)} = \$20$$
$$150\% \text{ (of cost)} = \$20$$
$$1.5 \times \text{Cost} = \$20$$
$$\text{Cost} = \$20 \div 1.5$$
$$\text{Cost} = \$13.33$$

Try these problems:

1. Betty Lou Dorr has a boutique. She marks up her clothing by 120%. How much do the dresses she sells for $100 cost her?

2. Alice Blythe marks up the stereo equipment she sells by 60%. If a set of speakers costs her $140, what does she charge for them?

3. Gomez Appliances buys lawn mowers for $120 and sells them for $199. What is the dollar markup, and what is the markup as a percentage of selling price?

5.1.2 Markup Based on Selling Price

More and more companies are starting to base their markup on a percentage of selling price instead of basing it only on cost. In Section 5.1.1, you learned that when you know cost and markup, you can find selling price. And when you know markup and selling price, you can find cost. Finally, when you knew cost and selling price, you can find markup. Although the markup concept is the same whether it is based on cost or selling price, you need three different equations to find the variable with markup based on selling price.

If you know the markup in dollars and the selling price and you want to find the markup percentage, you use this formula:

$$\text{Dollar markup} \div \text{Selling price} = \text{Percentage markup}$$

Suppose that the dollar markup is $3 and the selling price is $4. How much is the percentage markup? Here's how you figure it out:

$$\text{Dollar markup} \div \text{Selling price} = \text{Percentage markup}$$
$$\$3 \div \$4 = \text{Percentage markup}$$
$$0.75 = 75\% = \text{Percentage markup}$$

Consider the book example from the Section 5.1.1: You know the cost and the selling price, and you want to calculate the percentage markup based on selling price. You use the same formula in this situation, but first you have to find the dollar markup. Here's how you do it:

$$\text{Dollar markup} = \text{Selling price} - \text{Cost}$$
$$\text{Dollar markup} = \$6.99 - \$4$$
$$\text{Dollar markup} = \$2.99$$
$$\text{Percentage markup} = \text{Dollar markup} \div \text{Selling price}$$
$$\text{Percentage markup} = \$2.99 \div \$6.99$$
$$\text{Percentage markup} = .4278, \text{ or } 42.78\%$$

If you know the selling price and the percentage markup, you can find the dollar markup by using this equation:

$$\text{Selling price} \times \text{Percentage markup} = \text{Dollar markup}$$

Suppose the selling price is $50 and the markup is 20%. To find the dollar markup, you do this:

$$\text{Selling price} \times \text{Percentage markup} = \text{Dollar markup}$$
$$\$50 \times 0.2 = \text{Dollar markup}$$
$$\$10 = \text{Dollar markup}$$

Finally, if you know the selling price and the dollar markup, you can find the cost. Here's how:

$$\text{Selling price} - \text{Dollar markup} = \text{Cost}$$

If the selling price is $170 and the dollar markup is $40, what is the cost? Here's how you find it:

$$\text{Cost} = \text{Selling price} - \text{Dollar markup}$$
$$\text{Cost} = \$170 - \$40$$
$$\text{Cost} = \$130$$

Try these examples:

1. If the selling price is $20 and the dollar markup is $8, how much is the markup percentage?
2. The selling price is $130 and the dollar markup is $35. How much is the cost?
3. What is the cost if the markup is 60% of the selling price and if the selling price is $150?
4. If the selling price is $2,000 and the markup is 35%, find the dollar markup.

5.1.3 Markup Based on Cost vs. Markup Based on Selling Price

Are the two markups—markup based on cost and markup based on selling price—the same? No. But how are they different? That's a good question. To answer it, think about which is larger: a 20% markup on cost or a 20% markup on selling price?

Suppose a used Mini Cooper costs the dealer $10,000. How much is a 20% markup on cost? It's $2,000. So, what is the car's selling price? It's $12,000. Now, how much is a 20% markup on selling price if the selling price is $12,000. It's $2,400. So for a used Mini that sells for $12,000, a 20% markup on cost would be $2,000, but a 20% markup on selling price would be $2,400.

Here's an example that correlates the two types of markup: A pair of embroidered jeans costs a store $60. How much would the jeans sell for if the store used a cost-based markup of 40%? And how much would the store charge if it had a 40% selling price–based markup? To figure out how much the jeans would sell for if the store used a cost-based markup of 40%, you use the following equation:

$$\text{Cost} + \text{Dollar markup} = \text{Selling price}$$
$$\$60 + (\$60 \times 0.4) = \text{Selling price}$$

$$\$60 + \$24 = \text{Selling price}$$
$$\$84 = \text{Selling price}$$

To figure out how much would the store charge if it had a 40% selling price–based markup, you do the following:

$$\text{Selling price} - \text{Dollar markup} = \text{Cost}$$
$$\text{Selling price} - 0.4 \times \text{Selling price} = \$60$$
$$0.6 \times \text{Selling price} = \$60$$
$$\text{Selling price} = \$60 \div 0.6$$
$$\text{Selling price} = \$100$$

Here's another example: A microwave costs Sears \$160. How much would Sears charge if it used a selling-price–based markup of 50%? You figure it out like this:

$$\text{Selling price} - \text{Markup based on selling price} = \text{Cost}$$
$$\text{Selling price} - .5 \times \text{selling price} = \$160$$
$$.5 \times \text{selling price} = \$160$$
$$\text{Selling price} = \$160 \div .5$$
$$\text{Selling price} = \$320$$

FOR EXAMPLE

Cost Plus

Here's a real-life example that involves calculating both markup and cost: The manager of a running-shoe store decided to sponsor a racing team in order to better advertise his products. The manager recruited successful local runners to wear a team uniform that featured the store logo. Team members were offered three rewards for running on the team: a \$100 gift certificate once every year, free entry fees to all local road races, and all Nike shoes for 20% above cost. The store's markup, which is based on selling price, is 55%. If a member of the racing team goes to the store and wants to purchase an \$80 pair of Nike shoes, how much will she pay? To solve this problem, you first determine the store's markup on the shoes:

$$\text{Dollar markup} = \text{Selling price} \times \text{Percentage markup}$$
$$\text{Dollar markup} = \$80 \times 55\% = \$44$$

Then you determine the cost:

$$\text{Cost} = \text{Selling price} - \text{Markup}$$
$$\text{Cost} = \$80 - \$44 = \$36$$

If team members pay 20% above cost, they pay $\$36 + (\$36 \times 0.20) = \$36 + \$7.20 = \$43.20$. That's a pretty good deal for \$80 shoes!

Try these problems:

1. Tong sells kitchen sets that cost him $350. How much does he charge if he uses a selling price–based markup of 70%?
2. The Gap sets a 60% selling price–based markup on its jeans. If a pair of jeans costs the Gap $19, how much does it charge?

SELF-CHECK

- Define the terms **markup, cost,** and **selling price.**
- Describe the difference between dollar markup and percentage markup.
- Calculate markup, cost, and selling price when given certain information.

5.2 Markdown

Who can resist a bargain? Imagine a store offering **markdowns** (i.e., discounts) of 50%, 60%, or even 70%. Some markdowns! Usually, you see markdowns like this when a store is going out of business, when it's trying to get rid of fashionable clothes or shoes at the end of a season, when it's selling perishable items that are near or at their expiration date, or when it's selling items that are just not catching on with buyers. Occasionally, stores deeply discount a few items—and plan to lose money on those items—in order to get you into the store and, potentially, buy other items, as well. These items are called **loss leaders.**

The markdown equation is similar to the markup equations:

$$\text{Sale price} + \text{Markdown} = \text{Original price}$$

Suppose Roxanne's Camera Shop is having a clearance sale on all non-digital cameras, offering a 40% discount. If you go to the clearance sale and buy a camera for $160, what was its price before the sale? You figure it out like this:

$$\text{Sale price} + \text{Markdown} = \text{Original price}$$
$$\$160 + (0.40 \times \text{Original price}) = \text{Original price}$$
$$\$160 = 0.6 \times \text{Original price}$$
$$\$160 \div 0.6 = \text{Original price}$$
$$\$267 = \text{Original price}$$

Here's another example: A camera is marked down from $500 to $350. How much is the markdown amount and what is the markdown percentage?

Markdown amount = \$500 − \$350 = \$150

$$\text{Markdown \%} = \frac{\text{Markdown}}{\text{Original price}} = \frac{\$150}{\$500} = 30\%$$

Finally, some items are subject to **multiple markdowns.** For example, an air conditioner was selling for \$400 in April. In August, the store marked it down by 20%. In September, it was marked down an additional 20% from its sale price. How much was is selling for in September? You figure it out like this:

Original price − Markdown = Intermediate price

\$400 − (\$400 × 0.2) = Intermediate price

\$400 − \$80 = Intermediate price

\$320 = Intermediate price

Intermediate price − Markdown = Current price

\$320 − (\$320 × 0.2) = Current price

\$320 − \$64 = Current price

\$256 = Current price

Here's another example of multiple markdowns: A store marks down a flat-screen television by 25% from its original price of \$1,000. The television is then marked down two more times, first by an additional 25% and then by another 10%. What is the current price? Here's how you figure it out:

Original price − Markdown = First intermediate price

\$1,000 − (\$1,000 × 0.25) = First intermediate price

\$1,000 − \$250 = First intermediate price

\$750 = First intermediate price

First intermediate price − Markdown = Second intermediate price

\$750 − (\$750 × 0.25) = Second intermediate price

\$750 − \$187.50 = Second intermediate price

\$562.50 = Second intermediate price

Second intermediate price − Markdown = Current price

\$562.50 − (\$562.50 × 0.1) = Current price

\$562.50 − \$56.25 = Current price

\$506.25 = Current price

Try the following problems:

1. The Main Street gift shop has marked down its stuffed animals by 30%. If you bought a stuffed bear for \$14, what was its price before the sale?
2. A lawn mower is marked down from \$259 to \$199. How much is the markdown amount, and what is the markdown percentage?

FOR EXAMPLE

Figuring Multiple Discounts Correctly

Many consumers make the mistake of adding up all the multiple discounts on an item instead of figuring each discount off the previously discounted price. For example, if an item was first marked 40% off and then discounted another 30%, and then discounted a final 10%, some consumers believe the item will be 80% off. Not so. If the item cost $100, an 80% discount would be an $80 discount, making the item cost just $20. Instead, the first discount is $40 off, getting the cost down to $60. The second discount is $18 off, bringing the price to $42. The final discount is another $4.20 off, making the price $37.80. This makes the cumulative discount 62.2%, not 80%.

3. Cheryl's Beauty Supply has marked down its shampoos by 35%. If you bought a bottle of shampoo for $3.25, what was its price before the sale?
4. A shirt is marked down from $69.95 by 20%, then an additional 20%, and then 15% more. What is its current price?

SELF-CHECK

- Define **markdown**.
- Describe why stores offer substantial discounts to their customers.
- Discuss the idea of a loss leader to get customers into a store.
- Calculate multiple markdowns.

5.3 Taking Inventory

Almost every retail business carries a stock of inventory on its shelves and maybe also in a warehouse. Too little inventory makes for bad business because customers can't purchase the items they want. On the other hand, the more inventory a store carries, the more it costs the store. As a store owner, you might have tens or even hundreds of thousands of dollars tied up in inventory, not to mention all that valuable shelf space that's being used. Business owners need to find a balance, so they keep track of their inventories closely.

In this section, we focus on the three methods of inventory evaluation—weighted average, FIFO, and LIFO—as well as how to measure inventory turnover.

5.3.1 The Weighted Average Inventory Method of Taking Inventory

When businesses sell merchandise, they know exactly how much they charged for each unit. But they may have been holding some of their inventory for months before selling it, and might have, for example, bought some of the inventory in August for one price, in May for a different price, and in January for a third price. This can mean that identical items in inventory may have been purchased at different prices. This is especially true in a period of high inflation or if inventory was purchased from different suppliers. How do you place a value on such an inventory?

The **weighted average** method of inventory evaluation is calculated like so:

Step 1: Multiply the price per item by the quantity purchased for each purchase.

Step 2: Add the total of inventory purchases.

Step 3: Determine the number of items in the inventory.

Step 4: Divide the total of all purchases by the number of items in the inventory.

This is very much like figuring a grade point average. Suppose you took a four-credit-hour course and two three-credit-hour courses. You would multiply your grade in the four-credit-hour course by 4 and your grades in the three-credit-hour courses by 3. Then, after adding up these three products, you would divide that number by 10, which is the total number of credits. In the same way, using the weighted average inventory method, you multiply the cost of the inventory by the number of items purchased on that date. Then you add the total costs of inventory purchases and divide by the total number of units purchased.

Suppose that in September, a firm sold off some inventory that it had purchased in January, May, and August. Suppose the firm bought 100 units on January 1 at a cost of $2.50 each, 200 units on May 4 at a cost of $2.60 each, and 50 units on August 23 at a cost of $2.65 each. Suppose also that the firm sold those 350 units by September 6. First, you find the total cost for each set of units and then you add them all together, like this:

Date	Units	Cost	Total Cost
1/1	100	$2.50	$250.00
5/4	200	$2.60	$520.00
8/23	50	$2.65	$132.50
	350		$902.50

Then you find the average cost per unit, like this:

$$\text{Average cost} = \frac{\$902.50}{350} = \$2.58$$

Consider another example: NCD Corporation purchased 8 Serotta road bikes on June 15 at a cost of $8,365 each, 11 more on June 29 at a cost of $8,433 each, 9 more on July 3 at a cost of $8,509 each, and 15 more on July 29 at a cost of $8,531 each. What's the average cost of this inventory of bikes? First, you find the total cost for each set of bikes and then you add them all together, like this:

Date	Units	Cost	Total Cost
6/15	8	$8,365	$66,920
6/29	11	$8,433	$92,763
7/3	9	$8,509	$76,581
7/29	15	$8,531	$127,965
	43		$364,229

Then you find the average cost per bike, like this:

$$\text{Average cost} = \frac{\$364,229}{43} = \$8,470.44$$

5.3.2 The FIFO Inventory Evaluation Method of Taking Inventory

The **FIFO** (or first-in, first-out) inventory evaluation method makes two basic assumptions: (1) the oldest inventory is sold first, and (2) the current inventory is what was acquired most recently. You see the FIFO method of stocking inventory most often when buying perishable items, such as milk. The supermarket shelves are stacked such that newer milk is placed at the back of the case and older milk is place in the front. But other retailers use this method because using the FIFO inventory evaluation method is a very accurate means of determining how much the inventory is actually worth. Here's how it works:

Step 1: Determine which items are in the ending inventory by counting backward. If you have 10 items in ending inventory and your last purchase was 12 items, all the ending inventory comes from the last purchase. If you have 20 items in ending inventory and the last two purchases were 12 items and 10 items, you know that 12 items in ending inventory came from the last purchase, and 8 items in ending inventory came from the second-to-last purchase.

Step 2: Multiply the cost per item by the number of items and then sum to get the cost of ending inventory. If the last purchase cost $2 per item and 12 items came from the last purchase, that's worth $24. If the second-to-last purchase cost $1.50 per item, and 8 items came from that purchase, that's $12. Together, that's $36 as a total cost for ending inventory.

Step 3: Find the cost of goods sold by subtracting the value of the ending inventory from the cost of goods available for sale:

Cost of goods sold = Cost of goods available for sale − Ending inventory

Suppose the Life Is Good store has 36 ski hats in inventory as of March 1. Each of those hats had a cost of $10 each. On Mary 6, the store purchased 17 more hats at a cost of $8 each. On April 26, the store bought 19 more at $7 each. And on May 19, it purchased 23 more at $9 each. As of June 1, all told, 95 hats were available for sale, and 52 had been sold. This means there were 95 − 52 = 43 hats in ending inventory on June 1. If the store is following the FIFO method, those 43 hats must have come from the last three shipments: 23 from the May shipment, 19 from the April shipment, and 1 from the March shipment. That's step 1. For step 2, you total up the costs this way:

Date	Units	Cost	Total Cost	Ending Inventory
Beginning inventory	36	$10	$360	
3/6	17	$8	$136	1 × $8 = $8
4/26	19	$7	$133	19 × $7 = $133
5/19	23	$9	$207	23 × $9 = $207
	95		$836	43 items = $348

For Step 3, you find the cost of goods sold:

Cost of goods sold = Cost of goods available for sale − Ending inventory

Cost of goods sold = $836 − $348

Cost of goods sold = $488

5.3.3 The LIFO Inventory Evaluation Method of Taking Inventory

The **LIFO** (or last-in, first-out) inventory evaluation method makes the opposite assumption from the FIFO method. The two basic assumptions of LIFO are (1) the newest inventory is sold first, and (2) the current inventory was acquired earliest. Therefore, the cost of the ending inventory is based on the cost of the oldest stock.

You might be wondering why anyone would use this method, given that older milk, bikes, and hats would be getting moldy in the stockroom (or worse) while brand-new items are sold in stores. Keep in mind that a company doesn't *actually* have to stock items in the LIFO method; it simply has to declare to the IRS that it's using the LIFO method. And there is a great tax advantage to LIFO. Assuming that newer (and generally higher-costing) inventory is sold first raises the costs of the firm. The higher the costs, the lower the profits. And the lower the profits, the lower the taxes the firm will have to pay.

You use exactly the same steps in determining the costs of goods sold with the LIFO method as with FIFO, except that your remaining inventory is the old goods, not the new goods.

Here's an example: Circuit City has a beginning inventory of 78 earbuds for iPods, which cost $12 each. On July 15, the store received 50 more at $11 each. On August 1, it bought 32 more at $10 each. And on September 22, it purchased 41 more at $13 each. By October 1, Circuit City had sold 142 earbuds. Using the LIFO method, what's the cost of goods sold? If 142 of 201 units sold, ending inventory must be 59 units. Using the LIFO method, you would take all those out of beginning inventory, like this:

Date	Units	Cost	Total Cost	Ending Inventory
Beginning inventory	78	$12	$936	59 × $12 = $708
7/15	50	$11	$550	
8/1	32	$10	$320	
9/22	41	$13	$533	
	201		$2,339	59 item = $708

For Step 3, you find the cost of goods sold:

Cost of goods sold = Cost of goods available for sale − Ending inventory

Cost of goods sold = $2,339 − $708

Cost of goods sold = $1,631

5.3.4 Measuring Inventory Turnover

Carrying inventory is a major business expense, totaling tens (or even hundreds) of thousands of dollars for even small retail outlets. But carrying inventory is necessary for a successful retail operation. The trick is to move inventory as fast as possible: The faster a company can move its inventory, the more money it makes. Grocery stores usually have very high inventory turnover, whereas stores that sell consumer electronics, clothing, home furnishings, hardware, and appliances all have relatively low turnover rates.

Inventory turnover is the number of times a business firm replaces its inventory over a specific period of time. Two different rates can be calculated: (1) inventory turnover at retail and (2) inventory turnover at cost. To find inventory turnover at retail, you use the following formula:

$$\text{Inventory turnover at retail} = \frac{\text{Net sales}}{\text{Average inventory at retail}}$$

Consider a company that has the following inventory and sales figures:

Net sales	$117,400
Beginning inventory at retail	$62,000
Ending inventory at retail	$53,900
Cost of goods sold	$66,500
Beginning inventory (at cost)	$35,400
Ending inventory (at cost)	$30,500

First, you need to find the average inventory at retail:

$$\text{Average inventory} = \frac{\text{Beginning inventory} + \text{Ending inventory}}{2}$$

$$\text{Average inventory} = \frac{\$35,400 + 30,500}{2} = \frac{\$65,900}{2} = \$32,950$$

$$\text{Inventory turnover} = \frac{\text{Cost of goods sold}}{\text{Average inventory}}$$

$$\text{Inventory turnover} = \frac{\$66,500}{\$32,950} = 2.01$$

You use the same numbers to find the inventory turnover at cost. First, you find the average inventory at cost:

$$\text{Average inventory at cost} = \frac{\text{Beginning inventory} + \text{Ending inventory}}{2}$$

$$\text{Average inventory} = \frac{\$35,400 + 30,500}{2} = \frac{\$65,900}{2} = \$32,950$$

$$\text{Inventory turnover at cost} = \frac{\text{Net sales}}{\text{Average inventory at cost}}$$

$$\text{Inventory turnover} = \frac{\$117,400}{\$32,950} = 3.56$$

This means that the inventory cycles (i.e., is brought in as inventory and goes out to customers as sales) just over three times per year.

FOR EXAMPLE

Turns per Year

Most companies aim for 5 or 6 inventory turns per year. If you have low-cost items with little profit per item (trinkets, food items, and so on), you probably need more turns than that. For high-cost, low-volume, high-profit items (cars, boats, and the like), you can have fewer inventory turns. But at an average, you should aim for 5 or 6. Keep in mind, however, that a turnover rate of 5 or 6 doesn't mean that every item in a store will turn over 5 or 6 times per year because the rate is an average. Some items—usually very popular ones (e.g., best-selling books)—turn very quickly (maybe 10, 20, or even 30 times per year while the item is hot), whereas other items (e.g., copies of *The Catcher in the Rye*) are important to keep in inventory but may turn over only 1 or 2 times per year.

Try the following yourself. Using the following numbers, find inventory turnover at retail and inventory turnover at cost:

Net sales	$60,600
Beginning inventory at retail	$53,400
Ending inventory at retail	$58,700
Cost of goods sold	$41,600
Beginning inventory (at cost)	$36,800
Ending inventory (at cost)	$40,000

SELF-CHECK

- Define **weighted average method, FIFO inventory evaluation method, LIFO inventory evaluation method, inventory turnover.**
- Describe the various methods of measuring inventory.
- Discuss how to measure inventory turnover.

SUMMARY

Retail businesses focus heavily on inventory. The inventory they purchase must be marked up in order to cover their costs of doing business. The inventory in their stores must sometimes be marked down in order to make way for new merchandise. Inventory must also be measured and tracked so that store owners and managers know how much they have invested in inventory.

KEY TERMS

Cost	The amount a store pays to purchase an item.
FIFO	Stands for "first in, first out." An inventory evaluation method that is based on the assumption that (1) the oldest inventory is sold first, and (2) the current inventory is what was acquired most recently.
Inventory turnover	The number of times a company's inventory turns over in a year.
LIFO	Stands for "last in, first out." An inventory method that is based on the assumption that (1) the newest inventory is sold first, and (2) the current inventory was acquired earliest. Therefore, the cost of the ending inventory is based on the cost of the oldest stock.
Loss leader	An item that is heavily marked down in order to draw customers to a store.
Markup	The selling price of an item minus its cost. Markup can be measured in percentage or in dollars.
Markdown	The percentage of the original selling price by which a discounted selling price is reduced.
Multiple markdowns	Additional markdowns, in addition to the original markdown.
Selling price	The amount a store charges customers to buy an item, which is typically the cost of that item or service plus a profit margin.
Weighted average inventory evaluation	A method of calculating the value of identical items in an inventory that may have been purchased at different prices over the course of time.

ASSESS YOUR UNDERSTANDING

Go to www.wiley.com/college/slavin to evaluate your knowledge of markup, markdown, and inventory management.
Measure your learning by comparing pre-test and post-test results.

Summary Questions

1. Companies mark up their inventory to cover the cost of utilities and other expenses. True or False?
2. Multiple markdowns can be estimated by totaling all the percentage markdowns and multiplying that total by the original price. True or False?
3. The FIFO method of inventory evaluation:
   (a) averages out all the inventory, over time.
   (b) assumes that the current inventory is the latest inventory purchased.
   (c) assumes that the current inventory is the earliest inventory purchased.
   (d) all of above.
4. Define **turnover**.

Review Questions

1. Why do some retail stores, such as bookstores, have less control over markup than other stores?
2. In what instances do stores need to mark down their items?
3. In what situations is a turnover rate of one or two considered profitable?

Applying This Chapter

1. Johnson & Johnson sells aspirin to drug wholesalers at a 500% markup. If Johnson & Johnson receives $1 a bottle, how much does it cost the company to produce a bottle of aspirin?
2. Susie Wong sells world atlases. If she marks them up by 40% and they cost her $22, how much does she charge for them?
3. Chuck Stickney has a sandwich shop. If it costs him 80 cents to make a tuna sub, and he sells it for $2.25, what percentage is his markup?
4. If the selling price of an item is $195 and the dollar markup is $53, what is the cost?
5. If the selling price of an item is $65 and the dollar markup is $12, how much is the markup percentage?

6. If the selling price of an item is $550 and the markup is 40%, what is the dollar markup?

7. What is the cost if the markup is 40% of the selling price and if the selling price is $240?

8. A beach chair is marked down from $39.99 by 20% and then by another 15%. What is the current price of the chair?

9. A sport jacket is marked down from $119.95 by 25%, then 20%, and then another 20%. What is its current price?

10. A company has the following figures:

Net sales	$17,300
Beginning inventory at retail	$12,500
Ending inventory at retail	$13,000
Cost of goods sold	$9,100
Beginning inventory (at cost)	$6,900
Ending inventory (at cost)	$73,000

Find

(a) inventory turnover at retail.

(b) inventory turnover at cost.

11. A company has the following figures:

Net sales	$175,600
Beginning inventory at retail	$214,700
Ending inventory at retail	$202,400
Cost of goods sold	$101,900
Beginning inventory (at cost)	$122,800
Ending inventory (at cost)	$113,700

Find

(a) inventory turnover at retail.

(b) inventory turnover at cost.

InStyle Fashion

InStyle Fashion Store is excited about a fashion trend from the 1980s that is sure to be a big hit again: leg warmers. The store buyer purchases 300 pairs in October at $19.99 each and plans to mark them up 55%. In late December, 267 pairs still sit in inventory, so the manager marks them down 30%. A month later, with 127 pairs still in stock, they're marked down an additional 20%. Finally, at the beginning of March, they're marked down an additional 15%. All the leg warmers sell.

1. What was the original retail price?
2. What was the final markdown price?
3. Were the leg warmers a good investment for the company?

SFW Appliance Store

A low-end DVD recorder costs the SFW Appliance Store $140.

1. How much would SFW charge for the DVD recorder if it used a cost-based markup of 80%?
2. How much would SFW charge for the DVD recorder if it used an 80% selling price–based markup?

Markdown

At the end of the winter season, a fleece jacket is marked down from $69.95 by 20%, then an additional 20%, and then 15% more.

1. What is its current price?
2. Why doesn't the store just sell the jacket for 65% off the original price?

Sales Data

Consider the following sales data for a retail store:

Date	Units Purchased	Cost per Unit	Total Cost
Beginning inventory	216	$190	$41,040
5/10	173	$177	$30,621
7/1	156	$173	$26,988
9/29	180	$181	$32,580
	725		$131,229

As of October 1, a total of 519 units had sold.

1. Find the cost of goods sold, using the FIFO method.
2. Determine the inventory turnover.

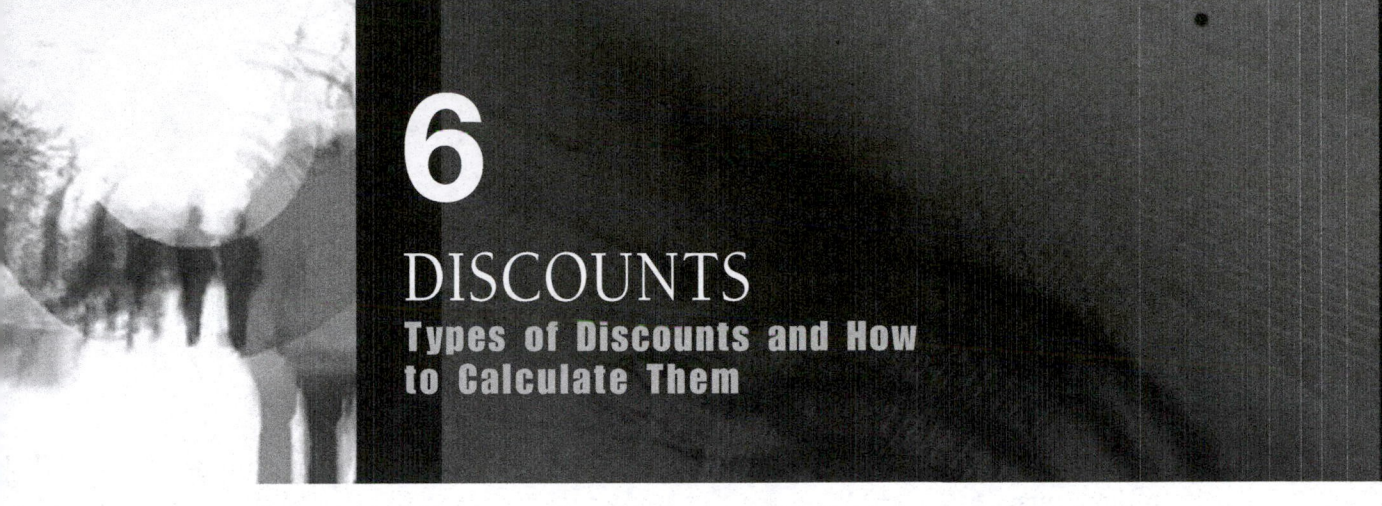

6

DISCOUNTS
Types of Discounts and How to Calculate Them

Starting Point

Go to www.wiley.com/college/slavin to assess your knowledge of the basics of discounts.
Determine where you need to concentrate your effort.

What You'll Learn in This Chapter

▲ What discounts are offered to customers buying in large quantities, called quantity discounts or trade discounts
▲ What discounts are given to retailers, which are also types of trade discounts
▲ What additional discounts (chain discounts) are offered to chain retailers
▲ The three types of cash discounts

After Studying This Chapter, You'll Be Able To

▲ Practice figuring simple quantity discounts
▲ Solve problems that involve retailers' discounts
▲ Calculate multiple discounts
▲ Apply various types of cash discounts

Goals and Outcomes

▲ Master the terminology of business discounts
▲ Compare various discount options available to suppliers
▲ Choose which day to pay an invoice that offers a cash discount

INTRODUCTION

Suppliers offer various types of discounts. Quantity discounts are offered to customers who order large quantities of goods. Retail discounts are given to retail stores that buy wholesale items and resell them at a retail price. Chain discounts are offered to retail outlets that order large quantities, and they include both a retail discount and a quantity discount. Cash discounts are offered to customers who pay their bills by a preset deadline. This chapter discusses the types of discounts available and also reveals how to calculate those discounts.

6.1 Quantity Discounts (Trade Discounts)

Because of shipping and handling costs, most suppliers offer **quantity discounts** to customers who buy in large quantities. Suppose, for example, that you run a beer distributorship. You make 20 stops a day and deliver 5 cases or kegs to each location. Imagine the effect on your business if, instead, you could make 1 stop and drop off 100 cases or kegs. You'd save planning time, driving time, gas, and more. So you'd likely be happy to offer a quantity discount to the customer who buys 100 cases.

Figuring quantity discounts is pretty simple. Here's an example. Suppose your beer distribution company offers a quantity discount on deliveries of at least 20 cases. You sell a case of beer to stores for $9 but offer a 10% discount to stores accepting delivery of 20 cases or more. How much do you charge a store that orders 25 cases? To figure that out, you use the following equation:

$$\text{Net price} = \text{Regular price} - \text{Discount}$$
$$\text{Net price} = \$9 - (0.1 \times \$9)$$
$$\text{Net price} = \$9 - \$0.90$$
$$\text{Net price} = \$8.10$$
$$\text{Total price} = \$8.10 \times 25 \text{ cases} = \$202.50$$

Here's another example: If Bazooka Corporation offers an 8% discount on deliveries of at least 20 cartons of gum and 10% on deliveries of at least 100 cartons, how much would your store pay for 20 cartons if the regular price were $22 a carton (for orders of under 20 cartons)? You again use this equation:

$$\text{Net price} = \text{Regular price} - \text{Discount}$$
$$\text{Net price} = \$22 - 0.08 \times \$22$$
$$\text{Net price} = \$22 - \$1.76$$
$$\text{Net price} = \$20.24$$
$$\text{Total price} = \$20.24 \times 20 \text{ cases} = \$404.80$$

FOR EXAMPLE

Wholesale Clubs

Wholesale clubs, such as Sam's and Costco, are good examples of how quantity discounts work. Suppose you want to make a tuna sandwich. If you go to your local grocer and buy one can of albacore tuna, you'll pay around $1.50 for the can. Before you got to the store, the grocer bought one or more cases of tuna, broke the individual cans out of the case packaging, stacked the cans on a shelf, threw away or recycled the case packaging, and labeled the shelf with the item and price. If you choose, instead, to go to a wholesale club, you'll have to buy a case of tuna, and the price per can will be much lower—perhaps $1 per can. Why? Because the wholesale club didn't have to hire someone to break out the cans from the cases, stack the cans, and throw away the packaging. By buying the case, you're taking care of that part of the job—it's your responsibility to get those cans out of the case, recycle the cardboard, and stack the cans in your pantry. When cases come in from Chicken of the Sea, the wholesale club has to simply move the cases from the Chicken of the Sea truck onto the warehouse floor and label the per-case costs. And that takes quite a bit less employee time than does breaking out all those individual cans.

Find the net price of each of the following purchases, given the quantity discount shown:

1. $300; 5%
2. $400; 4%
3. $5,000; $2\frac{1}{2}$%
4. $2,400; 20%

SELF-CHECK

- Define **quantity discount.**
- Calculate quantity discounts on cases.

6.2 Discounts for Retailers

When you buy a product from a retailer, you pay the **retail price,** or **list price.** For example, a Harry Potter novel might have a price of $29.99, which is printed right on the cover. Retailers earn a profit by buying their products at a discount and then selling them at a higher price.

How much do retailers pay for goods? Sometimes 20% less than list, sometimes as much as 50% less than list. Occasionally, trinkets—such as pens, stickers, magnets, and mugs sold at the point-of-sale (POS) terminal (i.e., the cash register) area of many retail outlets—are so inexpensive for retailers to buy that they may represent a 500% discount! The terms of the discount depend both on the retailers (what business they're in and what kind of volume they sell) and the suppliers.

Here's a simple example: If a college bookstore is offered a 20% discount on a textbook with a list price of $63.95, how much will the bookstore pay? To figure it out, you use this equation:

$$\text{Net price} = \text{List price} - \text{Discount}$$
$$\text{Net price} = \$63.95 - (0.2 \times \$63.95)$$
$$\text{Net price} = \$63.95 - \$12.79$$
$$\text{Net price} = \$51.16$$

FOR EXAMPLE

Where the Discount Goes

Are you starting to think that you're paying too much for your $80 Nikes? Keep in mind that most small retailers (non-chains that sell small goods such as books, clothing, and so on) get a 40% to 50% discount on their products. So, if you purchase a pair of Nike running shoes for $80, those shoes cost the retailer anywhere from $40 to $48. Suppose the store gets a 40% discount and hopes to make a profit of $5 on each pair of shoes; it has to meet all its expenses in selling that pair of shoes for $27 ($80 list price − $48 discount price − $5 profit = $27). This means a portion of the wages, building lease payment, utilities, displays, equipment (e.g., the cash register), and marketing must all be paid by the $27 difference. If the store sells 500 pairs of shoes each month (roughly 20 pair per day), it must be able to meet all its expenses of $13,500 per month. If it does this, it will show a profit of $2,500 per month, or $30,000 per year. However, if expenses are more than $13,500 per month or sales are lower than 500 pairs, profits will suffer unless the store can negotiate a better discount on those shoes.

Here's another example: Say you work at a car dealership that gets its cars at 18% off list. If a certain car lists for $25,000, how much does the dealer pay?

$$\text{Net price} = \text{List price} - \text{Discount}$$
$$\text{Net price} = \$25,000 - (0.18 \times \$25,000)$$
$$\text{Net price} = \$25,000 - \$4,500$$
$$\text{Net price} = \$20,500$$

Find the net prices for a retailer that makes the following purchases at the given rates of discount:

1. $55,000; 22%
2. $120,000; 17%
3. $68,000; $8\frac{1}{2}$%
4. $96,000; 23%

SELF-CHECK

- Define **retail price** (also called **list price**).
- Calculate discounts for retailers.

6.3 Chain Discounts

Sometimes, manufacturers, wholesalers, and other suppliers are feeling particularly generous because they want to move their inventories. Not only do they offer retailers (or other middlemen) the regular discount, but on top of that, they offer a quantity discount. These are known as **chain discounts.**

For example, suppose Levi Strauss Company offers a discount of 40% on its jeans to all suppliers. But if Goody's sells more Levi's than any other retailer, the Levi Strauss Company may offer an *additional* 10% discount to Goody's, for the same reason that a beer distributor gives an additional discount to a restaurant or convenience store buying 100 of its cases at one time. The discount is listed on the invoice as 40/10. Here's how this example works:

$$\text{Discounted price} = \text{List price} - \text{Discount}$$
$$\text{Discounted price} = \$45.95 - (0.4 \times \$45.95)$$
$$\text{Discounted price} = \$45.95 - \$18.38$$
$$\text{Discounted price} = \$27.57$$

$$\text{Net price} = \text{Discounted price} - \text{Additional discount}$$
$$\text{Net price} = \$27.57 - (0.1 \times \$27.57)$$
$$\text{Net price} = \$27.57 - \$2.76$$
$$\text{Net price} = \$24.81$$

Here's a shortcut for calculating multiple discounts (series of discounts). Convert each discount from a percentage into a decimal, like this:

$$40\% \text{ and } 10\% = 0.4 \text{ and } 0.1$$

Then subtract each from 1, to get this:

$$0.6 \text{ and } 0.9$$

Now multiply those together:

$$(0.6 \times 0.9 = 0.54)$$

And then multiply that result by the list price:

$$\$45.95 \times 0.54 = \$24.81$$

FOR EXAMPLE

The Wal-Mart/Harry Potter Phenomenon

Small, independent bookstores usually get between 40% and 42% discounts on their books. (The discount is sometimes higher than this, but when it is, the bookstore has to pay for shipping costs, and shipping books is pretty pricey, so the net discount usually sits between 40% and 42%.) This means that a retailer can buy a $29.99 Harry Potter book for about $17.99. So, with each release of the Harry Potter novels, these retailers have stocked up with as many books as possible, knowing they can make $12 on each book, from which they pay their expenses and earn a profit. Except that Wal-Mart and Sam's Club (which are owned by the same company) *sell* their books for $15.99, $2 less than the price for which small bookstores can even *buy* the books themselves. Independent bookstores can hardly compete if chains are selling products for less than they themselves can buy them. The solution? Small bookstores offer amenities that chains can't—such as late-night parties, Harry Potter sleepovers, and celebrity readings of the books the day they come out. And they have one more trick up their sleeves: Small bookstores order only enough to sell on the first night, and at midnight, they send out employees to buy up as many cartfuls of books as they can from Wal-Mart and Sam's Club. After the first day, bookstores are able to sell these Wal-Mart books and make $2 more profit on each one.

Find the net prices when given the following list prices and chain discounts:

1. $400; 20/10
2. $600; 15/10
3. $4,800; 10/5
4. $535; 12/6

SELF-CHECK

- Define **chain discount.**
- Figure multiple discounts that chain stores often receive.
- Find a shortcut for estimating multiple discounts.

6.4 Cash Discounts

Suppliers love to be paid on time. In fact, they're so anxious to see their money that they often offer their customers discounts (usually 2% off the bill) if they pay within 10 days. This is very attractive to companies that have funds available to pay their bills quickly, but many companies don't take advantage of these discounts. Why not? Some just don't have the money. Others would rather hold on to their money (which is invested and earning income) for as long as possible because that is worth more to them than getting a 2% discount. By not paying their bills early (or even on time), these companies get a no-interest loan from their supplies.

Suppliers generally offer three types of cash discounts: ordinary dating method, end-of-month (EOM), and receipt-of-goods (ROG) discounts.

6.4.1 Ordinary Dating Method Discounts

Suppliers commonly offer their customers a 2% discount if they pay within 10 days of the invoice date (also called the *billing date*). This is called the **ordinary dating method discount.** If customers choose not to take advantage of this discount, they usually have to pay the full amount within 30 days. These terms are written 2/10, n/30 and read, "two ten, net thirty." It is common practice if there is no net 30 mentioned in the terms then 20 days is the net payment date.

Suppose your company receives an invoice dated May 3. If you pay by May 13, you get a 2% discount. But if you don't take advantage of this discount, you must pay the full amount by June 2. That full amount probably reflects other discounts (such as retail discounts, quantity discounts, chain discounts, and so on), but it does not include the cash discount of 2%.

For example, say that Jason's Organic Grocery receives a bill dated July 9 with terms 2/10, n/30. The bill, which is for $538.75, is paid on July 15. How much does Jason's Organic Grocery pay? You figure it out like this:

$$\text{Cash discount} = \text{Invoice amount} - \text{Discount}$$
$$\text{Cash discount} = \$538.75 - (0.02 \times \$538.75)$$
$$\text{Cash discount} = \$538.75 - \$10.78$$
$$\text{Cash discount} = \$527.97$$

Although 2/10, net/30 is the most common cash discount offered, some suppliers offer more complex cash discounts, such as 3/10, 1/20, net/45. You read this discount as "three ten [3% off if you pay within 10 days], one twenty [1% off if you pay within 20 days], net forty-five [the full amount must be paid within 45 days]."

Suppose Allied Display Company receives an invoice dated September 1 for $9,164.87, with terms 2/10, 1/20, n/30. How much does Allied Signal pay if it pays the bill September 19? Here's how you figure it out:

$$\text{Cash discount} = \text{Invoice amount} - \text{Discount}$$
$$\text{Cash discount} = \$9,164.87 - (0.01 \times \$9,164.87)$$
$$\text{Cash discount} = \$9,164.87 - \$91.65$$
$$\text{Cash discount} = \$9,073.22$$

The Brown Shoe Company purchases leather with an invoice in the amount of $4,200, dated May 8, with payment terms of 3/10, n/30. Determine what amount is due if the bill is paid on the following dates:

1. May 12
2. May 17
3. June 7
4. June 10

6.4.2 End-of-Month (EOM) Discounts

Suppose your company receives a bill for $3,000, with the sales terms 2/10 EOM. The bill is dated April 18. **EOM** means that you receive an **end-of-month discount,** in this case, a discount of 2%, if you pay this bill on or before a certain day (in this case, the 10th day of the month) after the date of the bill. In other words, for this bill, you receive a 10% discount if you pay on or before May 10.

Note that there is an exception to this rule, and that's when the invoice is dated on or after the 26th of the month. In that case, the discount is allowed if the bill is paid within the first 10 days of the *second* month after the month dated on the invoice. This is easier than it sounds. An invoice dated April 18 is payable by May 10. An invoice dated April 28 is payable by June 10.

For example, an invoice dated October 3 for $3,999, with terms 3/15 EOM is paid on Oct 14. How much is paid? Here is how you figure it out:

$$3,999 \times .97 = 3879.03$$
$$1.00 - .03 = .97$$

Now try to solve the following:

1. An invoice dated December 1 for $699.95 has the terms 2/10 EOM. By what date must it be paid to get the cash discount?
2. Your college business office receives an invoice dated May 10 with the terms 2/10 EOM. What is the latest date the invoice can be paid to receive the discount?
3. What percentage of the invoice in Question 2 must be paid if the payment is forwarded within the discount period?

6.4.3 Receipt of Goods (ROG) Discounts

A supplier sometimes includes an invoice in the goods it ships (rather than mailing or emailing the invoice separately), which slows down its arrival date. For example, goods may ship on February 4, arrive February 15, with sales terms of 2/10, n/10, which means the recipient of the goods doesn't have a chance to take the discount. This is why some suppliers offer a 2/10 **ROG**, which means a 2% discount if the invoice is paid within 10 days after **receipt of goods.**

FOR EXAMPLE

Taking Unearned Discounts

One downside to suppliers' offering discounts for quick payment is that some companies take the discounts and still pay late. For example, if a bill needs to be paid by July 10 in order to receive a discount, a business might take the discount on July 14 and back-date the check. The check might then take three or four days to arrive via mail, which means the supplier might not have the check until July 18, eight days *after* the check was supposed to arrive if the discount was taken. At that point, the supplier's only recourse is to bill the customer for the 2% discount, but most customers won't pay it.

Solve the following:

1. A bill for $2,000 is dated July 3, with the terms 10/5 ROG. The product invoice arrives July 10. By what date must the bill be paid in order to get the cash discount?

2. How much should be paid on the bill in Question 1 to get the cash discount?

3. IKEA, a large global retailer, purchases furniture for resale that totals $28,450. It receives the furniture on November 3. The invoice dated November 5 arrives on November 15, with the terms 2/10 ROG, n/30. How much does IKEA need to pay if it pays the bill on November 20?

SELF-CHECK

- Describe the three types of cash discounts: **ordinary dating method discount**, **end-of-month discount**, and **receipt-of-goods discount**.
- Calculate the various cash discounts.
- Draw a basic conclusion about the fairest way to offer a cash discount.

SUMMARY

In addition to the goal of turning inventory into cash as fast as possible, a manufacturer or wholesaler is often interested in clearing its inventory for other reasons, such as making room for newer products, and will therefore offer a discount(s). Such discounts also have an incentive for the purchaser—namely, a savings. A retailer may take advantage of these discounts if it has the cash available because the true cost of the product may include the cost (or time value) of money.

KEY TERMS

Chain discounts	Two or more trade discounts that are applied in a series, often offered to large retail chains because they buy in volume.
End-of-month discount	A cash discount offered when customers pay within a set number of days (usually 10) from the end of the month in which the invoice is sent (dated).

EOM	End of month.
List price	The suggested retail price offered to the customer. The list price is the same as the retail price or sticker price.
Ordinary dating method discount	A cash discount offered if customers pay within a set number of days from the date of the invoice.
Quantity discounts	Discounts offered by suppliers (sellers) for ordering large quantities of goods.
Receipt-of-goods discount	A cash discount offered when customers pay within a set number of days from the day they receive the items. The discount period starts the day the goods are received, not from when they are ordered.
Retail price	The price customers pay for goods. *See also* list price.
ROG	Receipt of goods.

ASSESS YOUR UNDERSTANDING

Go to www.wiley.com/college/slavin to evaluate your assimilation of the basics of discounts.

Measure your learning by comparing pre-test and post-test results.

Summary Questions

1. A quantity discount is offered to retailers who place orders every day. True or False?
2. Retailers pay suppliers:
   (a) 20% below the retail price.
   (b) 30% below the list price.
   (c) 40% below the retail price.
   (d) all of the above.
3. Chain discounts are offered in addition to retailer discounts. True or False?
4. Define **cash discount**.

Review Questions

1. Grandma's Soup offers a quantity discount of 7% on all deliveries of more than 20 cartons. The regular price is $12.50 per carton. If Fairmont Grocery orders 30 cartons, how much does this order cost?
2. Goodyear gives a 27% discount off the list price on its tires. If Joe's Garage ordered 200 tires that listed at $45.99 each, how much would it have to pay?
3. The Smithtown Stationery Shop orders 10 boxes of Expresso fine-point pens. If these pens list at $0.99, and there are 10 pens in a box, how much does the store have to pay if it receives a 35% discount off the list price?
4. Neiman-Marcus received a shipment of 700 beaded camisoles that list for $69.99 each. How much did the company pay if it was entitled to a chain discount of 60/20 and it paid within 20 days?
5. The Buono Flooring Company received a $9,748.17 order on November 16. The invoice was dated November 12, and the terms of the sale were 2/10, 1/20, n/30.
   (a) If Buono paid on November 20, what was the amount due?
   (b) If Buono paid on November 29, how much was due?

6. An order for $3,704.56 dated April 27 was received on May 1. Sales terms were 3/10 EOM. The bill was paid June 9. How much was due?

7. Bill's Car Rentals gets a bill for $16,958.07, dated January 14. The order is received January 20, and sales terms are 2/10 ROG, n/30. If Bill's pays on January 28, how much is due?

8. Jake's Antique Wholesalers, Inc., received five restored tables on December 15. The invoice of $11,450 for these tables arrived on December 1, with terms of 2/15 ROG, n/30. How much must be paid if the bill is paid on December 28?

9. Peace a Pizza purchased a small pizza oven at a cost of $6,400. The oven was installed on June 17, and the invoice was delivered on June 13, with terms of 3/15 ROG, n/30. The owners decided to pay the bill on July 12. How much did it need to pay?

10. Joe's Donut Shop received a $400 invoice, dated January 12, with terms 3/10, 1/15, n/60. On January 24, Joe sent a check to pay the bill. What was the amount of his check?

11. A bill dated October 14 for $15,500 has a chain discount program of 3/10, 1/15, n/30. If payment is made on October 28, what is the amount due?

12. A wholesaler offers you a chain discount of 5/7 on a $3,400 invoice. What is the total discount?

13. An invoice of $59,400, dated November 28, had terms of 3/10 EOM and was paid in full on December 9.

    (a) What is the due date for the discount, and what is the discount amount?

    (b) What are the amount paid and the net payment date?

Applying This Chapter

1. The Poland Spring water company gives a 10% discount on deliveries of at least 50 gallons and a 15% discount on deliveries of at least 100 gallons. The regular price the stores pay for deliveries of less than 50 gallons is $0.80 per gallon.

    (a) How much would a store have to pay for 75 gallons?

    (b) How much would a store have to pay for 120 gallons?

2. Friendly Food Center gets a 23% discount off list price on all boxes of cereals it receives from a wholesaler. If a box of Quaker Oats retails for $2.49, how much does the store pay for two dozen boxes?

3. Gravesend Flag Company received a bill for 4,000 flags that list at $19.49 each. If the manufacturer provided a 40/15 discount, how much did

Gravesend pay? (To figure this out, use the shortcut method described in the text.)

4. Allsafe Ladder and Scaffolding Company receives an invoice dated January 17 for $12,315.62. The shipment arrives on January 28, and the sales terms are 3/10, 2/20, 1/30, n/45.

   (a) How much is due if the bill is paid on January 27?

   (b) How much is due if the bill is paid on February 1?

5. Boeing Air Manufacturing Corporation obtained delivery of and an invoice for 100 tires at $150 each. The trade discount is termed 10/5, and a cash discount is termed 2/10, n/30. The company pays within the discount period. What does Boeing pay?

6. The Philadelphia Eagles football team purchases three new copiers for the front office staff, at $349.95 each. The terms are 3/10, n/30. The bill is paid within the discount period. What is the amount due?

7. The associate dean of the student life office of a local college purchases five cell phones to be used by the various student organizations. Each phone lists at $230.95, with a 22.5% discount offered because of the quantity involved in the purchase. What is the amount paid? (Note that the college is sales tax exempt.)

8. Johnson Motors, Inc., received a $1,500 invoice July 6, with terms 2/10 EOM. It paid the bill on August 9. How much did it pay?

9. The head accountant for a company is training a new accounts payable staff member. The new hire is processing a bill for office supplies that is dated August 20, for $392.34, for goods delivered on August 24. If the terms are 3/10 ROG, how much needs to be paid if the bill is paid on September 6?

10. An Apple iPod has a list price of $299.95, with a chain discount of 7/7. Find the net price and the discount.

11. A hospital placed a requisition for 21 new cell phones for its emergency department staff doctors. The list price was $120 each, with a chain trade discount of 30/15. What net price did the hospital pay?

12. The accounts payable department of a major restaurant chain has been instructed to pay all invoices such that any and all discounts can be realized. However, its checking account has a balance of only $2,700. A $3,900 invoice presented for payment to the office is dated May 10, with the terms 2/10, n/30. The accountant determines to pay only $2,000 by May 15. What would be the credited amount?

13. A regional bank ordered and received furniture for its newest branch office from a small supplier located within the bank's service area. The list price was $8,755.95, and the terms were 5/10, 3/20. The invoice was dated October 22 and paid on November 20. Find the payment amount.

14. Your day-care center receives an invoice from the Jasper Toy Company in the amount of $25,988.99, with terms of 2/15 ROG. The invoice is dated August 5, and the toys are received on August 25. How much does your day-care center pay to the toy firm by check on September 3?

15. U.S. Foodservice, a large, full-service restaurant supplier, delivered $5,678.90 of paper products to your seasonal beach snack operations on May 10, with an invoice dated May 9 and terms of 3/10 EOM. What discount is available to you if you pay in full on or before June 7?

16. As a volunteer at an emergency ambulance service, you ordered high fire- and water-resistant boots for all new recruits, for an invoice price of $7,900.50. The invoice was dated April 9, and the boots were delivered on April 11 by FedEx. If the terms were 2/10 ROG, what dollar discount was available, if any?

Wal-Mart Discounts

Sony gives retailers a 40% discount off list price on all new plasma TVs. Wal-Mart receives an additional 15% discount because of its high-volume orders. Wal-Mart orders 3,000 TVs that list for $2,999 each, and they're delivered on July 23, along with an invoice that has the terms 3/10 EOM. Wal-Mart pays the bill on August 9.

1. In what amount is the check issued?
2. How much does Wal-Mart pay for each TV?

Hilton Hotel

Hilton Hotel in Seattle received a bill for $948, dated April 7, with terms of 2/10, 1/15, n/30.

1. What amount is due if the bill is paid on or before April 15?
2. What amount is due if the bill is paid on or between April 18 and April 22?
3. What amount is due if the bill is paid on or between April 23 and May 7?

Office Supplies

Sean O'Connell owed $400 on an office supplies invoice. Within the next week, Sean mailed a check for $80.

1. What credit should be applied to Sean's account at the office supply company?
2. What is the balance owed after Sean's payment?

Fitness Software

A large fitness company needs to buy an updated software system for its client records. A manufacturer is offering the product for $2,899, with a chain discount of 8/5 and no handling charge. Another supplier offers the same software for $3,000 with the terms 10/5 and a $50 FedEx delivery charge. Which is the better deal?

Golf Pros

The local golf pro shop, in preparing for the season, ordered $8,775 of new golf equipment. On March 23, the golf pro paid $5,000 as a partial payment on his account with a wholesaler for this equipment, with terms of 2/10, n/30.

1. How much credit does the pro receive?
2. What is the pro's discount amount?
3. What is the remaining balance on the account?

Seagram's Liquors

Seagram's offers a discount of 5% off all orders of $1,000 to $1,999 and 8% off all orders of more than $2,000.

1. If Buy-Rite Liquor Store places an order for $1,549, how much does it pay?
2. If Al's Liquors places an order for $3,712, how much does it pay?

Marcia's Jewelers

Marcia's Jewelers received a trade discount of 15% on a watch that lists at $39.95 in her wholesalers catalog.

1. What is the dollar amount of the discount?
2. What is the net price of the watch?

7

BANKING AND INSURANCE
Protecting Against Loss

Starting Point

Go to www.wiley.com/college/slavin to assess your knowledge of the basics of banking and insurance.

Determine where you need to concentrate your effort.

What You'll Learn in This Chapter

▲ How checking and savings accounts differ from one another
▲ How to reconcile a bank statement
▲ When and how you can insure yourself or your business

After Studying This Chapter, You'll Be Able To

▲ Illustrate various ways to make your money grow
▲ Demonstrate how debit cards are replacing paper checks
▲ Pay bills online
▲ Determine the cost of insurance

Goals and Outcomes

▲ Choose from among various banking options
▲ Protect yourself against identity theft and online fraud
▲ Understand risk and how to protect against it

INTRODUCTION

Banking and insurance may not, at first glance, appear to be related issues, but they are. Here's how: The purpose of insurance is to protect you against the risk of catastrophic financial loss. The purpose of banking is to protect you against the day-to-day financial loss that might come from the alternative (e.g., stashing your money under your mattress, get-rich-quick schemes) instead of earning or letting that money grow and therefore decreasing the effects of inflation on those dollars. The lines between checking and savings accounts are blurring more each day, as debit cards and online transactions replace paper checks. This chapter discusses these banking options and also discusses how to protect yourself against catastrophic financial losses through the purchase of various insurance products.

7.1 Savings Accounts

The purpose of a savings account is exactly what it sounds like it would be: to save money and earn interest. The idea is that you're putting money in the bank to save for a particular occasion, such as something you want to buy, Christmas presents you want to give, a vacation you want to take, tuition you'll need to pay in the future, a down payment you want to have to purchase a car or home, or a time when you won't be working as much (such as when having a baby) and will need to dip into your savings to pay your bills.

In addition to saving for a particular purpose, experts recommend saving from each source of income you receive to cushion against unexpected expenses (e.g., for saving 5% of receipts from your total receipts if you run a business or saving 5% from your paycheck if you're employed by someone else). By doing this month after month, you'll eventually build up a cushion for your household or business that will help you weather hard times.

Savings accounts are for short-term savings because their interest rates are fairly low—far lower than what is usually paid on longer-term investments, such as those in the stock market or in bonds. Therefore, people don't save for retirement through a savings account; instead, they invest in stocks or bonds, because they have many years to even out the volatility of the market (i.e., times when stock prices fall balance out against times when stock prices rise).

An understanding of how you earn interest on your money is fundamental to your ability to live in a competitive economic environment. It's your right under a free market system to acquire wealth, improve your quality of life, and provide for your heirs. A complete discussion of interest is provided in Chapter 9, but this chapter spends a few moments giving you a little idea of what you'll learn there.

A note for now: The concept of paying interest on interest is called *compound interest*. This method of determining interest earned or interest to be paid can be calculated periodically—daily, monthly, or quarterly—and then added to the principal for inclusion in the next period's interest determination. Again, see Chapter 9 for more on this.

Suppose you know the interest rate and the time over which the money will be (invested) in your savings account, and you want to find the amount of interest you would earn. You start with the simple interest formula and solve for I (interest) by multiplying p (principal; the amount deposited in the account) by r (the rate of interest paid by the bank) by t (the length of time the money is invested):

$$I = p \times r \times t$$

Try calculating interest by using the following facts with the simple interest formula:

1. Interest 5%, 1 year, $10,000 invested (deposited) in a bank account
2. Interest 8%, 1 year, $15,000 deposited
3. Interest $8\frac{1}{4}$%, 1 year, $2,200 deposited
4. Interest 10%, 1 year, $5,400 deposited
5. Interest $12\frac{1}{8}$%, 1 year, $25,000 deposited

7.1.1 Passbook Accounts

Passbook accounts are another name for savings accounts because some banks still issue **passbooks** with their savings accounts: booklets into which all deposits and withdrawals are recorded. Most banks, however, issue monthly statements (electronically, online, or on paper) instead of recording each transaction in a passbook, as was the norm in the past.

Passbook accounts tend to have few (if any) restrictions on the minimum balance ($5 to $25 is often the required minimum balance), which has traditionally made these accounts popular both with children and for specific types of savings, such as holiday savings accounts. In addition, funds can be removed without restrictions.

These accounts typically earn such a low rate of interest (i.e., rate of return) that they are not a popular way to save money for more than a few months at a time. However, **online banks** such as ING (see www.ingdirect.com) are revolutionizing the savings account market by offering relatively high rates of interest on their savings accounts (e.g., about $4\frac{1}{2}$% as of September 2006). Unlike traditional banks such as the ones in your neighborhood, online banks have almost no brick-and-mortar locations. Instead, they operate almost exclusively via the Internet, which means they don't pay for buildings, utilities, or salaries for tellers and managers.

The process of working with an online bank is simple: You register online, transfer money from your local bank's checking or savings account to the online bank, and transfer it back when you need it. Interest rates are often 2 percentage points higher than what local banks are paying. And with the "Fed" (i.e., the Federal Reserve System, the central bank in the United States) raising rates over the past 5 years or so, you need to have alternatives to continue to make your money grow in order to keep up with inflation.

7.1.2 Certificates of Deposit

Certificates of deposit (CDs) are another option for saving, and although they are considered short-term savings accounts, they lock in your money for a pre-determined amount of time, usually from 30 days to 5 years. With CDs, the interest rate depends on the length of the certificate but is often 1 to 3 percentage points higher than for a passbook account. However, if you withdraw the funds before the predetermined date (often called the **maturity date**), you usually forgo all interest earned *and* may have to pay an additional penalty. Banks are able to pay higher rates of interest on CDs because they know exactly how long they can use and invest the money. If you withdraw your money early, you essentially mess up your bank's plan for that money, and that is why you have to pay such hefty fees.

7.1.3 Government Bonds and Bills

Bonds and bills are both government savings vehicles (e.g., bonds, Treasury bills [T-bills], EE-savings, I-bonds). You can find out more about government savings accounts in Chapter 11.

FOR EXAMPLE

Federal Savings Bonds

A savings bond issued by the federal government is one of the oldest long-term savings vehicles in the United States. It's also one of the lowest-earning ways to save, but people tend to feel secure about purchasing savings bonds—much more so than with the most popular long-term savings option: buying stocks. Depending on which type of bond your purchase, you either pay less than the **face value** (i.e., the amount shown on the front of the bond, such as $50), and then when you redeem the savings bond, it is worth the face value, or you pay the face value, and upon redemption, the bond is worth more than the face value. Savings bonds vary in terms of the types offered, the length of time you must hold them before redeeming, and how much interest they earn (see Chapter 9 for more on interest). Check out www.savingsbonds.gov for details on purchasing savings bonds.

SELF-CHECK

- Discuss the uses of short-term savings accounts.
- Describe the types of savings accounts available.
- Describe how passbook accounts differ from CDs.

7.2 Checking/Debit Accounts

Checking and debit accounts differ from savings accounts in that they are designed to be continuously accessed. Your bank expects both regular deposits (e.g., paychecks, retirement checks, payments from customers/clients) and regular withdrawals (e.g., for rent or mortgage, utilities, car payment, tuition, food).

Most accounts today are both checking and debit accounts, which means you can use either paper checks or a debit card (i.e., check card). However, as more and more transactions take place with debit cards and online banking (see Section 7.3 for additional details), paper checks are decreasing in popularity.

Debit cards look very much like credit cards (see Chapter 11), but they actually subtract money from your checking account every time you use them; instead of writing a paper check for a purchase from, say, Wal-Mart, you swipe (or "blink") your debit card, and the amount of the purchase is automatically deducted from your checking account.

7.2.1 The Checkbook Register

The primary way of keeping track of checkbook transactions is with a **checkbook register.** Of course, today you can use the online banking services that most banks offer. This allows you to monitor your account(s) from anywhere, as long as you have an Internet connection. You start with the amount of funds you have in your account, add any deposits you've made, and subtract the amounts of any checks you've written, automated teller machine (ATM) withdrawals, debit card transactions, and any bank fees and **bank service charges.** In this way, you always know the current balance in your checking account.

Checkbook registers are, admittedly, low tech, but they've worked for generations of banking customers. Of course, sometimes you might forget to log a check, or you might add or subtract incorrectly, and this gives you an incorrect balance, which could result in a **bounced check** (i.e., **nonsufficient funds [NSF]**), which means that a check was written but funds weren't available in the account to cover the amount of that check. For this reason, many checking accounts offer **overdraft protection**, in which a savings account, secondary checking account, line of credit, or credit card is debited (i.e., charged) the amount of the check written if the balance in the checking account isn't sufficient to cover that check. But for the most part, checkbook registers allowed people to keep up with the balance in accounts. (Many people also use the online banking services provided by their financial institutions to monitor their accounts.)

One of the challenges of using a debit card is that it's more difficult to log the purchases you've made with a debit card than when you write a check. When you write a check, you have your checkbook register in front of you, and you input the amount of each check you write in that register. Keeping up with your balance in this way is pretty simple. But when you use a debit card, no register is in front of you, although many banking customers still use a checkbook register to keep track of debit card transactions.

7.2.2 Deposits and Withdrawals

A **deposit** is money put into an account to increase its balance. **Direct deposit** (using **electronic funds transfer [EFT]**) is a feature that many employers offer: Instead of receiving a paper check, the amount of your paycheck is deposited electronically into your account on your usual payday. This feature not only saves time and money but also allows you to allocate your paycheck into various accounts before you even touch the money. For example, you could allocate 10% of each paycheck to go into savings and then have the rest deposited into your checking account.

Withdrawals are made with checks, debit cards, or through online banking (see Section 7.3).

7.2.3 Reconciling a Register with a Bank Statement

Whether you use a checkbook register or find another way to keep track of withdrawals from your checking account (such as the online banking website for your financial institution), you must eventually **reconcile** your record keeping with the paper or electronic statement your bank sends you.

The bank's statement is, unfortunately, almost never up to date. This is understandable because of the timing of the postal service and the various types of transactions affecting your account(s). A bank statement shows a current balance as of the date of the statement, but it does not show debit card transactions made after that day, checks that might be floating around in the mail and therefore not presented to your bank for payment, or checks that the payees still haven't deposited (i.e., **outstanding checks**). You'd think people would want their money right away, but it often happens that some errant checks end up not being cashed, making the bank's balance in your account appear higher than it actually is.

The front of your bank statement lists the deposits made, checks cashed, service fees/charges, and other banking debits recorded between the date of the last statement and the date of this statement. In general, deposits and debits (i.e., charges) tend to be recorded within a few days of the actual transaction. Some deposits (i.e., deposits-in-transit) may not appear on a bank statement because they were made after the bank statement date. Checks can take some time to clear the bank, which is the main reason bank statements and checkbook registers don't match up.

The Check Clearing for the 21st Century Act is a federal law that became effective in 2004. This law, commonly referred to as Check-21, has greatly reduced this paper shifting problem by computerizing (i.e., digitizing) most checks. Have you noticed you do not get your canceled checks back from your bank anymore? That is a result of Check-21.

Figure 7-1 shows a small segment of a bank statement's listing of checks cashed.

Notice that one of the items in the listing has an asterisk next to it, indicating that the number sequence of checks has been interrupted. There are three explanations for this:

▲ A check was destroyed. Either you intentionally destroyed it because you filled it out incorrectly and tore it up or wrote "VOID" on it, or the check-processing equipment at a large utility company or credit card company accidentally destroyed the check.

▲ The check already cleared and appeared on last month's statement. If you have the statement handy, you can check to see whether this is the case.

▲ Your check is flying through space but will indeed land someday. You'll likely see it in the next month's statement.

Figure 7-1

CHECK	DATE PAID	AMOUNT
766	11/15	36.00
767	11/15	31.46
770*	11/16	115.12
771	11/16	58.38
772	11/17	61.50

A bank statement's listing of checks cashed.

On the back of your monthly bank statement are some well-intentioned forms for reconciling your account. Here's what to do:

1. Take the bank's total and write down the last check number. Put each number in the right place.
2. Look back at the bank's check listing and note which checks are missing (an asterisk or some other indicator will tell you when the number sequence has been interrupted).
3. Decide whether the checks missing in the bank's list have already been cashed, are really missing (destroyed), or just haven't landed yet (that is, by statement time).
4. If the checks missing from the list really are outstanding, write them in the spaces.
5. Get out your calculator and do the subtraction.

Figure 7-2 shows what the bank is trying to tell you.

If you find that your total and the bank's total don't match, you have to search the statement to find the reason. Were you charged a fee to use another

Figure 7-2

My own checkbook balance reconciliation form:

The bank thinks I have this much: $603.51

But they haven't seen these checks yet:

#455	$ 24.30
#517	$146.00
#518	$ 31.15
#519	$ 21.87
#520	$ 59.03
#	$

So the total is really this much, after check number #520 . $321.16

Typical statement balancing.

bank's ATM? Is there a monthly checking account fee (service fee) that you haven't added in? Did you fail to log in a debit purchase from the gas station? Did you fail to log a direct payment (i.e., EFT)? Did you transpose some numbers as you were adding and subtracting (e.g., you should have written $4.58 but mistakenly wrote $5.48)? Or did you accidentally slide a decimal point in the wrong direction? This happens frequently when you add several dollar numbers and don't place the decimal points in a line under each other (e.g., you intended to write $54.90 but slide the decimal so that you actually but incorrectly write $5.49). Transposing and sliding are common errors seen most often with employees who handle cash or deal with numbers once a day or so. You should take the time to figure out why your amounts don't match because if you don't, you'll likely overdraw your account, which could mean a $25 service fee. The bank isn't always right, but it thinks it is until you prove otherwise!

Try the following bank reconciliation situation:

1. Use the following information to reconcile the bank statement against the check register:

    (a) Statement balance, $~~$798.00~~ 698.00
        NSF service fees, $25.00
        Outstanding check, $45.00
        ATM fee, $3.00
        NSF check, $65.00 deposit
        Deposit in transit, $100.00
        Check register balance, $846

FOR EXAMPLE

Money Market Accounts

Money market accounts vary a bit from bank to bank, but in general, they tend to be a mixture of checking accounts and savings accounts. Like savings accounts, they earn a higher rate of interest than do checking accounts. Sometimes, the accounts are invested in mutual funds or stocks; in those cases, the rate of interest is usually very high, but, as with stocks, the accounts are not guaranteed and can also lose value. As with checking accounts, with a money market account, you're issued a checkbook from which you can withdraw funds, but the number of (free) checks you can write each month is limited—often to only three. Holders of money market accounts must often carry a high minimum balance in the account: $5,000 is not unheard of.

(b) Check register, $3,606.
   Service fees, $4.00
   ATM fees, $2.00
   Deposit in transit, $2,400.
   Bank statement, $1,200.

SELF-CHECK

- Consider the differences between paper checks and debit cards.
- Explain how to use a checkbook register and reconcile it with a bank statement.

7.3 Online Banking

The Internet introduced a streamlined method of banking that's commonly referred to as **online banking.** Secure connections and password-protected accounts allow customers to do from the comfort of their own homes what they used to have to drive to the bank to accomplish.

7.3.1 Online Deposits, Transfers, and Bill Paying

At its simplest, online banking allows banking customers to check balances and transfer money (e.g., between savings and checking accounts and vice versa). However, because funds can be transferred not only within one banking institution but also *between* banks, online banking allows for direct deposit, transfer from a checking account at one bank to a savings account at a different bank (e.g., a higher-earning online only bank such as ING; see www.ingdirect.com), and direct bill payment.

Online bill paying is simply a matter of transferring funds (i.e., EFT) from your bank account to the account of a utility company, credit card company, car company, and so on. Both businesses and individuals take advantage of online bill paying, which tends to work in two ways:

▲ You visit the Web site of the company to which you are paying money, such as a utility company. After registering and providing information about both your bank and your account with that bank, the utility company withdraws the funds from your account electronically.

FOR EXAMPLE

Identity Theft Statistics

According to the Federal Trade Commission and the Better Business Bureau, nearly 10 million people were victims of identity theft in 2003, resulting in $5 billion in losses for victims and almost $50 billion in losses for businesses. The average out-of-pocket loss for victims was $500; the average loss to businesses per victim was $4,800. Victims spent between 28 and 30 hours resolving the problems caused by identity theft, for a total of a whopping 297 million hours nationwide.

▲ Through your bank's Web site, you pay several different bills at one time, providing your bank with the account information of each bill you want to pay.

Check out these banks' Internet sites: www.bankofamerica.com and www.wachovia.com.

7.3.2 Protecting Your Identity

Identity theft (see www.consumer.gov/idtheft) is a crime in which, using information such as Social Security numbers, credit card numbers, and other financial information, criminals access your personal financial accounts and use those accounts for their own gain. Examples of identity theft include opening credit and bank accounts, taking out loans, buying merchandise online, and filling out rental or lease applications.

The most valuable way to protect your identity is to give out your Social Security number as little as possible. Although the federal government requires that you provide your Social Security number when you open a bank account, you should not put that number on your paper checks. In addition, you should resist attempts by your university or other institutions to use your Social Security number as a student ID number; ask instead to be assigned a different number. In addition, when banking online, use a non-obvious password—one that no one could possibly guess. Do *not* use the name of your pet, child, or boyfriend/girlfriend; your nickname; or anything else that is obvious.

Finally, you should not throw away any documents that include your Social Security number, birth date, credit card numbers, checking account numbers, and so on. Shred such information before allowing it to leave your home or business.

7.4 Insurance

The purpose of insurance is to protect you, your family, and your business against the risk of financial loss, a loss you may not be able to afford. People generally insure anything that's expensive to replace—a building, a vehicle, a business, the contents of a rented apartment or office—and even things that are difficult to put a value on, such as health. These and other forms of insurance are covered in this section.

For nearly all forms of insurance, a **policy** is written for a specific person, relating to a specific vehicle, home, office, and so on. Each policy has a specific rate or **premium** (i.e., the amount paid to put the policy in force). A **claim** is filed when damage to the property insured in the policy occurs. Most insurance is subject to a **deductible** (i.e., an amount that you pay out before your insurance begins paying for your loss) and a **cap** (i.e., an upper limit or maximum your policy will pay for each occurrence or over your policy's lifetime). The lower the deductible and the higher the cap, the more you pay in premiums (i.e., price).

7.4.1 Auto Insurance

Auto insurance, or insurance for a vehicle, is the most common type of insurance, primarily because it's required by most states. In fact, the amount you pay for auto insurance depends very much on where you live; states can dictate everything from how much insurance you must carry to how much of the other driver's expenses your insurance will have to pay if you're in an accident. For this reason, auto insurance is usually pretty expensive, even if your car is worth very little. For example, you may have to pay $400 every 6 months for a car that's worth only a few thousand dollars. Most of that $400 goes toward insuring against the injuries of other drivers and against lawsuits that may arise if you're at fault in an accident.

Your insurance has two major portions, each of which is separate from the other in terms of premium, deductible, and cap:

▲ **Collision:** The **collision** portion of an insurance policy covers damage to a car that occurs on the road—what we typically call an "accident." Typically, the insurance company for the person who is at fault in an accident ends up paying the collision damage.

▲ **Comprehensive:** The **comprehensive** portion of an insurance policy covers off-road claims (i.e., fire, theft, break-ins, vandalism, natural disasters). This coverage is often referred to as "act of God" coverage. This portion of an insurance policy covers, for example, a tree falling onto a car while it's parked in a driveway. Comprehensive claims also include damage from freak occurrences, such as a car that floods because the sunroof was left open while it went through a car wash and other non-collision claims. Because there's no one to blame for this type of incident, there's no other insurance company to go after for damages, so the insurance company of the person filing the claim has to cover all the costs of comprehensive damage.

Also, the medical payment provisions of the policy for most vehicle insurance is subject to a $100,000/$300,000 cap, meaning that injuries are covered at $100,000 per person and $300,000 per occurrence. So, if you're involved in an accident that was your fault, and one person receives injuries totaling $160,000, your insurance will likely pay $100,000 of that. However, if you're involved in a similar accident, but three people are injured, each with $95,000 injuries, your insurance will pay *that entire* amount. This $60,000 difference is known as a **gap** in insurance, which can be filled by an umbrella policy, as discussed in Section 7.4.6.

Auto insurance rates for personal and business policies are based on a number of factors besides the state in which you keep your car. The following factors can reduce your rates and keep them low:

▲ Infrequent driving and living close to your place of work
▲ Having a good driving record (i.e., no tickets or accidents)
▲ Having good credit (because people with good credit have been shown to be more responsible drivers)
▲ Owning a home (because homeowners tend to be more responsible than others)
▲ Insuring a home with the same insurance company that insures the vehicle (i.e., multiple-policy discount)
▲ Being a good student (some companies offer this discount because it shows responsibility)
▲ Being between the ages of 25 and 65
▲ Driving a car that has a car alarm system
▲ Driving a car that has a high safety rating
▲ Driving a car that is inexpensive to repair

In general, the less you drive (for work or pleasure), the older you are (before you reach senior citizen status), and the more responsible you are with both driving and handling money, the lower your insurance rates will be.

Conversely, the following factors can cause your rates to rise:

▲ Driving many miles each year
▲ Poor driving record
▲ Poor credit
▲ Renting an apartment or home
▲ Driving a car that tends to be targeted by thieves
▲ Driving a car that has a poor safety rating
▲ Driving a car that is expensive to repair (as is the case with some luxury imports)
▲ Being young or very old

Business vehicle insurance rates are based on either the personal data of the business owner or on the financial condition of the company. In addition, the amount of use a vehicle will get in the course of business has an impact on the insurance premium. For example, the insurance premium for a pizza-delivery vehicle driven by several different teenage drivers will tend to be much higher than the premium for a 40-year-old accountant who works in an office that's 5 miles from her home.

Look at the following facts about automobile accidents and calculate some of the claims and reimbursements on these claims:

1. You are in an accident with your new car that is insured with a policy containing a $500 deductible clause. If the repairs are to cost $2,200, how much can you expect your insurance policy to cover?

2. Your truck is backed into a pole, and the damages are $3,600. If you have a $500 deductible clause, how much will your insurance company cover?

3. You have a $4,000 accident in your car. Your automobile policy has a $250 deductible. What is the amount the insurance company will cover?

7.4.2 Homeowner's and Renter's Insurance

Property insurance, which is usually referred to as **homeowner's insurance**, insures against damage to a home, any outbuildings (e.g., a shed, a detached garage), and the contents inside those buildings. It usually does not, however, protect the real property itself. Why? Because land is difficult to damage. For example, if a fire destroys a home, a detached garage, a shed, and all the contents of the buildings, those buildings can all be rebuilt (and contents can be repurchased) on that same piece of real estate (i.e., property). Therefore, most homeowner's insurance covers *less* than the actual value of the home or office, outbuildings, and land because the cost of the land on which the house sits is subtracted. For this reason, it costs less to insure a small house on 100 acres than a mansion on a quarter acre, even if both would fetch the same price if sold by a real estate agent.

Besides the value of the home and land, other factors affect property insurance premiums:

▲ Distance to a fire hydrant or pond
▲ Distance to the nearest fire station (more than 5 miles causes premiums to rise considerably)
▲ Materials used to construct the building (e.g., steel and brick are less susceptible to fire damage than is frame or log)
▲ Whether smoke detectors, fire extinguishers, and sprinkler systems are in use in the building
▲ Whether the building is protected by a security system
▲ Whether an aggressive dog resides in the building
▲ Whether a business (even a home-based business) brings clients to the building
▲ Where the building is located (e.g., high-crime area, flood area)

Some insurance companies simply won't insure certain buildings, especially those in areas that are prone to crime, flooding, tornadoes, earthquakes, or hurricanes. Insurance companies also may insure a building but exclude claims related to burglary, floods, earthquake damage, or hurricane damage, or they may charge extra premiums to cover such events. Many people who are unable to afford these charges simply go without insurance.

Insurance rates for fire are usually quoted in dollar value based on $100 of insured property. The rate is then easily multiplied by the number of hundreds to determine the premium, or the cost (price) of the coverage.

Try figuring the following:

1. If you are quoted a rate of $0.256 per $100 of coverage on your business and you want/need $350,000 of coverage, how do you calculate this?
2. The rate is $0.731 per $100, and the insurer wants $560,00 in coverage. What is the premium?
3. Property is valued at $23,000, and the rate is $0.526 per $100. What is the cost of insurance on the property?
4. Your rate quote is $0.241 per $100 and you need $621,000 of coverage. What is the premium?

People who have put only a small down payment on a house and have a large mortgage may not have much incentive to buy insurance. After all, if something

FOR EXAMPLE

Hurricane Katrina

Some homeowners who suffered damage due to Hurricane Katrina found themselves only partially covered. For example, if a policy excluded flood damage but covered damage due to a hurricane, the torn-off roof and broken windows was covered, but the entire loss of the first floor and all its contents (due to flooding) was not. Many hurricane victims have found themselves caught in this insurance quagmire: protected against the loss they thought they might suffer (a hurricane) but not against the one that caused the most damage (flooding). In some cases, policyholders, unable to afford total coverage, had to choose between two very expensive insurance options—hurricane or flood—and they chose the event they felt was most likely.

happened to the house, the bank, not the homeowner, would suffer losses. For this reason, banks and other mortgage lenders will not finalize the paperwork on any home until an entire year of insurance has been purchased on the home. If the homeowner ever cancels the policy, the bank is notified immediately of the lapse in coverage.

Renter's insurance is for people who need to insure only the contents of a home or office but not the building itself. For example, when you rent an apartment, the owner of the building is responsible for insuring against damage to the building itself—due to fire, an act of God, poor construction, and so on. If a fire destroyed the building, the insured owner would be given money to rebuild. However, the contents of the apartments (e.g., sofas, chairs, beds, tables, desks, electronics, clothes) would *not* be covered under the building owner's policy. That's where renter's insurance comes in; it covers everything you own *inside* a rented building. Because people tend to own less "stuff" than property, renter's insurance tends to be pretty inexpensive compared to a homeowner's policy.

Note that with either type of policy (homeowner's or renters), certain items can be excluded and must be listed separately, with an extra premium paid for each listed item. **Exclusions** generally include jewelry, equipment used in a home-based business, and portable electronics (e.g., laptop computer, iPod, cell phone, personal digital assistant, digital camera). Note that having receipts and photos (or a video) of the items in your home, office, or apartment helps speed up claims processing. Be sure, however, to keep the receipts, photos, and/or video off-site, such as in a safe-deposit box at your bank; if they are destroyed along with the items, they won't help you.

7.4.3 Business Insurance

Business insurance is a catch-all phrase for any type of insurance that relates to a business. An auto insurance policy that's for a company car is business insurance, as is property insurance for a business location. Of course, the big question is How much is a business's property worth? There are three methods to determine this value.

1. **Actual cash value approach:** This method places the value at the replacement cost minus any accumulated depreciation. For example, say that a law school graduate opened an office several years ago. She purchased a desk suite for $4,700, but over the years, the desk has depreciated by 50% (see Chapter 11 for additional information). If damage occurs now, the insurance will cover only $2,350.
2. **Replacement approach:** This method places the value at the amount needed to completely replace the damaged property. Using the example above, the lawyer would get a new desk or the money to purchase one, which would probably be more than she paid for the original desk.
3. **Agreed-amount approach:** This method usually applies to art works, wine collections, and other rather unique property. The amount covered is the amount agreed to at the writing of the policy.

Let's practice using the information provided so far with the following insurance situation: Mrs. Bricks and Mr. Sticks are owners of similarly constructed business properties built in the 1990s with basic wood studs and drywall construction, with insurance replacement costs determined to be $450,000. Mrs. Bricks took the advice of her insurance agent and purchased a policy with an 80% replacement cost clause. Mr. Sticks, trying to keep the premium cost low, had a policy written with 50% replacement cost.

Both structures had $30,000 damage to their roofing systems during a recent storm. Because Mrs. Bricks was insured for 80%, she will be fully reimbursed for her loss minus the amount specified in any deductible clause. But Mr. Sticks did not have the 80% coverage, and therefore, his insurance carrier will reimburse only $18,750, calculated at the greater amount of either the actual cash value to fix the roof or that proportion of the cost of the roof repair. The second approach here involves the fact that a coinsurance penalty comes into play because Mr. Bricks was not adequately insured (i.e., he did not have at least 80% coverage). Assume that the roof systems were at least 15 years old and carried a 25-year warranty. To figure out how much is actually covered, first, you need to calculate the actual cash value of the damage:

$$1 - \tfrac{15}{25} \times \$30,000 = \$12,000$$

Next, you calculate the proportional cost of the roof repair:

$$\text{Insured amount} \div 80\% \text{ of Replacement cost} \times \text{Damage}$$
$$\$225,000 \div (0.8 \times 450,000) \times 30,000$$
$$\$225,000 \div 360,000 \times 30,000 = \$18,750$$

Two types of insurance that tend to be unique to business are the following:

▲ **Disability insurance:** This type of policy covers employees against a debilitating illness or accident. In the event that a covered person can no longer work, he or she continues to receive regular paychecks, although usually for a lower amount (usually 60%) than the full salary earned before the disability. (This is because, in theory, expenses tend to decline when one is no longer working; for example, a disabled person may no longer need a car or may not have to pay for dry cleaning or a professional wardrobe. Of course, in practice, many disabled people find that their expenses increase due to additional care needs.)

▲ **Malpractice insurance:** Any company that provides a product or service runs the risk of getting sued if that product or service does not perform as expected or causes problems for the client. The likelihood of an expensive event happening affects the expense of malpractice rates. (Think, for example, of the potential problems associated with brain surgery versus those with copier repair service.) In fact, recent sharp increases in malpractice insurance have forced many doctors who specialize in obstetrics and gynecology to leave their practices. They simply cannot generate enough income to cover their skyrocketing insurance premiums.

7.4.4 Medical Insurance

These days, most people get their **medical insurance** through their work: Employers contract with an insurance provider (e.g., Blue Cross/Blue Shield) to cover their employees' medical costs. The employer and employees generally share the cost of coverage, and employees generally also pay a deductible.

However, many Americans are not covered by employer-sponsored medical insurance, for a variety of reasons (e.g., they're not currently working; they're working part time; their employers don't offer insurance [many small firms—those with 20 or fewer employees—cannot afford to offer medical insurance for their employees]). For these reasons, more and more insurance companies are offering medical insurance to individuals. Most individual policies have high deductibles, exclude preexisting conditions for at least 1 year, and do not include dental, vision, or maternity coverage. In addition, many people cannot get coverage through individual policies at all because of preexisting conditions.

It's worth a minute to explain the issue of health insurance deductibles. A deductible is the amount a policyholder must pay prior to the health insurance company paying anything. This is usually a yearly amount per insured member of the covered family (e.g., $1,000, with a maximum of $3,000). Once this amount is reached, the policy's coinsurance enters the mix. For example, if you have a policy with a $1,000 deductible and 80% coinsurance, once you have paid out $1,000, you will only have to pay 20% of any additional charges. This 20% payment usually has a cap of a few thousand dollars.

Although individual medical insurance is expensive, such plans do protect against unexpected medical costs, which can be staggering. In fact, about half of all bankruptcies are due to medical expenses that have drained family finances. For this reason, of all the insurance policies available to you or your business, medical insurance is, arguably, the most important. To go without is a risk that could wipe you out financially.

Try to figure out these examples.

1. You have health coverage that includes a deductible of $400 per person and 80% coinsurance. What is your out-of-pocket cost for a $670 health charge?

2. Your medical insurance policy has 80% coinsurance with a $700 deductible. What is your cost for a $950 medical problem?

For many individuals and families, a more important coverage number than the deductible is the maximum or the aggregate total out-of-pocket coverage per family in a covered year. As mentioned above, this aggregate is the amount of out-of-pocket services the individual or family pays for prior to the max being reached. For example, say that your family policy includes a $500 family deductible and coinsurance of 80%, up to a max of $5,000. Now assume the following:

▲ On May 5, your youngest son has a medical procedure that costs $8,000. The cost to you is $1,500 (because you first pay the $500 deductible and then pay 20% of the remaining $7,500).

▲ On June 5, your older son has a procedure that costs $7,000. The cost to you is $1,400 (because the deductible has been met, so now you must pay 20% of $7,000).

▲ On August 10, you have a medical problem that costs $15,000. The cost to you is $2,100 (because the deductible has been met and the coinsurance brings the amount down to $3,000, but you have an out-of-pocket max of $5,000, of which $2,900 has already been met).

▲ On November 20, your daughter has a procedure for $9,500. The cost to you for this is 0 (because you have already met your out-of-pocket max).

7.4.5 Life Insurance

Life insurance protects the people the policyholder leaves behind when he or she dies. Benefits are paid to a **beneficiary** (i.e., the person the policyholder designates to receive the value of the policy) upon the policyholder's death, and that money can be used to pay for everything from funeral expenses to mortgage payments. Life insurance generally comes in two flavors:

▲ **Term life: Term life** covers the life of the policyholder during a particular term (usually 1 year), and the policy is usually renewable at the end of the year. However, rates often increase every year or in 5-year chunks (staying stable between the ages of 50 and 54, for example, but then increasing at age 55). To protect against annual increases, many companies offer **level-term** policies, in which the annual premiums remain the same (level) for a set period—usually 20 or 30 years. Although policyholders pay a little more in the first few years than they would with a non-level-term policy, the assurance of knowing the premiums will not increase for several decades makes the initial cost increase worthwhile to many consumers.

▲ **Whole life: Whole life,** also called a permanent insurance policy, is like a term life policy that's combined with a savings account. Part of the premium goes to pay for a life insurance policy that pays benefits to a beneficiary—just like term life insurance. In addition, part of the premium goes into an account, into which the policyholder builds up a **cash value**, money that the policyholder can withdraw or borrow against. Because some of the premium is going toward the cash value account, to get the same size benefit, the premium is usually larger than for term insurance. One major difference between whole life and term life insurance is that term life often isn't available after a certain age, such as 70 or 75 years. If a person has locked into a whole life policy, however, he or she can continue to renew it until any age.

Life insurance policy premiums vary dramatically, based on a number of statistical factors:

▲ **Age:** Life insurance when you're 25 years old is substantially less expensive than when you're 65.

▲ **Sex:** Women live longer than men and, therefore, pay less than men for otherwise identical policies.

▲ **Smoking:** Smokers pay substantially more for life insurance than non-smokers.

▲ **Lifestyle:** If you hang glide, parachute, pilot a plane, drive a motorcycle, or engage in any other hobbies that are considered risky, you pay more for life insurance.

▲ **Existing conditions:** Any condition that will limit your lifespan forces you to pay more for life insurance.

The premiums for life insurance policies are usually quoted in units of $1,000. If a policy is quoted as $2.50 per $1,000, you would pay $2.50 per year for $1,000 coverage.

Try using the following situations to figure out the premiums required:

1. The rate presented to you per $1,000 is $3.50. You want $12,000 coverage. What is the premium?
2. A term life policy is calculated as $2.98 per $1,000. If you want $200,000 in coverage, what is the premium?
3. Your whole life policy uses a $5.20 rate per $1,000. You need $50,000 in coverage. What is the premium charged?
4. The quote from your term insurance agent is $6.11 per $1,000 of coverage. If you what a $75,000 policy, what is the premium?

7.4.6 Umbrella Policies

An **umbrella policy** (also called **excess liability**) is meant to provide additional coverage beyond what your homeowner's or auto policy offers. Ranging from $1 million to $5 million in coverage (more for commercial umbrella policies), these policies protect you from accidents that exceed the limits of your other policies. An umbrella policy is especially helpful if you're sued. With many insurance companies, in order to purchase an umbrella policy, you must already have a homeowner's or auto insurance policy in place.

7.4.7 Travel Insurance

Travel insurance, also called **trip-interruption insurance,** protects you from forfeiting the cost of a trip if you're unable to travel because of illness, injury, or family emergency. This insurance covers only one particular trip and may cover the cost of an entire tour or cruise. On the other hand, some travel insurance covers only the transportation portion (i.e., airfare, cruise ship fare) of a nonrefundable fare because many hotel and spa accommodations can be cancelled without penalty until the day of arrival. Travel insurance is available through travel agents, travel Web sites, cruise lines, airlines, and tour groups; costs for travel insurance vary, depending on the provider and the cost of the trip covered.

> ## FOR EXAMPLE
>
> ### Free Insurance Benefits
>
> The Discover card offers cardholders a travel accidental death insurance policy, but it's pretty specific. If you purchase airline tickets with your Discover card, a life insurance policy automatically kicks in, even for your spouse and children, if you also purchase their tickets with your Discover card. The fine print is that, in order to be able to make a claim, the accident has to involve the airplane, a death has to be involved, the death has to be accidental, and the death has to occur within 1 year of the airline-related accident. If you meet all those criteria, policy amounts are $150,000 to $500,000, depending on what kind of card you have (e.g., regular, platinum). But if your card is not in good standing (i.e., you're not paying your bills), the policy is voided. Other credit card companies offer similar policies, but few offer so much coverage.
>
> Some credit cards also offer collision damage when you rent a car so that you can waive that additional (and annoying) fee from a car-rental company. Should you be in an accident, the credit card company will pay for any collision damage not covered by your regular auto insurance company.

7.4.8 Extended Warranties

When you purchase appliances and electronics, you're almost always asked whether you want to purchase an **extended warranty,** which is essentially an insurance policy that covers the cost of repairing or replacing the item after its original warranty expires (usually 90 days to 1 year). The cost of extended warranties is usually a percentage of the cost of the item and is based on the number of additional years purchased: A 3-year extended warranty on a 42-inch flat-screen TV will be significantly higher than a 1-year extended warranty on an iPod Shuffle. Many extended warranties have a deductible clause similar to those in other insurance products.

Have you ever seen a home with a for sale sign, with a sign attached that the house will be sold to you with a warranty? This warranty covers many of the appliances and certain operational aspects of the house, such as the water heater, the furnace and air-conditioning systems, and the garage door opener. Before you buy a home warranty, you should think about how much it will really save you. For example, say that your dishwasher stops working. The home warranty policy covers up to $75 for a service call charge and up to $250 for parts. If the repair service costs $395, even with the policy, you have to pay $70 out of pocket to repair the dishwasher ($395 − [$75 + $250]).

SELF-CHECK

- Describe the main variables used in determining auto insurance rates.
- Discuss the difference between homeowner's and renter's insurance.
- Explain how people obtain medical insurance coverage.
- Consider the implications of lifestyle and existing medical conditions on life insurance rates.
- Explain how umbrella policies add coverage to existing policies.
- Describe short-term insurance options such as travel insurance and extended warranties.

SUMMARY

Banking and insurance serve the same purpose: They both protect you from financial loss. Savings and checking accounts offer a way for you to earn interest, manage your finances, and keep your money safe, and insurance protects you from the risk of accidents, acts of God, medical problems, and so on.

KEY TERMS

Auto insurance	Insurance for a vehicle
Bank service charge	A fee that a financial institution charges for a service, such as covering a bounced check or printing checks.
Beneficiary	The person a policyholder designates to receive the value of a life insurance policy.
Bounced check	A check for which funds are unavailable in the account.
Cap	An upper limit a policy will pay for each occurrence or over the policyholder's lifetime. For example, most vehicle insurance is subject to a $100,000/$300,000 cap.
Cash value	Money in a life insurance account that the policyholder can withdraw or borrow against.

Certificates of deposit (CDs)	A savings account that locks in money for a predetermined amount of time, usually from 30 days to 5 years.
Checkbook register	A system for keeping track of checkbook transactions that is useful in maintaining an accurate balance.
Claim	Paperwork filed if damage is done to property, vehicle, or person insured by a policy.
Collision	The portion of auto insurance that covers accidents that occur on the road.
Comprehensive	The portion of auto insurance that covers off-road claims. Often referred to as "act of God" coverage.
Debit card	A card that looks like credit card but operates like a paper check.
Deductible	An amount that a policyholder pays out before the insurance company begins paying for losses.
Deposit	Money that is put into an account to increase its balance.
Direct deposit	A feature offered by employers that electronically deposits a person's pay into his or her account on payday.
Disability insurance	Insurance that covers employees against debilitating illnesses or accidents.
EFT	Stands for electronic funds transfer; provides for electronic collections and payments.
Excess liability	*See* umbrella policy.
Exclusion	Categories of claims that cannot be made against a policy.
Extended warranty	A low-cost insurance policy that prolongs the standard warranty on appliances and electronics.
Face value	The amount shown on the front (or face) of a bond.
Gap	The difference in the amount of an insurance claim and the cap on the policy.
Homeowner's insurance	Insurance for a building, usually a home.

Identity theft	A crime in which criminals access personal financial accounts and use those accounts for their own gain.
Level-term	Term life insurance that has leveled premiums, which stay the same for a set period—usually 20 or 30 years.
Life insurance	Insurance that pays beneficiaries when a person dies.
Malpractice insurance	Insurance that protects against lawsuits arising from mistakes a company or person makes.
Maturity date	Predetermined date for withdrawal of money on a CD.
Medical insurance	Insurance that covers the costs of illness and injury.
Money market account	A higher-earning account that allows limited check writing and requires a high minimum balance.
NSF	Insufficient funds in an account to cover transactions. Stands for nonsufficient funds.
Online bank	A bank that has no (or few) brick-and-mortar locations.
Online banking	Conducting banking business using a computer instead of at a brick-and-mortar banking location.
Online bill paying	Transferring funds from a bank account to the account of the companies that are owed money.
Outstanding checks	Checks written on an account but not shown on a bank statement.
Overdraft protection	A feature offered by banks in which a savings account, secondary checking account, or credit card is debited the amount of the check written if the balance in the primary checking account is not high enough to cover the check.
Passbook	A booklet in which all deposits and withdrawals for an account are recorded.
Passbook account	Another name for a savings account.

Policy	Insurance coverage relating to a specific person, vehicle, home, office, and so on.
Premium	The amount paid to put an insurance policy in force.
Reconciliation	Matching a checkbook register with a monthly banking statement. Also called bank reconciliation.
Renter's insurance	Insurance on the contents of a home or an office but not the building itself.
Term life	Basic life insurance that covers a person for a particular term, usually 1 year.
Travel insurance	Insurance that protects the policyholder if he or she becomes ill or is otherwise unable to travel. Also known as trip-interruption insurance.
Trip-interruption insurance	*See* travel insurance.
Umbrella policy	Insurance that provides additional coverage, up to $5 million. Also known as excess liability.
Whole life	Traditional life insurance, plus a cash value account. Also called straight life.
Withdrawal	A transaction that reduces the balance of an account.

ASSESS YOUR UNDERSTANDING

Go to www.wiley.com/college/slavin to evaluate your knowledge of the basics of banking and insurance.

Measure your learning by comparing pre-test and post-test results.

Summary Questions

1. Online banks have virtually no brick-and-mortar locations. True or False?
2. Debit cards work exactly like credit cards. True or False?
3. Certificates of deposit:
   (a) offer higher interest rates than savings accounts.
   (b) lock in your money for set amount of time.
   (c) charge a penalty for early withdrawals.
   (d) all of the above.
4. Your monthly bank statement always reflects the most up-to-date information about your account. True or False?
5. The purpose of insurance is to protect you against losses you can't afford. True or False?
6. Define **act of God.**
7. In general, people who have good credit tend to be better risks for insurance companies. True or False?
8. Most general renter's and homeowner's policies do not cover jewelry and portable electronics. True or False?
9. Term life insurance is an insurance policy plus a savings account. True or False?

Review Questions

1. Describe the purpose of a savings account.
2. Describe the differences between checking accounts, savings accounts, and CDs.
3. What is the key point to remember when reconciling a bank statement?
4. What is identity theft?
5. Discuss the primary ways to protect yourself against identity theft.
6. What are the primary types of insurance?
7. Does someone have to die for the beneficiaries to collect on a life insurance policy?
8. Why buy whole life instead of the less expensive term insurance?

9. Under a term life policy, who will receive money when the policyholder dies?

10. Based on what this chapter says, what is the most important form of insurance?

11. What is the major challenge that debit card users face?

12. Explain the two ways in which bills are paid online.

Applying This Chapter

1. Use the simple interest formula to figure out the following:

   (a) Bob Norman deposited $2,000 for 1 year at a rate of 7%. Determine the interest paid.

   (b) The Philadelphia Eagles football team owners deposited $3 million for 1 year at $4\frac{1}{2}\%$. What was the interest paid to the team owners?

   (c) Find the principal of a $500,000 check deposited by you at your bank if the interest rate is 6% for 1 year.

   (d) Frank's bank statement reflects deposits of $15,000 over the last year at $8\frac{1}{2}\%$. How much interest did this account earn?

   (e) Using the simple interest formula, what was the principal amount deposited 2 years ago in an account that earns $4\frac{1}{4}\%$ and is now worth $42,519.

   (f) Use the simple interest formula to calculate the interest earned on $10,790 deposited in a bank for 7 years at a rate of $5\frac{3}{4}\%$.

   (g) Your Great Uncle George will lend you college tuition, with the understanding that in 4 years, you will return the $25,000 to him with a simple interest payment of $4\frac{1}{4}\%$. How much will you return to Uncle George after 4 years?

2. How much is the annual fire insurance premium on an old brick building that is covered for $170,000 at a rate of $0.695 per $1,000?

3. The rate for insuring your newly constructed garage is $0.246 per $100 of coverage. What is the annual premium for $35,000 of insurance coverage?

4. An older restaurant in the city has a fire insurance policy for $250,000. What is the cost if the rate used to calculate the premium is $0.519 per $100?

5. The van used in delivery of all your company's manufactured parts was involved in a collision that caused $10,952 in damages to the van. If the deductible is $500, how much will you receive for the insurance claim?

6. On your newly refurbished food court, a fire insurance agent quotes a rate of $0.391 per $100 in coverage. If you have an insurable interest of $2,009,000, how much will this policy cost you?

7. Your son's new Ford Focus has a $500 deductible. He backs the car into a pizza shop exterior wall, causing $7,905 in damage to the car. How much will the insurance company pay?

8. Your employer offers you a term life insurance policy for $1.79 per $1,000 of life coverage. It also offers to deduct this cost over the 26 pay periods in the next year. What is the total annual premium for a $175,000 policy?

9. A term life policy was offered to your spouse for $3.49 per $1,000. You want him to have $100,000 coverage. What is the premium?

10. Your home is valued at $1,200,000, and the house itself represents $1,000,000 of that amount. With homeowner's insurance rates at $0.263 per $100, what is the cost of coverage?

11. In a local fabricating factory's business office, a $5,000 desk was completely destroyed by mold after a water leak. The property insurance policy used the actual cash value approach to determine the amount of the claim. If the desk was 7 years old and depreciated by 50% at the time of the damage, what was the amount covered?

12. You are in an accident with your Honda, which is insured with a policy that has a $500 deductible. If the repairs are to cost $1,200, how much can you expect your insurance policy to cover?

13. Your Volvo is backed into a pole, and the damages are $5,600. Your insurance company will reimburse you how much, if you have a $200 deductible?

14. Your cash value life insurance for your spouse is a $250,000 policy. If the rate is $3.79 per $100, what is the cost to you?

15. A college van used for student club activities was in an accident. The deductible on the policy is $200, and the damages were $2,953.96. What was the amount the insurance paid the body shop?

16. If you are quoted a rate of $0.562 per $100 of coverage on your car wash business and you need $350,000 of coverage, what is the cost?

17. The insurance company quotes you a rate of $0.331 per $100 of coverage, and you want $560,000 in coverage. What is the premium?

18. A recently renovated catering facility has opened in your town. The property, for insurance purposes, is valued at $1,023,000, and the rate is $0.126 per $100. What is the cost of this coverage?.

YOU TRY IT

Bank Reconciliation

Reconcile your bank account, using the following information:

- Bank statement = $870
- Deposit in transit = $100
- Outstanding check = $56
- Check register = $943
- Service fee = $25
- ATM fee = $4

Out-of-Pocket Expense

What is your out-of-pocket expense for a health problem that costs $5,800 if you have a policy with an 80% coinsurance clause, a max of $1,000, and a $500 deductible?

Brand-New Account

You've just taken a new job, moved to a new town, and are shopping for a new bank. You need a way to pay your monthly bills, but you don't want the hassle of paper checks, if you can avoid them. You also want to start a rainy-day fund that will eventually total 3 months' salary. What sort of account(s) will you open?

Avoiding Financial Loss

The purpose of insurance is to reduce your risk of financial loss. Describe how you could limit your loss in the following scenario: You're in a serious accident in which you're at fault. You're injured, your car is totaled, and you'll be out of work for 4 months. The passenger in the other car is also injured and has medical bills alone that total $275,000, plus an additional loss of work.

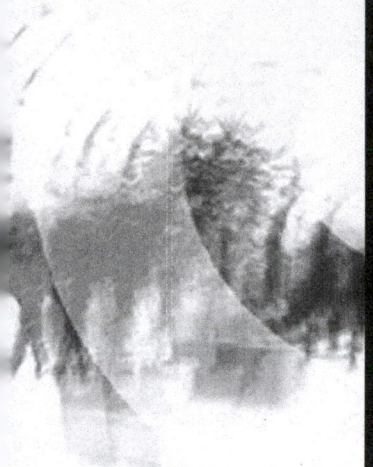

8

TAXES
Personal, Sales, and Property Taxes

Starting Point

Go to www.wiley.com/college/slavin to assess your knowledge of the basics of taxes.
Determine where you need to concentrate your effort.

What You'll Learn in This Chapter

▲ The various taxes on income
▲ Sales taxes and how they vary from state to state
▲ How real estate property is taxed
▲ What **use tax** means

After Studying This Chapter, You'll Be Able To

▲ Describe the various ways to report and pay income tax
▲ Identify the key sections of a pay stub
▲ Determine whether sales taxes are a fair form of taxation
▲ Question the practice of taxing the use of purchased items
▲ Determine whether property taxes unfairly tax the fixed-income elderly

Goals and Outcomes

▲ Understand the implications of taxing income, property, and retail sales
▲ Evaluate the fairest and least fair forms of taxes
▲ Choose the form of tax you feel is the most effective for raising revenue and argue for it

INTRODUCTION

Taxes come at you from all angles: You pay taxes on your income, on your home, on items you purchase (whether a new car or a box of cotton swabs), and sometimes on items you already own and are using. You're taxed on property you own, cars you drive, other retail items you buy, and the roads on which you drive. This chapter helps you sort through all of the ways you are taxed. You may find the following IRS webpage of frequently asked questions of interest: www.irs.gov/faqs/index.html.

8.1 Personal Income Taxes

Your employer—or at least the payroll software your company uses—does some interesting math on your **wages** before issuing you or directly depositing a paycheck. This chapter helps you understand the calculations your employer does each pay period to figure out how much money to take out of your earned wages and send to the government to pay taxes on your income.

This section explains how personal federal and state income taxes are determined and what (if anything) you can do to improve your bottom line (i.e., taxable situation). Employers use software from various companies to prepare their payroll (e.g., www.payroll.com/quickpayroll/, www.peachtree.com/payroll/)

8.1.1 Form W-4 (Employee's Withholding Allowance Certificate)

All income tax deductions from your paycheck begin with the W-4. If you're employed (i.e., you're not an independent contractor and aren't running your own business), you were given a **W-4 form** your first day on the job (see Figure 8-1). With this form, you communicate to the Internal Revenue Service (IRS) what you think your tax burden will be at the end of the year, and you ask your employer to remove the appropriate amount in taxes. If you live in a state that has a state income tax, you might also fill out a similar form for your state.

An employer can use IRS Publication 15: *Circular E, Employer's Tax Guide* (www.irs.gov/pub/irs-pdf/p15.pdf) to determine the amount of deduction its employees are allowed.

The simplest way to figure your W-4 is to follow the instructions and fill out the worksheet the IRS provides with the form. You're asked to determine your filing status; namely, whether you're single or married, whether you're the head of a household, how many dependents you can claim on your tax return, and how many jobs you have (or you and your spouse have between you; refer to Figure 8-1). These are called *exemptions*, and you do not have to pay income tax on that portion of your pay.

Figure 8-1

Cut here and give Form W-4 to your employer. Keep the top part for your records.

Form **W-4**
Department of the Treasury
Internal Revenue Service

Employee's Withholding Allowance Certificate

► **Whether you are entitled to claim a certain number of allowances or exemption from withholding is subject to review by the IRS. Your employer may be required to send a copy of this form to the IRS.**

OMB No. 1545-0074
2006

1 Type or print your first name and middle initial. | Last name | 2 Your social security number

Home address (number and street or rural route) | 3 ☐ Single ☐ Married ☐ Married, but withhold at higher Single rate.
Note. If married, but legally separated, or spouse is a nonresident alien, check the "Single" box.

City or town, state, and ZIP code | 4 **If your last name differs from that shown on your social security card, check here. You must call 1-800-772-1213 for a new card.** ► ☐

5 Total number of allowances you are claiming (from line **H** above **or** from the applicable worksheet on page 2) 5
6 Additional amount, if any, you want withheld from each paycheck . . . . 6 $
7 I claim exemption from withholding for 2006, and I certify that I meet **both** of the following conditions for exemption.
• Last year I had a right to a refund of **all** federal income tax withheld because I had **no** tax liability **and**
• This year I expect a refund of **all** federal income tax withheld because I expect to have **no** tax liability.
If you meet both conditions, write "Exempt" here . . . . ► 7

Under penalties of perjury, I declare that I have examined this certificate and to the best of my knowledge and belief, it is true, correct, and complete.
Employee's signature
(Form is not valid unless you sign it.) ► **Date** ►

8 Employer's name and address (Employer: Complete lines 8 and 10 only if sending to the IRS.) | 9 Office code (optional) | 10 Employer identification number (EIN)

For Privacy Act and Paperwork Reduction Act Notice, see page 2. Cat. No. 10220Q Form **W-4** (2006)

Form W-4.

What the employer is trying to figure out with the W-4 is how much you're likely to owe in taxes at the end of the year. The goal is for your employer to withdraw the amount you will owe—not too much, and not too little. If you pay too much, you get a refund next year, but you don't have access to that money throughout the current year. Even if all you'd do with that money is stick it in a savings account at 2% interest, that's interest you won't be able to earn. You don't want to pay too little because you'll owe the balance at the end of the year *and* may have to pay an underpayment penalty.

If you're under- or overpaying your taxes (i.e., you owe money or you get a large refund), you can talk to your payroll department and adjust your W-4. If you're paying too much, you should increase the number of dependents you claim. If you're paying to little, you should either reduce the number of dependents (you can even claim zero) or specify an additional amount you'd like withheld from each paycheck. Try this IRS site, which helps you calculate how much to claim on Form W-4: www.irs.gov/individuals/page/0,id=14806,00.html.

8.1.2 Social Security, Medicare, and Withholding Tax

In addition to state and local taxes, the federal government requires your employer to remove three types of taxes from each paycheck:

- **Withholding tax: Withholding** tax is the tax we commonly think of as "income tax." When you complete your tax form at the end of the year, the amount you owe should be the amount you paid in withholding tax. When you adjust your W-4, it is this tax that is affected. Withholding tax is also known as *federal income tax (FIT)* and *federal withholding tax (FWT)*.

▲ **Social Security:** The **Social Security** tax funds the Social Security payment you'll receive in your retirement years. The amount you pay in Social Security tax depends on how much you earned (see www.ssa.gov/mystatement/fica.htm). Social Security tax is also known as FICA, for the Federal Insurance Contributions Act.

▲ **Medicare:** The **Medicare** tax funds, as you might expect, the Medicare program that pays a portion of the medical expenses for elder citizens. This tax is also dependent on how much you earn (www.medicare.gov).

The amounts of these taxes change from year to year. This chapter uses the 2006 tax rates and provides you with some payroll problems that test your ability to perform simple math using these rates. So for the sake of this material, use the following tax information when calculating any problems in this chapter.

▲ The Social Security tax rate is 6.2% (or .062) on the first $94,200 of your gross earnings (i.e., the amount of wages/salary you earned before deductions). *Note:* You may be entitled to certain adjustments to this amount if you participate in a flexible benefit plan or plans at work (see www.treasury.state.tn.us/flex/flex-1.htm).

▲ Medicare tax is 1.45% (or .0145) on all wages/salary.

Based on these tax rates, try to determine the amounts to be deducted for Social Security and/or Medicare under the following conditions:

1. If your total yearly salary prior to the paycheck of November 1, 2006, is $57,600 and you are paid 24 times per year, how much Social Security and how much Medicare are taken from the November 1 check?

2. If your total pay for the year up to July 1, 2006, is $23,750 and you are paid $789 per week, how much Medicare tax is deducted each week?

3. If you're paid weekly, and your total pay prior to your pay of December 1, 2006, is $94,876, what is the Social Security tax owed from your last paychecks in December?

8.1.3 Reading a Pay Stub

Pay stubs differ widely from company to company, but all generally show the following information:

▲ **Gross wages:** The **gross pay** is how much you earned during the pay period. If you work for a salary, this amount will be the same from paycheck to paycheck. If you are paid hourly, paid for **piecework** (i.e., by the number of pieces you produce), or paid **commission** (i.e., you get a percentage of the products you sell), your wages will likely change from one paycheck to another. Also, you may receive your pay under different pay periods, such as

▲ **Weekly:** 52 checks a year.

▲ **Biweekly:** 26 checks per year.

▲ **Semimonthly:** 24 checks per year, twice a month (e.g., on the 1st and 15th of each month).

▲ **Monthly:** 12 checks per year

We'll look at how to figure out gross pay in Section 8.1.6.

▲ **Taxes:** This is the amount of your wages deducted to cover your tax burden. It is usually broken down by federal withholding (FWT), Social Security (FICA), Medicare, state income taxes (SWT), and local income taxes (often called occupancy tax).

▲ **Insurance:** If you pay all or a portion of your medical, life, or other insurance, that amount will be reflected on your pay stub and deducted from your wages.

▲ **Union dues:** If you're a part of a union, your dues are usually subtracted from your wages.

▲ **Retirement:** If you pay all or a portion of your retirement—including 401(k) contributions—this amount will appear on your pay stub and will be taken out of your wages.

▲ **Parking/train pass/bus pass:** Many companies offer their employees low-cost transportation passes to get to and from work. To simplify matters, the cost of these passes is removed from the employee's wages, and the pass is given to the employee.

▲ **Day-care/fitness center:** Whether on site or off site, some employers pay all or part of the expenses for a day-care facility and/or fitness center. If the employee pays any amount for these services (which is common), that amount is subtracted from the wages and is reflected on the pay stub.

For each of these categories, most paychecks show not only the **current amounts** but also the **year-to-date (YTD)** amounts, which total up all that you've earned or taxes paid since the January 1.

8.1.4 W-2s and 1099s

Employers and clients send forms to the government at the end of each year; employers send W-2, and clients send 1099s. This is how the government tracks your income: The IRS double-checks your tax return against your W-2s or 1099s to ensure that you're not underreporting your income.

A **W-2** is essentially a summary of your pay stub. The form must be sent to the IRS (with a copy for you, the employee) by January 31 of each year, giving you time to make corrections before the April 15 annual tax-filing deadline. Figure 8-2 shows what a typical W-2 form looks like; it lists your personal information, income for the year, any tips you reported to your employer, withholding tax paid, Social Security/Medicare payments made, and state/local taxes paid. The W-2 also details whether you have a retirement plan or other plan into which you made contributions; plans like this often save you money because they reduce the amount of income you made by the amount you contributed, and when you reduce your income, you also reduce the amount of tax you owe.

A **1099** (see Figure 8-3) looks very much like a W-2, but it is sent by any company or individual that pays $600 or more for your services in one year. So, if you start a pet-sitting company on the weekends, and you charge $15 per day for each client, you're probably not going to receive a 1099 because you will not have earned at least $600 from any *one* client. But if one of your pet-sitting clients goes to Europe for two months and pays you $900 for your services, that client needs to file a 1099 for you, sending a copy to the IRS and another to you.

Technically, a 1099 does *not* ensure that you will adequately report your income to the IRS. For example, in your pet-sitting business, you may earn $2,000 per year but not have a single client that pays you more than $100 or $200 for the year. In this case, you wouldn't have a single 1099 filed on your behalf and could, if you wanted to, not report your pet-sitting income and underpay your taxes (i.e., cheat). However, the 1099 does encourage everyone with self-employment income to accurately report earnings.

Note: Using the Internet to file personal income taxes is now popular. You can use sites as www.turbotax.com and www.taxcut.com.

Figure 8-2

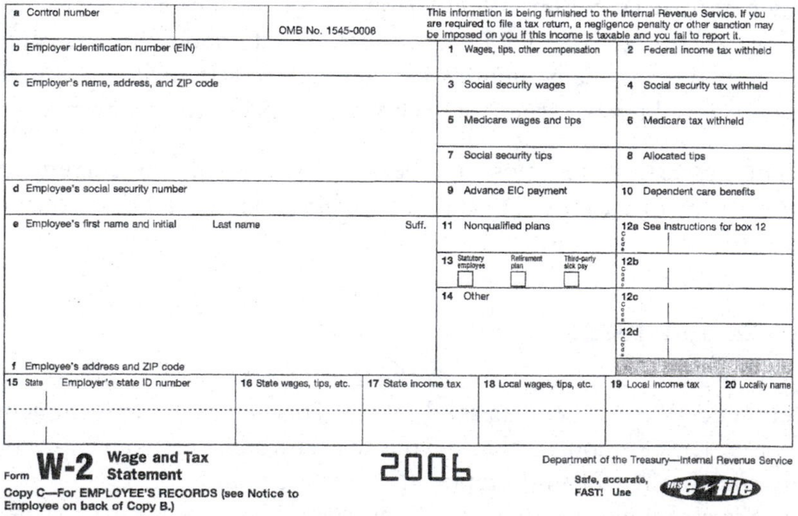
a Control number
OMB No. 1545-0008
This information is being furnished to the Internal Revenue Service. If you are required to file a tax return, a negligence penalty or other sanction may be imposed on you if this income is taxable and you fail to report it.
b Employer identification number (EIN)
1 Wages, tips, other compensation
2 Federal income tax withheld
c Employer's name, address, and ZIP code
3 Social security wages
4 Social security tax withheld
5 Medicare wages and tips
6 Medicare tax withheld
7 Social security tips
8 Allocated tips
d Employee's social security number
9 Advance EIC payment
10 Dependent care benefits
e Employee's first name and initial Last name Suff.
11 Nonqualified plans
12a See instructions for box 12
13 Statutory employee Retirement plan Third-party sick pay
12b
14 Other
12c
12d
f Employee's address and ZIP code
15 State Employer's state ID number
16 State wages, tips, etc.
17 State income tax
18 Local wages, tips, etc.
19 Local income tax
20 Locality name
Form W-2 Wage and Tax Statement
2006
Department of the Treasury—Internal Revenue Service
Safe, accurate, FAST! Use IRS e-file
Copy C—For EMPLOYEE'S RECORDS (see Notice to Employee on back of Copy B.)

Form W-2.

Figure 8-3

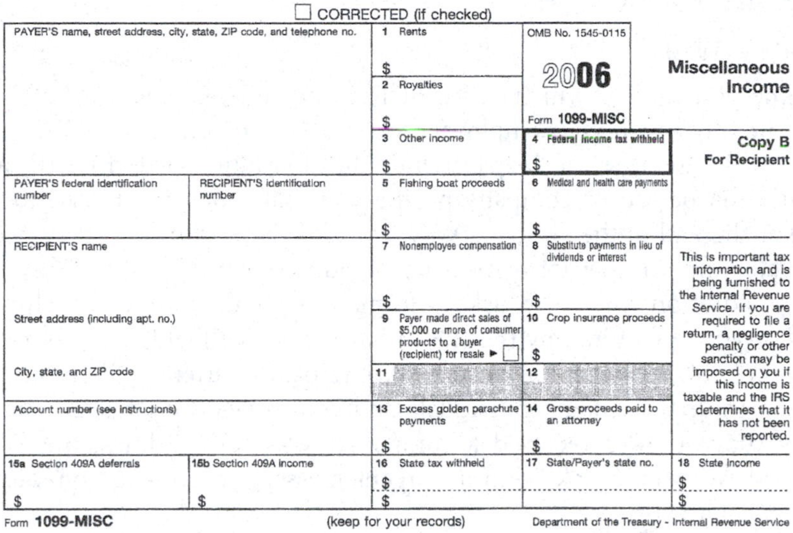

☐ CORRECTED (if checked)

PAYER'S name, street address, city, state, ZIP code, and telephone no.

1 Rents $

2 Royalties $

3 Other income $

OMB No. 1545-0115

2006

Form 1099-MISC

Miscellaneous Income

4 Federal income tax withheld $

Copy B For Recipient

PAYER'S federal identification number

RECIPIENT'S identification number

5 Fishing boat proceeds $

6 Medical and health care payments $

RECIPIENT'S name

7 Nonemployee compensation $

8 Substitute payments in lieu of dividends or interest $

This is important tax information and is being furnished to the Internal Revenue Service. If you are required to file a return, a negligence penalty or other sanction may be imposed on you if this income is taxable and the IRS determines that it has not been reported.

Street address (including apt. no.)

9 Payer made direct sales of $5,000 or more of consumer products to a buyer (recipient) for resale ► ☐

10 Crop insurance proceeds $

City, state, and ZIP code

11

12

Account number (see instructions)

13 Excess golden parachute payments $

14 Gross proceeds paid to an attorney $

15a Section 409A deferrals $

15b Section 409A income $

16 State tax withheld $ $

17 State/Payer's state no.

18 State income $ $

Form 1099-MISC (keep for your records) Department of the Treasury - Internal Revenue Service

Form 1099.

8.1.5 Self-Employment (SE) Taxes

Suppose you start a personal training business, or you sell Mary Kay or Arbonne, or you run some other small business. Do you pay tax on the income you make from that business? Of course you do! After subtracting your expenses related to running that business, you pay taxes much as you would if you were an employee. However, unlike employees, whose taxes are withdrawn from each paycheck, if you're self-employed, you pay your taxes four times per year (for a tax year that runs from January to December): April 15, June 15, September 15, and January 15. At each date, you determine how much money you've made so far in the year, estimate how much you're likely to make for the entire year, calculate your taxes due for the year, and pay the portion of tax that's due at that time.

In addition to paying withholding taxes, if you're self-employed, you must also pay Social Security tax, and the amount you owe may seem like too much—much more, anyway, than you pay when you're an employee. This is because you're paying both portions of the Social Security tax: the portion normally paid by the employer (but when you're self-employed, that's you), and the portion paid by the employee (that's also you). When you're employed by someone else, you pay only *half* of the total amount being paid to the Social Security Administration on your behalf; your employer pays the other half. The SE tax is the equivalent to both employee and employer taxes, namely 12.4% for FICA and 2.9% for Medicare; however, you do get to deduct half of that tax as a business expense (i.e., deduction). See www.irs.gov/businesses/small/article/0,,id=98846,00.html.

FOR EXAMPLE

What's a W-9?

Anytime you earn or win (i.e., in a lottery or raffle) more than $600 from someone other than your employer, you're asked to complete a **W-9,** which is called the Request for Taxpayer Identification Number and Certification. Because the person or company paying you that money will need to file a 1099 at the end of the year, the W-9 provides the information they need to adequately fill out that form: your name, address, and Social Security number. In addition, the form asks information about your citizenship and whether you're required by the IRS to have taxes withheld from your check (generally, this happens only if you haven't paid quarterly self-employment taxes in the past). Often, individuals and companies don't release payment to you until they've received a completed W-9; other times, the W-9 is enclosed with the check, with an urgent message for you to complete the form and return it.

8.1.6 Determining Your Gross Pay

Let's compare how your paycheck would appear, prior to deductions (i.e., gross pay), if you were paid using different pay periods.

Let's first determine the gross pay for each paycheck if you received a $31,500 yearly salary under the following pay period formats:

▲ **Monthly:** $31,500 divided by 12 = $2,625 per month
▲ **Weekly:** $31,500 divided by 52 = $605.77 per week
▲ **Biweekly:** $31,500 divided by 26 = $1,211.54 (rounded) every other week

You might not receive a salary but instead be paid by the hour, called an *hourly rate.* Your pay might also include any overtime. This type of arrangement is subject to a federal law, the Fair Labor Standards Act (FLSA; see www.dol.gov/esa/whd/flsa/), and most states have such laws as well. These laws cover overtime pay for work performed over the 40 hours in one 7-day period. By law, the overtime rate must be at least $1\frac{1}{2}$ times your regular hourly rate.

Now you can try to calculate a paycheck by using various hourly rates. Figure out the gross pay of employees earning the following hourly rates:

1. 40 hours at $7.15 per hour
2. 30 hours at $8.25 per hour
3. $38\frac{1}{2}$ hours at $9.25 per hour
4. 8 hours at $14.95 per hour

Now try a few with overtime hours:

1. 45 hours at $8.00 per hour
2. 50 hours at $23.00 per hour
3. 48 hours at $12.00 per hour
4. 56 hours at $9.00 per hour

As mentioned earlier, some people receive a commission based on the sales they generate during their work day. Let's assume that a store pays a 5% commission to you if you make total sales today of $1,000. How much would your commission be if you sell $1,000 in goods today? It would be .05 multiplied by $1,000, which is $50. This amount would be added to your hourly rate of pay or your salary, if you are paid in either of these methods.

Now you can try a few commission problems. Determine the total gross pay in the following situations:

1. You receive $10 per hour and a commission of 3% on all sales. Sales were $1,500 today, and your worked a full 8-hour shift.
2. You are paid a weekly salary of $670 plus a 1% commission on total stores sales, which this week were $68,000.
3. Your hourly rate is $12.50 and you also earn 2% on the $2,100 sales during your 8-hour shift today.
4. You earn a salary of $21,000 plus a 5% commission on all sales above $100,000. Sales are $670,000.

Now let's consider those working and paid under the piecework method, which involves being paid for each item made. For example, if you are paid $12 for every oil change you perform at a vehicle service station and you do 7 jobs today, your pay is $12 × 7, which is $84 for the day.

Now try to calculate the daily pay under the following situations, where the employee works under a piecework method:

1. An employee earns $0.15 per unit for meat cuts at a butcher department, and during the day she handled 150 meat cuts.
2. A repair technician at the rental car depot is paid $24 for every wheel alignment he performs on his shift. If he does 23 during a busy day, what is his payment?
3. A seamstress is paid $0.02 per button, and she works on 12,000 buttons during the shift. What pay does she earn?
4. A painter of new kitchen cabinet doors is paid $4 for each door. How many doors did he paint if he earns $224 today?

- Consider the implications of increasing the number of dependents on a W-4 form.
- Describe the main forms used to determine taxes and report income.
- Explain what appears on a pay stub.

8.2 Sales Taxes

Sales tax is a tax on retail purchases, such as purchases of clothing, electronics, and cars. Sales tax is considered one of the fairest ways to tax people because it usually taxes non-essential or less-essential items. Most states do not, for example, charge sales tax on groceries (although they may tax prepared foods from restaurants), prescription drugs, or apartment rent. A few states also don't charge sales tax on clothing or over-the-counter drugs.

Some states have no sales tax, but most hover around the 3% to 4% mark. A few states—such as California (7.25%), Mississippi (7%), Rhode Island (7%), Tennessee (7%), and Pennsylvania (6%)—have much higher sales tax rates. Some also allow an additional local tax. For example, in some areas of Tennessee, the sales tax rate is 9.75% because local taxes of 2.75% are added to the 7% state rate. This means that you have to add nearly 10% to every retail purchase you make. However, Tennessee residents don't pay a state income tax.

You calculate sales tax by using the following formula:

$$\text{Sales tax} = \text{Price} \times \text{Tax rate}$$

Now you're ready to try a few sales tax calculations. Solve the following:

1. If the sales tax is 6% on an item that costs $19.95, how much is the tax, and what is the total amount paid?
2. Sales tax is 4% and the price is $670. What is the tax amount?
3. Sales tax is 10% on a bookcase priced at $1,200. What is the tax amount?
4. Sales tax is 6% on a textbook that costs $98. What is the total cost of the book to you?

In addition to sales tax, some states charge a **tourism tax** or a **luxury tax** on items such as hotels (called a bed tax), restaurants, and expensive items, such as luxury cars. Two groups of people pay these taxes—tourists and the wealthy—and taxpayers love to tax tourists (who don't live in the area and, for the most part, have money to spend) and the wealthy.

FOR EXAMPLE

Thinking of Dodging the Sales Tax by Shopping Online?

Suppose you live in a state with a combined 9% state and local sales tax rate and want to purchase an iPod at $300. You find the iPod online, at a site that offers free shipping, and discover that no sales tax will be charged. (Online stores charge you sales tax only if they operate brick-and-mortar locations in your state. Otherwise, they do not charge you sales tax.) You figure you've just saved yourself $27 ($300 × 9%) and are feeling pretty smug about the whole thing. Hang on there, tax-dodger. When you pay your yearly state income tax, you'll be asked how much you purchased that year from out-of-state retailers and—you guessed it—you'll be required at that time to cough up the amount of sales tax you avoided paying earlier in the year. Even if you live in a state with no state income tax (and, therefore, you don't file taxes each year with the state), you're probably required to file a form each year in which you pay for any state sales tax you've avoided paying throughout the year. Don't be surprised if, in the near future, all online purchases will be subject to sales tax.

The bed tax is usually 1% to 12% of the total hotel room charge and is often used to fund the local visitors/tourism office in the county or state. This tax may be in addition to the sales tax, often 6%, on a hotel room. Check your lodging receipt next time you travel for itemization of these taxes.

Try these problems:

1. You stay at the Treetop Lodge in Williamsburg, Virginia, where a 9% bed tax is charged and a 6% occupancy (sales) tax is added to your bill, based on a room charge of $215. What is the total amount owed?

2. The Hilton in your town charges $75 per hotel room plus a bed tax of 12%. What is your total bill for 3 nights?

3. If the motel room rate is $79.50 and there is a tax of 6%, what is the total bill?

SELF-CHECK

- Describe and calculate total price, including sales taxes.
- Explain luxury and tourism taxes.
- Consider the implications of buying taxable items online.

8.3 Property, Excise, and Use Taxes

Property taxes are levied on physical property you own: a house, an apartment, a condominium, an office building, acreage, and so on. (However, if you rent property, you do not pay the property tax for it; the property manager or owner does.) The annual tax for the property is based on the **assessed value** of the house (an amount, usually a percentage of the actual market value, used for taxing purposes). Then each county or other taxing authority sets its own assessment tax rate, which is then multiplied by the assessed value to determine the actual property tax.

To derive the actual tax due, deductions for living in the house and/or having a mortgage (to more heavily tax those with second homes or who have paid off their homes) are first subtracted from the assessed value. Then the following formula is used to take a percentage of that amount and multiply it by an assessment tax rate:

$$\text{Assessed value} = \text{Assessment rate} \times \text{Market value}$$

The tax rate, which may be stated in terms of **mills** (i.e., $\frac{1}{1000}$ of a dollar), is applied to this assessed value of the property. For example, a rate of 5.45% would be presented as .0545 (mills).

For example, if your house has a market value of $210,000 and the assessment rate is 30% of this value, then you have an assessed value of $63,000. If the millage is .0545, you multiply this by the assessed value to determine your tax due:

$$\$63,000 \times .0545 = \$3,433.50$$

Try these problems:

1. Your property has a current market value of $560,000, and the county is using a 25% assessment rate and a .0640 mill rate. What are your taxes due?
2. Your local school district has a property tax of .0534 mills on assessed value and an assessment rate of 30% of the market value. What is your tax obligation if the property has a market value of $189,000?

One of the biggest challenges related to property tax is how to tax someone who has lived in a house for 40 or 50 years—a house that may now be worth a great deal more than it once was but might belong to someone who is on a limited income. This challenge has caused taxpayers to question the fairness of property taxes because being "land rich" (i.e., owning valuable property) does not mean one is, indeed, wealthy. Wealth that is tied up in real estate is often impossible to access, so someone with a property tax bill of $10,000 or $20,000 may simply not have enough income to cover the tax. For this reason, some counties do not change the assessed value for a property until it is sold, thus keeping the tax low for a long-time resident. As an additional measure, many states are enacting

FOR EXAMPLE

Toll Roads

One of the simplest forms of use tax is a road **toll**: You pay to use the road on which you drive. Road tolls are one of the fairest forms of tax because only the people who use the toll roads pay for them. Non-toll roads are paid for and maintained using county or state taxes that everyone pays (whether they use those roads or not), but toll roads are paid for and maintained solely by the drivers who use those particular roads. Companies that use toll roads, such as trucking firms that are hauling lettuce to your local grocer, simply pass along the toll to their customers, so, again, the system is fair. Fair as this system is, however, toll roads aren't very popular among drivers, mostly because they slow down traffic and make the morning commute that much longer.

legislation to permit casino gambling in an attempt to reduce taxes, particularly the heavy property tax on elderly and low-income property owners.

Use taxes are taxes that charge you for using something: a car, a boat, a road, and so on. Each year you receive a form, asking you to detail what you own, and later, you receive a bill for the use tax you owe. This tax is highly unpopular because it strikes people as being too much: First you're taxed on the income you make, and then you're taxed when you buy an item, and then you're taxed for using that item! As a result, states are finding other ways to raise tax revenue.

SELF-CHECK

- Define **assessed value** and how it relates to property tax.
- Describe how use taxes are charged.
- Consider whether tolls are fair taxes.

SUMMARY

No matter who you are or where you live, you pay taxes. You pay when you make money, when you spend money, when you use what you have bought, and even when you're just sitting in your home, enjoying the sunset. In the end, you get something in return for what you pay: politicians to make and uphold laws, a military to protect the country, squadrons of police, free public schools, free libraries, well-maintained roads and parks, free or low-cost museums, free research on issues of public health and safety, and on and on. Taxes pay for services that add to the quality of our lives.

KEY TERMS

1099	An IRS form that clients send to report self-employment income for the year.
Assessed value	The estimated price (value) of real estate's worth in today's market.
Commission	Income that is based on a percentage of the goods or services sold.
Gross pay	Total wages earned, before deductions.
Luxury tax	Tax on luxury items that is meant to be paid by the wealthy.
Medicare	The tax that funds the Medicare program.
Mill	$\frac{1}{1000}$ of a dollar (e.g., 43.10 mills is 4.31%). Mills are used in real estate tax determination.
Piecework	Income that is based on the number of pieces produced.
Property tax	A tax on real estate.
Sales tax	Tax on retail purchases.
Social Security	The tax that funds the Social Security program. Also known as *FICA (Federal Insurance Contributions Act)*.
Toll	A tax on some roads, interstates, and highways.
Tourism tax	A tax on hotels and restaurants.
Use tax	A tax on the use of items you own.
W-2	An IRS form that employers send to report employee income and taxes withheld for the year.
W-4	An IRS form that an employer uses to determine federal withholding for an employer.
W-9	A form used to gather information to prepare a 1099 form.
Wages	Income earned from an employer.
Withholding tax	Tax withheld from income to cover a person's income tax liability. Also known as *federal income tax (FIT)* and *federal withholding tax (FWT)*.
YTD	The amount made or paid since January 1 of the current year. Stands for *year-to-date*.

ASSESS YOUR UNDERSTANDING

Go to www.wiley.com/college/slavin to evaluate your assimilation of the basics of taxes.

Measure your learning by comparing pre-test and post test results.

Summary Questions

1. *Withholding tax* is another term for Social Security tax. True or false?
2. Which form does an employer use to report employees' annual wages to the IRS?
   (a) W-4
   (b) 1099
   (c) W-2
   (d) W-9
3. Year-to-date (YTD) amounts on your pay stub total your wages since January 1. True or False?
4. Self-employed workers pay taxes:
   (a) once per month.
   (b) once per quarter.
   (c) twice per year.
   (d) once per year.
5. Many states exempt prescription drugs from sales tax. True or False?
6. Excise tax usually taxes use of a home or an apartment. True or False?
7. You use IRS form 1099 to file your excise tax information. True or False?

Review Questions

1. Self-employed taxpayers pay a higher tax on their income than do those who are employed by someone else. Explain why.
2. Why are luxury taxes popular among taxpayers?
3. Describe why a toll is considered a fair form of taxation.
4. What is the advantage of listing income tax, Social Security tax, and Medicare tax separately on pay stubs and W-2 forms?
5. In what ways do taxpayers avoid paying their fair share of tax burdens?
6. Taxes that tend to adversely affect the poor and/or elderly are known as *regressive*. Which type of tax is more likely to be regressive: property tax, sales tax, or income tax?

7. Describe why taxes on tourism-related items—namely hotels and high-end restaurants—tend to be popular with taxpayers.

8. What is the disadvantage of rising real estate values to an elderly home-owner on a tight budget?

Applying This Chapter

1. If the sales tax is 6% in your state, what is the total you pay for a new iPod priced at $135.95?

2. A restaurant check for $73.50 had a 6% sales tax added, and you wanted to charge the total amount, plus a 20% tip, to your credit card. What is the total charged?

3. You are paid a 5% commission for your sales yesterday of $1,010. What is the commission?

4. Your pay for a week is $567. How much Social Security and Medicare taxes do you pay from that check?

5. The head of your marketing department, Paul, is paid a salary, and he receives biweekly checks for $6,908 gross pay. What is Paul's annual salary?

6. A new phone system for your office costs $530.95, plus a 6% sales tax. If you buy this system online, from an out-of-state company, charging the purchase to the company's Visa card, what is the total cost?

7. Your first position after college is as banquet/catering supervisor at the newest riverfront hotel in the city. Your compensation package is explained as a combination of salary ($625 per week), a commission on food and beverage sales of $\frac{1}{4}$%, and $1 for every whole bottle of wine sold during catered events. You are paid biweekly. During one two-week period, sales were $76,900 and your department sold 24 cases (12 bottles per case) of wine. What is your gross pay for the period?

8. Your staff members in problem 7 earn an hourly wage as well as a 12% commission on the total sale of food and beverage (which appears as a service charge to the customer). If Walter, a waiter, earns $5.50 per hour and works 87 hours during the same two-week pay period as in problem 7, what is his gross pay?

9. An employee earns $8.25 per hour and $12\frac{1}{2}$ cents on each beef cut when cutting meat at a boutique hotel. During a day, she handles 250 meat cuts. What would her gross pay be for an 8-hour shift?

10. A slot machine technician at a casino is paid $17 for every machine he works on during his shift. If he works on 43 machines during a busy day, what is his wage?

11. A seamstress is paid $1\frac{1}{4}$ cents for each button she replaces on a security company's uniforms. If she works on 13,450 buttons during a shift, what is the gross pay she earns?

12. A carpenter painting kitchen cabinet doors on an apartment remodeling project is paid $4 for each door. How many doors did he paint if he earned $234 today?

13. David receives $13.45 per hour and a commission of 2% on all sales. His sales today were $2,500, and he worked an 8-hour shift. What is his gross pay?

14. Jane is paid a weekly salary of $970 plus a $1\frac{1}{2}$% commission on total store sales, which this week were $468,000. What is her gross pay?

15. You pay each of your employees an hourly rate of $12.50, and you also pay them a 2% commission if sales top $4,000. During an 8-hour shift today, what do you pay one employee if sales targets are reached?

16. David's salary in 2005 was $61,700, plus he earned a 4% commission on all sales above $100,000. Sales in 2005 were $670,000.

    (a) What was David's gross pay?

    (b) How much were David's Social Security and Medicare taxes?

17. If your total yearly salary prior to the paycheck of December 1, 2006, is $87,690 and you are paid 24 times per year, how much Social Security and how much Medicare are taken from the your first check in December?

18. If George is paid a total salary of $43,000 for the year up to July 1, 2006, and he is paid $895 per week, how much Medicare tax is deducted each week?

19. Your total pay prior to your pay of December 1, 2006, was $194,800.91. How much Social Security tax do you owe from your last paycheck in December?

YOU TRY IT

State and Local Taxes

If your state sales tax is 6% and your local tax is an additional 1.5%, how much will you pay for

1. a $3,000 Vespa scooter?
2. $290 in prescription drugs?
3. a $400 pair of Jimmy Choo shoes?
4. a $120 grocery bill?

Commission Pay

You are paid a commission plus a salary. Your commission is 2% of sales over $15,000 per month. You are paid a $1575 monthly salary, and sales were $65,970

1. What was your gross pay?
2. If your total wages for the year were less than $90,000, what was the total deducted from your pay for Social Security plus Medicare?

Alice's Sandwich Shop

Your sandwich maker, Alice, earns $10.25 per hour and works 35 hours the last pay week in March.

1. What is her gross pay for the week?
2. Alice works 47 hours the next week. What is her gross pay for that week?

3. Assuming that Alice earns less than $23,000 per year, calculate the Social Security tax on Alice's first check in April.

Consultant's Salary

Ann Morgan, a regional manager with a moderate-sized consulting firm in suburban Atlantic City, New Jersey, earns a salary of $3,590 per pay period and a commission of 1% on sales over $45,000. Say she is paid monthly and the total sales for a month are $2,608,000.

1. What is her gross pay?
2. How much are her Social Security and Medicare deductions?

Pastry Wages

You own a five-star restaurant in New York City. You pay your pastry chef, Claude Bennett, $18.75 per hour and guarantee him 8 hours of overtime each week.

1. What is Claude's normal gross pay?
2. An apprentice to Claude earns $7.75 per hour and is paid per unit produced, at a rate of $2 per cake or pie. If on this past Saturday the apprentice baked 35 items, what was his total earned for his 8-hour shift?

9

CALCULATING INTEREST
Simple and Compound Interest

Starting Point

Go to www.wiley.com/college/slavin to assess your knowledge of the basics of simple interest and consumer credit.
Determine where you need to concentrate your effort.

What You'll Learn in This Chapter

▲ How to relate simple interest to maturity value
▲ How to read compound interest tables
▲ The present value and future value of money

After Studying This Chapter, You'll Be Able To

▲ Calculate simple interest when given certain variables
▲ Manipulate the simple interest formula to solve for the variables
▲ Describe the importance of compound interest on the future value of money
▲ Compute the present value of money, given a dollar value in the future

Goals and Outcomes

▲ Master the terminology, understand the procedures and perspectives, and recognize the tools used to calculate interest
▲ Understand the implications of compound interest on the value of money
▲ Use tools and techniques to compare simple and compound interest
▲ Estimate the future and present values of money
▲ Describe what effect inflation has on the future value of money

INTRODUCTION

Consumer credit is based on the idea of buying something now and paying for it later. A bank savings account is based on the opposite idea: saving money now and receiving **interest** on that money from the bank. In order for companies to have an incentive to lend you money to pay for goods now (but not receive payment for those goods until some point in the future), they charge interest. Similarly, when you deposit money in a savings account or another savings vehicle, the bank pays you interest because it wants to give you an incentive to keep your money there. The first section in this chapter discusses simple interest; the second section explains compound interest, the third discusses the concept of present value, and the final section discusses basic consumer credit.

9.1 Simple Interest

What is **simple interest?** Suppose you put $100 in the bank for 1 year, and the bank pays 4% simple interest. At the end of the year, you have $104—the $100 you started with (called the **principal**), and the $4 simple interest you earned during the year. The total amount (in this case, $104) is called the **maturity value.**

There is another type of interest—called compound interest—that is discussed later in this chapter.

9.1.1 Solving for the Unknown

The formula for finding simple interest is

$$\text{Interest} = \text{Principal} \times \text{Rate} \times \text{Time}$$

or

$$I = p \times r \times t$$

In the **simple interest formula,**

▲ **Principal** is the original investment or borrowed amount, represented by p.

▲ **Rate** (or **interest rate**) is the percentage charged to lend or borrow money, represented by r.

▲ **Time** is the length of the investment or loan, expressed in years, months, or days, represented by t.

Simple interest is the amount paid or received, calculated on the principal. Maturity value is the value of the investment after a period of time, calculated using the following formula:

$$MV = p + I$$

For example, how much interest is earned if $1,000 is loaned for 2 years at 6%? To figure this out, you use the following equation:

$$I = p \times r \times t$$
$$I = \$1,000 \times 0.06 \times 2$$
$$I = \$1,000 \times 0.12$$
$$I = \$120$$

As another example, how much interest is earned if $100 is invested at 8% for 6 months? (Remember to calculate 6 months as half a year, or 0.5 year.) You figure this out as follows:

$$I = p \times r \times t$$
$$I = \$100 \times 0.08 \times 0.5$$
$$I = \$100 \times 0.04$$
$$I = \$4$$

Use the simple interest formula to solve the following loan problems:

1. Paul Adams borrowed $2,000 for 1 year, at a rate of 7%. Determine the interest paid.
2. The Detroit Lions football team owners borrowed $3,000,000 for 1 year at $4\frac{1}{2}$%. What was the interest paid?
3. Find the MV of a $500,000 debt owed to SoftwarePays, Inc., at 6% for 1 year.
4. A loan matures in 1 year, from a loan of $15,000 at $8\frac{1}{2}$%. What was the interest amount?
5. Determine the time (in years and days) it would take for a $36,000 loan at a rate of 3% to cost the borrower $400 in interest.

Remember that you can calculate the maturity value with this equation:

$$MV = p + I$$

For example, what is the maturity value of a loan of $100 at 7% interest for 1 year? You calculate this as follows:

$$MV = p + I$$
$$MV = \$100 + I$$

Remember that to find the interest amount, you calculate the following:

$$I = p \times r \times t$$
$$I = \$100 \times 0.07 \times 1$$
$$I = \$100 \times 0.07$$
$$I = \$7$$

Now you can find the maturity value, like this:

$$MV = \$100 + \$7$$

$$MV = \$107$$

Calculate the interest earned for the following:

1. $500 loan at 3%
2. $15,000 loan at 3.2%
3. $16,000 loan at 3.25%
4. $17,000 loan at 4%
5. $8,500 loan at 8%
6. $10,400 loan at $8\frac{1}{4}$%
7. $300 loan at $7\frac{3}{4}$%

9.1.2 Solving for the Principal

Suppose you know the interest amount, the interest rate, and the time over which the money will be invested or loaned out. You want to find the principal. To do so, you start with the interest formula and solve for p by dividing both sides of the equation by $r \times t$:

$$I = p \times r \times t$$

$$\frac{I}{r \times t} = p$$

Suppose you paid $85 interest on a 1-year loan on which the rate of interest was 10%. How much did you borrow? In this case, you're looking for p, and you know I ($85), r (10%, or 0.10), and t (1). You substitute these numbers into the equation and then solve for p, rounding to the nearest cent:

$$p = \frac{I}{r \times t}$$

$$p = \frac{\$85}{0.10 \times 1}$$

$$p = \frac{\$85}{0.10}$$

$$p = \$850$$

Here's another example: Jim paid $117.40 in interest on a 6-month loan for which the rate of interest was 12%. How much money did he borrow? You figure this out as follows:

$$p = \frac{I}{r \times t}$$

$$p = \frac{\$117.40}{0.12 \times 0.5}$$

$$p = \frac{\$117.40}{0.06}$$

$$p = \$1,956.67$$

Calculate the principal amount, given the following:

1. Interest of 5%, over 1 year, with total interest paid of $72.00
2. Interest of 8%, over 2 years, with total interest paid of $145.25
3. Interest of $8\frac{1}{4}$%, over 1 year, with total interest paid of $212.00
4. Interest of 10%, over 6 months, with total interest paid of $321.00
5. Interest of $12\frac{1}{8}$%, over 3 years, with total interest paid of $499
6. Interest of 15%, over 5 years, with total interest paid of $1,245.80
7. Interest of 1.6%, over 1 year, with total interest paid of $14.89
8. Interest of $21\frac{1}{2}$%, over 10 years, with total interest paid of $4,305.90

9.1.3 Solving for the Rate of Interest

It is possible to solve for the rate of interest, r. The analysis in this section is virtually the same as that in the last section, in which you solve for the principal. To solve for the rate of interest, you simply solve for r by dividing both sides by $p \times t$:

$$I = p \times r \times t$$

$$\frac{I}{p \times t} = r$$

You're ready to solve a problem for the rate of interest.

If Helen borrowed $4,000 for 6 months and paid $200 interest, what rate of interest did she pay? You're looking for r, and you know p ($4,000), t (0.5), and I ($200). You need to use this formula:

$$r = \frac{I}{p \times t}$$

$$r = \frac{\$200}{\$4,000 \times 0.5}$$

$$r = \frac{\$200}{\$2,000}$$

$$r = 0.10, \text{ or } 10\%$$

Here's another example: Stephanie paid $372.63 on a 2-year, $7,500 loan. What interest rate was she charged? You figure it out like this:

$$r = \frac{I}{p \times t}$$

$$r = \frac{\$372.63}{\$7,500 \times 2}$$

$$r = \frac{\$372.63}{\$15,000}$$

$$r = 0.0248 \text{ or } 2.5\%$$

Solve for the interest rate, given the following variables:

1. Bob paid $59.71 on a 2-year loan of $10,000
2. Jean paid $456.90 on a 5-year loan of $25,000
3. Mr. Amati paid $2,450.76 on a 3-year loan of $31,750.90
4. Juan paid $4,507.87 on a 1-year loan of $21,599
5. Frank paid $4,500 on a 2-year loan of $34,980
6. Susan paid $3,100 on a 6-year loan of $24,595
7. Angelo paid $45.91 on a 1-year loan of $4,300
8. Mrs. Hughes paid $7,890.31 on a 5-year loan of $35,000

9.1.4 Solving for the Time

Similarly to solving for principal and rate, you can also solve for time. To do that, you need to isolate t in the simple interest equation:

$$I = p \times r \times t$$

$$\frac{I}{p \times r} = t$$

For example, say that Alexandra borrowed $20,000 at 9%. If she paid $2,700 in interest, for how long was the loan? You're looking for t, and you know I ($2,700), p ($20,000), and r (0.09). Here's what you do:

$$t = \frac{I}{p \times r}$$

$$t = \frac{\$2,700}{\$20,000 \times 0.9}$$

$$t = \frac{\$2,700}{\$1,800}$$

$$t = 1.5 \text{ years, or 18 months}$$

Here's another example to try: Dana borrowed $10,000 at 7.5% and paid $375 in interest. For how long was the loan? You figure it out as follows:

$$t = \frac{I}{p \times r}$$

FOR EXAMPLE

Simple Interest as a Quick Estimation

There are almost no uses in the business and banking worlds for simple interest either being paid or earned. But calculating simple interest is a fast, easy way to estimate what you might earn on investments or pay on a loan, especially in short-term situations. For example, suppose you're thinking about buying a new car that costs $18,000. The promotional interest rate is 4%, and you want to pay for the car over 3 years, or 36 payments. You could use the quick calculation $18,000 \times 1.04 \times \$18,720 \div 36 = \$520$ per month. The actual payments would be $531.43 each, but the simple calculation gets you pretty close. Note: Over the long term, such as with retirement investments or with a 30-year mortgage, simple interest does not provide a very good estimation because the effects of compounding have years to take effect.

$$t = \frac{\$375}{\$10,000 \times 0.75}$$

$$t = \frac{\$375}{\$750}$$

$$t = 0.5 \text{ year, or six months}$$

Solve the following to determine the length of each loan:

1. Bob's loan was $14,000 at 8%; he paid $42.50 in interest
2. Barbara's loan was $120,000 at $4\frac{1}{2}$%; she paid $459.80 in interest
3. Howard's loan was $31,000 at 7%; he paid $367.90 in interest
4. Kerry's loan was $1,200,000 at 6%; she paid $4,509.00 in interest
5. Linda's loan was $31,000 at $8\frac{1}{2}$%; she paid $456.90 in interest
6. Paula's loan was $65,000 at $7\frac{3}{4}$%; she paid $6800 in interest
7. Simon's loan was $22,000,000 at 4%; he paid $45,700 in interest
8. Kelly's loan was $15,798 at $7\frac{1}{4}$%; she paid $1,600.23 in interest

SELF-CHECK

- Define **simple interest**.
- Calculate simple interest when you know the principal, rate, and time of the loan or investment.
- Solve for other variables in the simple interest formula.

9.2 Compound Interest

Compound interest is calculated periodically—daily, monthly, or quarterly—and then added to the principal for inclusion in the next period's interest determination.

9.2.1 Simple Interest vs. Compound Interest

Your bank pays compound interest, and because it does, your money grows faster than it would if the bank paid only simple interest. To see why, think about this: If your bank paid 8% simple interest, and you put $1,000 in your savings account today, how much money would be in your account 1 year from now? Here's what you need to do to figure this out:

$$MV = p + I$$
$$MV = \$1,000 + I$$

To figure out I, you need to use the following formula:

$$I = p \times r \times t$$
$$I = \$1,000 \times 0.08 \times 1$$
$$I = \$1,000 \times 0.08$$
$$I = \$80$$

Then you insert the value of I into the maturity value formula, like this:

$$MV = \$1,000 + \$80$$
$$MV = \$1,080$$

So, if your bank paid 8% simple interest, at the end of 1 year, your $1,000 balance would rise to $1,080.

But what would happen to your $1,000 deposit if your bank compounds interest quarterly? Believe it or not, you can find out by using the simple interest formula. You begin by calculating simple interest for the first quarter (i.e., 3 months):

$$I = p \times r \times t$$
$$I = \$1,000 \times 0.08 \times 0.25$$
$$I = \$1,000 \times 0.02$$
$$I = \$20$$

Then you insert the value of I into the maturity value formula:

$$MV = p + I$$
$$MV = \$1,000 + \$20$$
$$MV = \$1,020$$

Next, you calculate simple interest for the second quarter:

$$I = p \times r \times t$$

$$I = \$1,020 \times 0.08 \times 0.25$$
$$I = \$1,000 \times 0.02$$
$$I = \$20.40$$

Then you insert the value of I into the maturity value formula:

$$MV = p + I$$
$$MV = \$1,020 + \$20.40$$
$$MV = \$1,040.40$$

Next, you calculate simple interest for the third quarter:

$$I = p \times r \times t$$
$$I = \$1,040.40 \times 0.08 \times 0.25$$
$$I = \$1,040.40 \times 0.02$$
$$I = \$20.81$$

Then you insert the value of I into the maturity value formula:

$$MV = p + I$$
$$MV = \$1,040.40 + \$20.81$$
$$MV = \$1,061.21$$

Next, you calculate simple interest for the fourth quarter:

$$I = p \times r \times t$$
$$I = \$1,061.21 \times 0.08 \times 0.25$$
$$I = \$1,061.21 \times 0.02$$
$$I = \$21.22$$

Finally, you insert the value of I into the maturity value formula:

$$MV = p + I$$
$$MV = \$1,061.41 + \$21.22$$
$$MV = \$1,082.43$$

You see the difference? If you bank paid simple interest, your $1,000 deposit would grow to $1,080. With compound interest, your $1,000 deposit would grow to $1,082.43.

Many banks pay interest that is compounded (i.e., calculated) daily, which means you make even more money than with monthly or quarterly compounding. That same $1,000, compounded daily, would be worth a bit more at the end of a year: $1,083.28.

9.2.2 Compound Interest Tables

In Section 9.2.1, you calculated the maturity value of $1,000 deposited in a bank savings account for 1 year if that bank paid 8% interest, compounded quarterly. It came to $1,082.43.

If you deposited $1,000 in that same bank and left it there for 4 years, how much would its maturity value be? Could you just multiply that $82.43 in interest by 4 and tack it on to the $1,000? No, because of the effects of compounding.

You could find the maturity value by calculating the simple interest over the 4-year-period, quarter-by-quarter, for 16 quarters. Luckily, there's a much better way: You can simply look up the answer in the **compound interest tables.** To find out the maturity value of $1,000 with interest compounded quarterly for 4 years, you can find the answer in Table 9-1. Notice that this table is arranged in terms of periods, with interest compounded each period. In the problem you're working on now, interest is compounded quarterly, so there are four periods each year.

Using the information you have, you plug in the numbers that fit into this formula, and then you find the rate per period:

$$\text{Rate per period} = \frac{\text{Annual rate}}{\text{Number of periods per year}}$$

$$= \frac{8\%}{4}$$

$$= 2\%$$

This means that you can find 8% compounded quarterly in the compound interest tables under a rate of 2%. You need more information before you can use the tables. First, you need to know how many periods there are. You're looking at the interest compounded quarterly over 4 years, which is 16 quarters. If each

Table 9-1: The Maturity Value of $1 at Compound Interest Rates of .5%, 1%, 1.5%, and 2%

Period	0.5%	1.0%	1.5%	2.0%
1	1.0050	1.0100	1.0150	1.0200
2	1.0100	1.0201	1.0302	1.0404
3	1.0151	1.0303	1.0457	1.0612
4	1.0202	1.0406	1.0614	1.0824
5	1.0253	1.0510	1.0773	1.1041
6	1.0304	1.0615	1.0934	1.1262
7	1.0355	1.0721	1.1098	1.1487
8	1.0407	1.0829	1.1265	1.1717
9	1.0459	1.0930	1.1434	1.1951
10	1.0511	1.1046	1.1605	1.2190
11	1.0564	1.1157	1.1780	1.2434

Table 9-1: *Continued*

Period	0.5%	1.0%	1.5%	2.0%
12	1.0617	1.1268	1.1960	1.2682
13	1.0670	1.1381	1.2135	1.2936
14	1.0723	1.1495	1.2318	1.3195
15	1.0777	1.1610	1.2502	1.3459
16	1.0831	1.1726	1.2690	1.3728
17	1.0885	1.1843	1.2880	1.4002
18	1.0939	1.1961	1.3073	1.4282
19	1.0994	1.2081	1.3270	1.4568
20	1.1049	1.2202	1.3469	1.4859
21	1.1104	1.2324	1.3671	1.5157
22	1.1160	1.2447	1.3876	1.5460
23	1.1216	1.2572	1.4084	1.5769
24	1.1272	1.2697	1.4295	1.6084
25	1.1328	1.2824	1.4510	1.6406
26	1.1385	1.2953	1.4727	1.6734
27	1.1442	1.3082	1.4948	1.7069
28	1.1499	1.3213	1.5172	1.7410
29	1.1556	1.3345	1.5400	1.7758
30	1.1614	1.3478	1.5631	1.8114
31	1.1672	1.3613	1.5865	1.8476
32	1.1730	1.3749	1.6103	1.8845
33	1.1789	1.3887	1.6345	1.9222
34	1.1848	1.4026	1.6590	1.9607
35	1.1907	1.4166	1.6839	1.9999
36	1.1967	1.4308	1.7091	2.0399
37	1.2027	1.4451	1.7348	2.0807
38	1.2087	1.4595	1.7608	2.1223
39	1.2147	1.4741	1.7872	2.1647
40	1.2208	1.4889	1.8140	2.2080

quarter is a period, you need to look up an interest rate of 2% for a period of 16 quarters. Now, a glance at Table 9-1 gives you the answer.

In Table 9-1, you find the maturity value of $1 at the appropriate rate and over the correct period. But you need to find the maturity value of $1,000 instead of $1. Here's how you do it: You multiply $1.3725 by 1,000, which means moving the decimal point three places to the right. So you get $1,372.50. (See Chapter 1 for more on fast multiplication.)

Here's an example: If $100 were left in a bank account for 5 years, and the account paid 6% interest compounded quarterly, what would that $100 be worth at the end of 5 years? Here's how you figure it out:

$$\text{Rate per period} = \frac{\text{Annual rate}}{\text{Number of periods per year}}$$

$$= \frac{6\%}{4}$$

$$= 1.5\%$$

How many periods are there in 5 years? If each period is one quarter, there are four periods in 1 year, so there are 20 in 5 years. When you look up 1.5% interest in Table 9-1, you find that in period 20, the maturity value of $1 is $1.3469. You're dealing with a deposit of $100, and that $100 has grown to $100 \times $1.3469 = $134.69

Tables 9-2 through 9-6 contain the same information as in Table 9-1, but for higher rates of interest.

Table 9-2: The Maturity Value of $1 at Compound Interest Rates of 2.5%, 3%, 3.5%, and 4%

Period	2.5%	3.0%	3.5%	4.0%
1	1.0250	1.0300	1.0350	1.0400
2	1.0506	1.0609	1.0172	1.0816
3	1.0769	1.0927	1.1087	1.1249
4	1.1038	1.1255	1.1475	1.1699
5	1.1314	1.1593	1.1877	1.2167
6	1.1597	1.1941	1.2293	1.2653
7	1.1887	1.2299	1.2723	1.3159
8	1.2184	1.2668	1.3168	1.3686
9	1.2489	1.3048	1.3629	1.4233
10	1.2801	1.4339	1.4106	1.4802
11	1.3121	1.3842	1.4600	1.5395

Table 9-2: *Continued*

Period	2.5%	3.0%	3.5%	4.0%
12	1.3449	1.4258	1.5111	1.6010
13	1.3785	1.4685	1.5640	1.6651
14	1.4130	1.5126	1.6187	1.7317
15	1.4483	1.5580	1.6753	1.8009
16	1.4845	1.6047	1.7340	1.8730
17	1.5216	1.6528	1.7947	1.9479
18	1.5597	1.7024	1.8575	2.0258
19	1.5986	1.7535	1.9225	2.1068
20	1.6386	1.8061	1.9898	2.1911
21	1.6796	1.8603	2.0594	2.2788
22	1.7216	1.9161	2.1315	2.3699
23	1.7646	1.9736	2.2061	2.4647
24	1.8087	2.0328	2.2833	2.5633
25	1.8539	2.0938	2.3632	2.6658
26	1.9003	2.1566	2.4460	2.7725
27	1.9478	2.2213	2.5316	2.8834
28	1.9965	2.2879	2.6202	2.9987
29	2.0464	2.3566	2.7119	3.1187
30	2.0976	2.4273	2.8068	3.2434
31	2.1500	2.5001	2.9050	3.3731
32	2.2038	2.5751	3.0067	3.5081
33	2.2588	2.6523	3.1119	3.6484
34	2.3153	2.7319	3.2209	3.7943
35	2.3732	2.8139	3.3336	3.9461
36	2.4325	2.8983	3.4503	4.1039
37	2.4933	2.9852	3.5710	4.2681
38	2.5557	3.0748	3.6960	4.4388
39	2.6196	3.1670	3.8254	4.6164
40	2.6851	3.2620	3.9593	4.8010

Table 9-3: The Maturity Value of $1 at Compound Interest Rates of 4.5%, 5%, 5.5%, and 6%

Period	4.5%	5%	5.5%	6%
1	1.0450	1.0500	1.0550	1.0600
2	1.0920	1.1025	1.1130	1.1236
3	1.1412	1.1576	1.1742	1.1910
4	1.1925	1.2155	1.2388	1.2625
5	1.2462	1.2763	1.3070	1.3382
6	1.3023	1.3401	1.3788	1.4185
7	1.3609	1.4071	1.4547	1.5036
8	1.4221	1.4775	1.5347	1.5938
9	1.4861	1.5513	1.6191	1.6895
10	1.5530	1.6289	1.7081	1.7908
11	1.6229	1.7103	1.8021	1.8983
12	1.6959	1.7959	1.9012	2.0122
13	1.7722	1.8856	2.0058	2.1329
14	1.8519	1.9799	2.1161	2.2609
15	1.9353	2.0789	2.2325	2.3966
16	2.0224	2.1829	2.3553	2.5404
17	2.1134	2.2920	2.4828	2.6928
18	2.2085	2.4066	2.6215	2.8543
19	2.3079	2.5270	2.6756	3.0256
20	2.4117	2.6533	2.9178	3.2071
21	2.5202	2.7860	3.0782	3.3996
22	2.6337	2.9253	3.2475	3.6035
23	2.7522	3.0715	3.4261	3.8197
24	2.8760	3.2251	3.6146	4.0489
25	3.0054	3.3864	3.8134	4.2919
26	3.1407	3.5557	4.0231	4.5494
27	3.2820	3.7335	4.2444	4.8223

Table 9-3: *Continued*

Period	4.5%	5%	5.5%	6%
28	3.4297	3.9201	4.4778	5.1117
29	3.5840	4.1161	4.7241	5.4184
30	3.7453	4.3219	4.9839	5.7435
31	3.9139	4.5380	5.2581	6.0881
32	4.0900	4.7649	5.5472	6.4534
33	4.2740	5.0032	5.8523	6.8406
34	4.4664	5.2533	6.1742	7.2510
35	4.6673	5.5160	6.5138	7.6861
36	4.8774	5.7918	6.8721	8.1472
37	5.0969	6.0814	7.2500	8.6361
38	5.3262	6.3855	7.6488	9.1542
39	5.5659	6.7047	8.0695	9.7035
40	5.8164	7.0400	8.5133	10.2857

Table 9-4: The Maturity Value of \$1 at Compound Interest Rates of 6.5%, 7%, 7.5%, and 8%

Period	6.5%	7%	7.5%	8%
1	1.0650	1.0700	1.0750	1.0800
2	1.1342	1.1449	1.1556	1.1664
3	1.2079	1.2250	1.2423	1.2597
4	1.2865	1.3108	1.3355	1.3605
5	1.3701	1.4026	1.4356	1.4693
6	1.4591	1.5007	1.5433	1.5869
7	1.5540	1.6058	1.6590	1.7138
8	1.6550	1.7182	1.7835	1.8509
9	1.7626	1.8385	1.9172	1.9990
10	1.8771	1.9672	2.0610	2.1589
11	1.9992	2.1049	2.2156	2.3316

Table 9-4: *Continued*

Period	6.5%	7%	7.5%	8%
12	2.1291	2.2522	2.3818	2.5182
13	2.2675	2.4098	2.5604	2.7196
14	2.4149	2.5785	2.7524	2.9372
15	2.5718	2.7590	2.9589	3.1722
16	2.7390	2.9522	3.1808	3.4259
17	2.9170	3.1588	3.4194	3.7000
18	3.1067	3.3799	3.6758	3.9960
19	3.3086	3.6165	3.9515	4.3157
20	3.5236	3.8697	4.2479	4.6610
21	3.7527	4.1406	4.5664	5.0338
22	3.9966	4.4304	4.9089	5.4365
23	4.2564	4.7405	5.2771	5.8715
24	4.5330	5.0724	5.6729	6.3412
25	4.8277	5.4274	6.0983	6.8485
26	5.1415	5.8074	6.5557	7.3964
27	5.4757	6.2139	7.0474	7.9881
28	5.8316	6.6488	7.5760	8.6271
29	6.2107	7.1143	8.1442	9.3173
30	6.6144	7.6123	8.7550	10.0627
31	7.0443	8.1451	9.4116	10.8677
32	7.5022	8.7153	10.1175	11.7371
33	7.9898	9.3253	10.8763	12.6761
34	8.5091	9.9781	11.6920	13.6901
35	9.0622	10.6766	12.5689	14.7854
36	9.6513	11.4239	13.5116	15.9682
37	10.2786	12.2236	14.5249	17.2456
38	10.9467	13.0792	15.6143	18.6253
39	11.6583	13.9948	16.7854	20.1153
40	12.4161	14.9744	18.0443	21.7245

Table 9-5: The Maturity Value of $1 at Compound Interest Rates of 8.5%, 9%, 9.5%, and 10%

Period	8.5%	9%	9.5%	10%
1	1.0850	1.0900	1.0950	1.1000
2	1.1772	1.1881	1.1990	1.2100
3	1.2773	1.2950	1.3129	1.3310
4	1.3859	1.4116	1.4377	1.4641
5	1.5037	1.5386	1.5742	1.6105
6	1.6315	1.6771	1.7238	1.7716
7	1.7701	1.8280	1.8876	1.9487
8	1.9206	1.9926	2.0669	2.1436
9	2.0839	2.1719	2.2632	2.3579
10	2.2610	2.3674	2.4782	2.5937
11	2.4532	2.5804	2.7137	2.8531
12	2.6617	2.8127	2.9715	3.1384
13	2.8879	3.0658	3.2537	3.4523
14	3.1334	3.3417	3.5629	3.7975
15	3.3997	3.6425	3.9013	4.1772
16	3.6887	3.9703	4.2719	4.5950
17	4.0023	4.3276	4.6778	5.0545
18	4.3425	4.7171	5.1222	5.5599
19	4.7116	5.1417	5.6088	6.1159
20	5.1121	5.6044	6.1416	6.7275
21	5.5466	6.1088	6.7251	7.4002
22	6.0180	6.6586	7.3639	8.1403
23	6.5296	7.2579	8.0635	8.9543
24	7.0846	7.9111	8.8296	9.8497
25	7.6868	8.6231	9.6684	10.8347
26	8.3401	9.3992	10.5869	11.9182
27	9.0491	10.2451	11.5926	13.1100
28	9.8182	11.1672	12.6939	14.4210

Table 9-5: *Continued*

Period	8.5%	9%	9.5%	10%
29	10.6528	12.1722	13.8998	15.8631
30	11.5583	13.2677	15.2203	17.4494
31	12.5407	14.4618	16.6663	19.1944
32	13.6067	15.7634	18.2495	21.1138
33	14.7633	17.1821	19.9833	23.2252
34	16.0181	18.7284	21.8817	25.5477
35	17.3797	20.4140	23.9604	28.1025
36	18.8569	22.2513	26.2367	30.9127
37	20.4598	24.2539	28.7291	34.0040
38	22.1989	26.4367	31.4584	37.4044
39	24.0858	28.8160	34.4470	41.1448
40	26.1331	31.4095	37.7194	45.2593

Table 9-6: The Maturity Value of $1 at Compound Interest Rates of 10.5%, 11%, 11.5%, and 12%

Period	10.5%	11%	11.5%	12%
1	1.1050	1.1100	1.1150	1.1200
2	1.2210	1.2321	1.2432	1.2544
3	1.3492	1.3676	1.3862	1.4049
4	1.4909	1.5181	1.5456	1.5735
5	1.6474	1.6851	1.7234	1.7623
6	1.8204	1.8704	1.9215	1.9738
7	2.0116	2.0762	2.1425	2.2107
8	2.2228	2.3045	2.3889	2.4760
9	2.4562	2.5580	2.6636	2.7731
10	2.7141	2.8394	2.9699	3.1058
11	2.9991	3.1518	3.3115	3.4785
12	3.3140	3.4985	3.6923	3.8960

Table 9-6: *Continued*

Period	10.5%	11%	11.5%	12%
13	3.6619	3.8833	4.1169	4.3635
14	4.0464	4.3104	4.5904	4.8871
15	4.4713	4.7846	5.1183	5.4736
16	4.9408	5.3109	5.7069	6.1304
17	5.4596	5.8951	6.3632	6.8660
18	6.0328	6.5436	7.0949	7.6900
19	6.6663	7.2633	7.9108	8.6128
20	7.3662	8.0623	8.8206	9.6463
21	8.1397	8.9492	9.8349	10.8038
22	8.9944	9.9336	10.9660	12.1003
23	9.9388	11.0263	12.2271	13.5523
24	10.9823	12.2392	13.6332	15.1786
25	12.1355	13.5855	15.2010	17.0001
26	13.4097	15.0799	16.9491	19.0401
27	14.8177	16.7386	18.8982	21.3249
28	16.3736	18.5799	21.0715	23.8839
29	18.0928	20.6237	23.4948	26.7499
30	19.9926	22.8923	26.1967	29.9599
31	22.0918	25.4105	29.2093	33.5551
32	24.4114	28.2056	32.5683	37.5817
33	26.9746	31.3082	36.3137	42.0915
34	29.8070	34.7521	40.4898	47.1425
35	32.9367	38.5749	45.1461	52.7996
36	36.3950	42.8181	50.3379	59.1356
37	40.2165	47.5281	56.1267	66.2318
38	44.4392	52.7562	62.5813	74.1797
39	49.1054	58.5593	69.7782	83.0812
40	54.2614	65.0009	77.8027	93.0510

> ## FOR EXAMPLE
>
> ### The Higher the Investment, the More Compounding Matters
>
> The difference between quarterly and daily compounding isn't very noticeable when you invest $100 or even $1,000. But if the investment were $1,000,000, the difference between quarterly and daily compounding would be substantial. $1,000,000, invested at 8% compounded quarterly, is worth $2,208,039.66 in 10 years. That same amount, compounded daily, is worth $2,225,345.85. That's a difference of $17,306.19, simply for compounding daily instead of quarterly! Check with your bank as to how it determines your interest.

Try a problem using the compound interest tables: You deposit $500 for 10 years. If the annual rate of interest is 3.5% and the interest is compounded annually, what is the maturity value of your $500 at the end of 10 years. (Hint: Use Table 9-2.)

In this case, you don't need to use the rate-per-period formula because the interest is compounded annually. Using Table 9-2, you find the maturity of $1 after 10 periods—it's $1.4106. Then you multiply that by $500, to get $705.30.

Determine the maturity value for each of the following situations if the interest is compounded quarterly:

1. $5,000 deposited for 10 years at 4%
2. $10,000 deposited for 6 years at 3%
3. $1,000,000 deposited for 1 year at 10%
4. $4,500 deposited for 5 years at 6%
5. $98,000 deposited for 10 years at 6%
6. $90,000 deposited for 2 years at 4%
7. $1,000 deposited for 3 years at 4%
8. $1 deposited for 6 months at 10%

SELF-CHECK

- Define **compound interest.**
- Calculate compound interest using compound interest tables.
- Discuss the difference between simple and compound interest.
- Consider the implications of yearly versus quarterly compounding.

9.3 Present Value

Economists are fond of saying that $1 today is worth more than $1 you will have in the future. Part of the reason is **inflation**, the general upward price movement of goods and services in an economy. (In other words, a loaf of bread or gallon of gasoline costs more now than it did 10, 20, and 100 years ago.)

However, even if inflation didn't occur, $1 today would still be worth more than $1 you received some time in the future. That's because people (namely, banking institutions) are willing to pay interest for the use of your money. And if you wanted to borrow money, you would still be charged interest—with or without inflation.

You can think of the numbers you've calculated so far in this chapter as the **future value** of money; that is, you've calculated what a set (i.e., fixed) amount of money, invested now for a certain period of time, will be worth in the future. Figuring the **present value** is similar: If you know the future value of an investment, you can calculate its value today, in the present.

The formula to determine the present value of $1 received 1 year from now is

$$\frac{1}{1 + r}$$

where r is the interest rate.

For example, what is the present value of $100 in 1 year, when the interest rate is 5%? You figure it out like this:

$$\frac{1}{1 + r} = \frac{1}{1 + 0.05}$$
$$= \frac{1}{1.05}$$
$$= 95.24 \times \$100 = \$95.24$$

You can also use a general formula for the present value of dollars held any number of years into the future:

$$\text{Present value of a dollar received } n \text{ years from now} = \frac{1}{(1 + r)^n}$$

Substituting the rate of interest for r and the number of years for n, you have a simple arithmetic problem.

Here's an example: What is the present value of $1,000 received 2 years from now if the interest rate is 3%? You figure it out like this:

$$\text{Present value of a dollar received } n \text{ years from now} = \frac{1}{(1 + r)^n}$$

$$\frac{1}{(1 + r)^n} = \frac{1}{(1.03)^2}$$

$$= \frac{1}{(1.03) \times (1.03)} = \frac{1}{1.0609} = 0.942 \times \$1,000 = \$942$$

Here's another example: If the interest rate is 6%, and $10,000 will be paid to you in 5 years, what's the present value of that $10,000? Here's how you figure it out:

$$\text{Present value of a dollar received } n \text{ years from now} = \frac{1}{(1 + r)^n}$$

$$\frac{1}{(1 + r)^n} = \frac{1}{(1.06)^5} = \frac{1}{(1.06) \times (1.06) \times (1.06) \times (1.06) \times (1.06)}$$

$$= \frac{1}{1.3382} = 0.7472 \times \$10,000 = \$7,472$$

FOR EXAMPLE

The Present Value of Retirement Money

The most common use for calculating present value is when preparing for retirement or some other large financial need in the future (e.g., buying a home or business, expanding a business, or planning for tuition payments). In such cases, you can figure out how much money you'll need in the future and then find the present value of that money, so that you know how much you need to start investing today.

Here's an example: If you plan to accumulate $3 million for retirement, how much would you need to invest today to have that money available in 40 years? Are you thinking you'd need to invest $1 or $2 million? Think again. If you put away $291,666.56 (that's less than $300,000) and invested it for 40 years at 6%, compounded annually, you'd have $3 million in 40 years. If you compounded quarterly, monthly, or daily, you'd have substantially more. Does that motivate you to start saving for retirement? Remember that present value is the amount you need to be invested today at a given compounding rate in order to accumulate a certain future value.

- Define **present value.**
- Draw a basic conclusion about the effects of inflation on the future value of money
- Explain how to calculate present value.

SUMMARY

Calculating interest involves a number of variables: the principal amount invested or financed, the interest rate, and the length of the investment or loan. Knowing these three variables also allows you to calculate the future value of money; if you know the future value, you can calculate the present value. In addition, the rate at which the principal is compounded affects the total amount paid or earned.

Key Terms

Compound interest	Interest that is calculated periodically and then added to the principal.
Compound interest tables	Tables that help you calculate compound interest.
Future value	How much $1 invested or borrowed today is worth in the future.
Inflation	The general upward price movement of goods and services in an economy.
Interest	An amount paid in order to borrow money or received for lending money.
Interest rate	A percent charged for lending or borrowing money.
Maturity value	The money you get when a loan matures; it is equal to Interest + Principal.
Present value	How much $1 received at some date in the future is worth today. It is the amount needed to be invested today at a given compounded

	rate in order to accumulate to a certain future value.
Principal	The amount of money originally deposited, borrowed, or loaned; represented by p.
Rate	The interest rate charged or earned; represented by r.
Simple interest	Money paid for the use of principal; represented by I.
Simple interest formula	A formula for determining simple interest; Interest = Principal × Rate × Time.
Time	The length of an investment or a loan, usually expressed in years or months; represented by t.

ASSESS YOUR UNDERSTANDING

Go to www.wiley.com/college/slavin to evaluate your knowledge of the basics of calculating interest.
Measure your learning by comparing pre-test and post-test results.

Summary Questions

1. *Maturity value* is how much $1 received at some point in the future is worth today. True or False?
2. $1 today is worth more than $1 tomorrow because of:
   (a) inflation.
   (b) the payment or charging of income.
   (c) both of the above.
   (d) none of the above.
3. If you know the principal amount, the interest rate, and the length of the investment or loan, you can calculate the interest that will be charged or earned. True or False?
4. Interest compounded monthly results in higher earnings than interest compounded daily. True or False?

Review Questions

1. What is the maturity value of a loan of $25,000 at 10% interest for 1 year?
2. Clay borrowed $6,000 for 3 months and paid $150 in interest. What rate of interest did he pay?
3. Louise borrowed $15,000 at 12% and paid $450 in interest. For how long was the loan?
4. If Shari paid $713.26 in interest on an 18-month loan for which the interest rate was 9%, how much money did she borrow?
5. What is the maturity value of a loan of $15,000 at 8.5% interest for 6 months?
6. If the interest rate is 4%, what is the present value of $1,000 that will be paid to you in 5 years?

Applying This Chapter

1. Juan invests in a certificate of deposit at his bank, depositing $5,000 for 5 years at 10% interest, which is compounded semiannually. What is the

maturity value of the deposit after 5 years? Use the compound interest tables and the following formula:

$$FV = p \times (1 + I)/\text{Number of periods}$$

2. Katie needed to take out three loans:

   (a) First, Katie paid $596.24 in interest on a 9-month loan for which the rate was 11%. How much money did she borrow?

   (b) A year later, Katie borrowed $10,000 for 3 months. If she paid $225 in interest, what rate of interest did she pay?

   (c) Finally, Katie borrowed $12,000 at 10% interest. If she paid $600 in interest, for how long was the loan?

3. If you were to deposit $12,000, and the bank paid you 6% interest compounded quarterly, what would the maturity value of your deposit be at the end of 9 years? To solve this problem, you use the following formula:

$$MV = p \times (1 + r)^{36}$$

4. If the interest rate is 8%, what is the present value of $10,000 that will be paid to you in 3 years?

5. What is the present value of $500,000 that will be paid to you at the end of this year if the interest rate is tied to the Fed Fund rate of 6.5%.

6. Using the compound interest tables, figure out the maturity value of your savings account, which is currently (at summer's end) $3,400, if you work all next summer at the New Jersey beaches and are able to bank an additional $4,000. The bank pays interest quarterly, at 4%. (Hint: You make no deposits until the end of summer and earn no interest the second summer.)

7. What is the maturity value of your IRA account of $45,000 if you hold it for 10 more years, at a quarterly interest rate of 8%?

8. What is the length of a loan that matured from $1,000 to $2,685.10 at a quarterly interest rate of 10%?

9. Your certificate of deposit matured to $1,359 in 1 year. If the bank paid interest quarterly on its CDs, at a 10% interest rate, how much did you invest?

10. Mary Cassatt put $10,000 into her pension fund for her retirement at age 60. Mary is now 50. The rate of return is 5% compounded on semi-annually. Determine the value of this pension money at Mary's retirement.

11. If the bank rate is 4%, and you want to have about $20,000 for a down payment on your first house in 1 year, what amount would you deposit today at a bank paying quarterly interest?

12. You have an opportunity to purchase bonds in one of two corporations. Corporation A is offering 6% interest, paid quarterly for 4 years, and

the Corporation B is offering 8% interest, compounded semiannually for 4 years. Which is the preferred investment for you?

13. Robert Gana has a daughter who will attend college in 6 years. If he puts aside $25,000 for her college tuition at 7% interest, compounded annually, how much will he have accumulated?

14. Hakim wants to buy a house in 3 years and knows he will need a down payment of $40,000. If he can earn 4% in a certificate of deposit that compounds quarterly, how much should he invest now to have $40,000 in 3 years?

Jay & Bee, Inc.

Jay & Bee, Inc., charges 1.5% per month simple interest on any past-due invoices. If your company were in arrears for 6 months on a $12,500 bill, what interest would it pay to Jay & Bee?

Broadway Productions, LLC

Broadway Productions, LLC, borrows $70,000 at $9\frac{1}{2}$% simple interest for $2\frac{1}{2}$ years. How much total interest will be due?

The Vanilla Factory

The Vanilla Factory, an importer of fine confections, places $60,000 in a CD that pays 6% simple interest. Calculate the amount of interest that will be earned after 4 full years.

Lottery Win

In a recent lottery, Mr. Piazza won $100,000 to be paid today or the option of $145,000 paid over the course of 5 years. Which would give the greater yield if he could invest the $100,000 for the first year at 8% simple interest?

Money Market Funds

Two investors each deposit $4,000. One invests in the Banjo Money Market Fund, and the other invests in the Casino Money Fund. The Banjo investor receives a return of 8%, compounded semiannually for 2 years. The Casino investor receives 8%, compounded quarterly for 18 months. Which is the better investment?

Tuition Calculations

Say that your Uncle Charles loans you tuition money of $15,000 at simple interest of $\frac{1}{4}$ point above the prime rate, which is currently $7\frac{1}{2}$%, for each of the 4 years of college. How much will you return to your uncle if calculations begin September 1 of your freshman year and you expect to pay off the entire loan on the first anniversary of your June college graduation? (**Hint:** $15,000 is loaned each September.)

Sorority Sums

A university sorority receives $11,000 from an alum. The sorority members plan to paint the sorority house but want to set aside enough money to landscape the outside of the building in 1 year. The landscaping will cost $7,000. How much of the $11,000 must be set a side today to pay for that work if the money can earn 10%, compounded semiannually?

Casino Renovation

How much would a casino corporation have available for renovation projects commencing in 4 years if the rate is 8%, compounded semiannually, and the corporation places $700,000 in a capital budget fund today?

Café Cutlery

To buy new cutlery for her café, the owner borrows $11,200 for 4 years and pays $1,200 in simple interest on this loan. What is the interest rate?

Evergreen Landscaping

Evergreen Landscaping needs to purchase three new 52-inch lawn mowers. The partners in the company borrowed $6,000 at 12% simple interest per year from their father. If they paid $110 in interest, what was the duration of the loan?

Zenith Light Co.

The Zenith Light Co. agreed to loan money to the Gliding Light Lamp Company, with a simple interest rate of 8%, on a condition that Gliding would borrow sufficient funds to earn Xenith a total of $12,000 in interest over a 3-year period. What is the minimum amount that Gliding must borrow?

10

LOANS AND CONSUMER CREDIT
Promissory Notes, Mortgages, and Credit Cards

Starting Point

Go to www.wiley.com/college/slavin to assess your knowledge of loans and consumer credit.
Determine where you need to concentrate your effort.

What You'll Learn in This Chapter

▲ How interest is determined on a discounted note
▲ The various ways mortgages can be structured
▲ How annual percentage rate works
▲ How to tabulate the interest charged on installment loans and credit cards

After Studying This Chapter, You'll Be Able To

▲ Discuss relationship between Treasury bills (T-bills) and discounted notes
▲ Identify the critical factors in shopping for a business or home mortgage
▲ Calculate the interest rate, given the other terms of the debt or loan
▲ Describe a list of important factors when agreeing to an installment loan

Goals and Outcomes

▲ Master the terminology, understand the procedures and perspectives, and recognize the tools of loans and other forms of consumer credit
▲ Understand the implications of charging or receiving interest on a note
▲ Identify the main issues affecting whether to apply for a 15-year or 30-year mortgage
▲ Use tools and technique to analyze how much interest credit card companies charge

INTRODUCTION

Loans and other forms of consumer credit can make your life easier—or lead you down the path of financial trouble. Whether you are creating a legal document for a simple IOU, buying a car, building a home, buying an expensive china cabinet, or paying off your credit card debt, you probably want to pay the least amount of interest possible. This chapter helps you calculate the interest you pay on various types of loans and other forms of debt.

Chapter 9 describes the basics of calculating interest. In order to understand the details of this chapter, be sure you have mastered the calculations you are asked to do in Chapter 9.

10.1 Notes

A **note** is a legal document that requires a borrower to repay a loan at specific intervals and at a specific interest rate. In other words, a note is a legal IOU, which is why it's sometimes called a **promissory note** (in that you "promise" to pay it back). The difference between a note and an IOU between you and your brother, however, is that most notes are interest bearing, so you must pay the amount borrowed, plus some amount of interest.

The major distinction between a note and other types of loans is that with a note, the interest is often deducted from the amount lent. So, for example, if you have a $10,000 note that is charging you $800 in interest, you will likely receive not $10,000, but $9,200—the note amount (or **face value**) minus the interest. This type of note is called a **discount note.** The most popular form of discount note is a U.S. Treasury bill (also called a T-bill), which is, essentially, a loan you make to the federal government for a short period of time—from a few days to 6 months. T-bills are sold at a discount from their face value (e.g., you may pay $950 for a $1,000 bill); the difference between the price you pay and the face value is the interest. You can check the financial section of your local newspaper for the rates on these issues or try the *New York Times* website, at http://marketwatch.nytimes.com/custom/nyt-com/html-rates.asp.

You can calculate the interest on a note by using the simple interest formula from Chapter 9:

$$I = p \times r \times t$$

Here's an example. What would be the purchase price for a $10,000, 91-day T-bill paying 4% interest? You're looking for I, the interest rate, and you know p ($10,000), r (0.04), and t (one quarter of a year). You simply solve for I, like this:

FOR EXAMPLE

Tips

A relatively new type of government investment is called *Treasury Inflation-Protected Securities* (TIPS). These securities are tied to the consumer price index (CPI). This means that when the CPI rises (as it does with inflation), the principal on TIPS increases. If there is deflation (which rarely happens but can occur), the principal decreases. TIPS can be purchased in 5-year, 10-year, and 20-year terms, and each pays interest every 6 months, based on a fixed rate that's applied to the changing principal. Because interest is paid twice per year, each interest payment is one-half the interest rate multiplied by the principal at that time. Hint: Check out www.publicdebt.treas.gov/sec/seciis.htm.

$$I = p \times r \times t$$
$$I = \$10,000 \times 0.04 \times \frac{1}{4}$$
$$I = \$100$$

The purchase price is the face value minus the interest:

$$\$10,000 - \$100 = \$9,900$$

Calculate the purchase prices of the following:

1. $20,000 note at 9% for 60 days
2. $75,000 note at 12% for 90 days
3. $28,500 note at $9\frac{1}{4}$% for 4 months
4. $60,000 note at 6.7% for 150 days

SELF-CHECK

- Define **note, promissory note,** and **discount note.**
- Determine the purchase price of a note.
- Explain how to determine the interest paid on a note.

10.2 Loans

Like other products, loans come in all shapes and sizes. They are offered by banks, savings and loans, mortgage lenders, employers, not-for-profit organizations, retail stores, wholesalers (to other businesses), and so on. This section discusses the loans most consumers apply for in their lifetimes.

10.2.1 Real Estate Loans (Mortgages)

Real estate loans, also called **mortgages,** vary substantially in how they are structured. The most common mortgage is a fixed-rate mortgage that lasts for 30 years, but other mortgages are available for shorter terms, such as 10 years, 15 years, or 20 years. A mortgage may also have a variable rate. Check rates at www.bankrate.com/brm/ratehm.asp.

▲ A **fixed-rate loan** has an interest rate that does not change over the life of the loan.

▲ A **variable-rate,** or adjustable-rate, **loan** has an interest rate that changes at fixed intervals, usually every 6 months or a year. When the Federal Reserve Board changes its rates, the interest rate on a variable-rate mortgage changes, too; when rates go up, the monthly payments goes up, and when rates go down, the monthly payment goes down. When interest rates are very high, you can consider a low-interest variable-rate loan. If you know you will be in your house for only a few years, a variable-rate loan makes sense.

Table 10-1 shows the monthly payments for a $100,000 loan, at various fixed interest rates, for 15- and 30-year mortgages. Using this table and the following formula, you can calculate the monthly payment for virtually any loan amount:

Monthly payment = Monthly payment from table at a given interest rate
× (Actual loan amount ÷ $100,000)

To determine the payment for a $100,000 loan for 15 years at 7%, you simply use Table 10-1 to find the value: $899. Compare that to the payment for a 30-year loan at 7%, and you see that your payments are $234 less per month. However, in the end, you will have paid $899 × 180 = payments = $161,820 for the 15-year mortgage and $665 × 360 payments = $239,400 for the 30-year mortgage. That's a difference of $77,580! And keep in mind that the interest rate on 15-year mortgages is usually slightly lower (for example, $\frac{1}{2}$%) than for 30-year loans. So although you pay more per month, you pay far less in interest, and your house is completely paid off in 15 years instead of 30.

But what if you want to figure the payment for a $220,000 loan for 30 years at 7%? You have to do a little math:

Table 10-1: Monthly Payments for a $100,000 Loan

Interest Rate	Monthly Payment for 30 Years	Monthly Payment for 15 Years
4%	$ 477	$ 740
5%	$ 537	$ 791
6%	$ 600	$ 844
7%	$ 665	$ 899
8%	$ 734	$ 956
9%	$ 805	$1,014
10%	$ 878	$1,075
11%	$ 952	$1,137
12%	$1,029	$1,200

Monthly payment = Monthly payment from table at a given interest rate
× (Actual loan amount ÷ $100,000)

Monthly payment = $665 × (220,000 ÷ $100,000) = $1,463

Now suppose that you want to calculate a different interest rate, such as 8.25%, for a $139,500 loan over 30 years. First, you have to interpolate the interest rate, which isn't exact but does get you close. The 8% payment is $733, and the 9% payment is $805. The different between these values is $72. Half that difference again is $36. So, if you add $36 to $733, you can approximate the extra $\frac{1}{4}$%: $733 + $36 = $769. Plug $769 into the formula, and you get the following monthly payment:

Monthly payment = $769 × (139,500 ÷ $100,000) = $1,073

Find the monthly mortgage payments, given the following terms and using Table 10-1:

1. $1,000,000 at 7% for 30 years
2. $235,000 at 8% for 15 years
3. $190,000 at 11% for 30 years

Two other types of real estate loans are **home equity loans** and **home equity lines of credit.** With one of these types of loans, you borrow against the paid-off portion of your mortgage (the **equity**). So if you've lived in your home for 10 years, you've been paying *down* the mortgage principal, and the value of the house has *risen* (**appreciated**) at the same time. This means you may be living in a $250,000 home and have only a $100,000 mortgage. A home equity loan or line of credit allows you to borrow against the $150,000 value of your home. A home equity loan gives you a fixed amount of cash, which you repay over a certain number of years. A home equity line of credit gives you a certain amount that you can borrow, but you dip into the line only when you need it. You repay when you use the line, your monthly payments then begin, and they increase if you draw from the line of credit again in the future. The interest may be a variable rate, so the monthly payment may change as the rate changes.

A **reverse mortgage** is another form of home equity loan, and it is usually reserved for seniors who have a paid-off home but relatively little monthly income. A bank (or mortgage banker) pays the homeowner a set amount each month, but the homeowner can stay in the home until he or she dies or moves to a nursing home. At that time, the bank owns the home free and clear, with certain exceptions to the heirs.

10.2.2 Personal Property Loans

Personal property loans are those that are not tied (i.e., collateralized) to real estate. A car loan falls under this category, as does a loan for a boat, a flat-screen TV, a hot tub, and so on. The terms on personal property loans are usually fairly short (5 years or less), and the loan is tied to the item, so if you **default** on the loan (i.e., you don't make your payments), the item can be **repossessed.**

An **unsecured personal loan** is one in which you are given money to use as you wish for example, to start a small business, pay off credit cards, do some remodeling to your home, and so on. The bank gives you the loan based on your **creditworthiness** (how well you've managed your credit and finances in the past) and has very little recourse if you don't pay back the loan because there's nothing to repossess, as there would be with a car or house. For this reason, unsecured personal loans are difficult to obtain until you have an excellent credit rating.

10.2.3 Early Payoff of Loans

Most mortgages, car loans, and personal loans allow you to pay off the loan early and, therefore, pay less in interest. (There may be a prepayment penalty, so always ask before signing any loan documents.) A popular option for mortgages is to agree to a 30-year mortgage but make the payments as though you were paying for 15 years. If you do this, the loan will be paid off in 15 years, just as if you had signed up for a 15-year loan in the first place.

Another common way to pay off loans early is to put any unexpected income toward the loan in a lump-sum payment. So, suppose you win $2,000 in a local charity raffle; you could put that money toward your mortgage principal.

FOR EXAMPLE

Loan Calculators

One of the coolest tools available on the Internet is the multitude of loan calculators you can find. Go to any search engine, and type in what you're looking for: *mortgage loan calculator* or *credit card calculator,* for example. With these and other loan calculators, you can run through several what-if scenarios and see the differences instantly.

With a mortgage calculator, you type in the principal amount, the interest rate, and the length of the loan, and the calculator tells you the monthly payment. This is a good way to compare a 15-year mortgage to a 30-year mortgage or to calculate the difference between a 10% down payment and a 20% down payment. By using a mortgage loan calculator, you can also get information that's a lot more difficult to calculate on your own, such as any additional payment you want to make, either added to each month's payment or in a lump sum at the end of each year. And you can discover the amount of your mortgage balance each year of the loan.

With a credit card calculator, you type in your credit card balance and interest rate, and then you either type in the number of months in which you want to pay it off (and the calculator tells you how much your monthly payments need to be) or type in the monthly payment you plan to make (and the calculator tells you how long it will take you to pay off the loan).

SELF-CHECK

- Understand the various types of loans available.
- Calculate monthly mortgage payments.
- Consider the implications of a 15-year versus 30-year mortgage.
- Explain the benefits of paying off a loan early.

10.3 Other Forms of Consumer Credit

You have probably seen signs like this: "No down payment and no payments until next year!" or "Buy now, pay later." What's the catch? Well, in exchange for not having to make any payments for some period of time (from a few months to a year), you generally pay quite a bit in interest when the payments do start. (**Note:** Some companies really do let you use their money for free. If you pay off the entire amount at the end of the "no payment" period, you can sometimes avoid paying any interest at all.)

The following sections discuss how to calculate interest and look at the cost of installment buying and credit card debt.

10.3.1 Annual Percentage Rate (APR)

The most important feature of consumer credit is the **annual percentage rate (APR)** of interest charged to the consumer.

Keep in mind that there is a major difference between consumer credit and notes or loans. With consumer credit, we are no longer talking about borrowing a fixed amount of money for a fixed amount of time. With notes and loans, the amount of interest paid is pretty straightforward: You borrow $1,000 for 1 year at 8% interest, which means you pay back the loan along with $80 in interest. With buying on installment or using credit cards, you pay off the debt over a period of time that may not even be set, at a monthly amount that you determine. This makes calculating the interest rate rather challenging. Here's how you calculate the APR:

$$\text{APR} = \frac{2 \times \text{Number of payment periods in one year} \times \text{Finance charge}}{\text{Amount of loan} \times (\text{Total number of payments} + 1)}$$

Suppose you borrow a total of $1,000 at the stated interest rate of 10%. You are to pay off the loan in 12 equal monthly payments. You want to find the APR to the nearest $\frac{1}{10}$%. First, you find the finance charge:

$$\text{Finance charges} = \$1,000 \times 0.10 = \$100$$

Then, you calculate the APR as follows:

$$\text{APR} = \frac{2 \times \text{Number of payment periods in one year} \times \text{Finance charge}}{\text{Amount of loan} \times (\text{Total number of payments} + 1)}$$

$$\text{APR} = \frac{2 \times 12 \times \$100}{\$1,000 \times (12 + 1)}$$

$$\text{APR} = \frac{24 \times \$100}{\$1,000 \times 13}$$

$$\text{APR} = \frac{\$2,400}{\$13,000} = 18.5\%$$

As you can see, the APR is a lot higher than 10%. This is because you don't have the use of the $1,000 for a full year. As you pay off the loan, you have the use of a **declining principal.** (We examine this concept in greater detail in Section 10.3.2)

Determine the APR for each of the following scenarios.

1. Finance charges of $5,000 on a $100,000 purchase for 1 year
2. Finance charges of $67.40 on a $395 purchase for 2 years
3. Finance charges of $740 on a $9,250 purchase for 1 year
4. Finance charges of $3,300 on a $6,900 purchase for 1 year

10.3.2 Installment Buying

Installment buying is just what it sounds like: You buy a good or service and pay for it over a period of months, or even years, one installment at a time.

Installment buying didn't exist prior to 40 or 50 years ago. Before that time, if you didn't have enough money to buy something, you saved up for it, or you used a layaway plan. Under the layaway plan, you pay out what you owe in installments, and when you make your last payment, you can take the product home. You don't get to use the product while you make the payments, but you also don't pay any interest. With installment buying, the price you pay for being able to use the product right away is that you usually pay a high rate of interest (so check the fine print). Retailers like installment plans because they take the focus off the total cost of the product and off the interest rate; instead, consumers tend to focus only on the now "affordable" monthly payment.

Consider this common example of a used-car advertisement: "Here's a fantastic deal on a pickup truck—just $1,000 down and $300 per month for 3 years." If you want to pay cash for this same deal, you owe $9,500. Under the installment plan, how much are you paying in interest, and what's the APR? To find out how much you pay in interest, you simply add up all the payments and subtract the cash price:

$$\$1,000 + (\$300 \times 36) = \$11,800 - \$9,500 = \$2,300 \text{ in interest}$$

That's pretty steep: Under the installment plan, you pay $11,800 for the same vehicle you could purchase for $9,500 cash. Next, you figure the APR:

$$APR = \frac{2 \times \text{Number of payment periods in one year} \times \text{Finance charge}}{\text{Amount of loan} \times (\text{Total number of payments} + 1)}$$

$$APR = \frac{2 \times 12 \times \$2,300}{\$10,800 \times (36 + 1)}$$

$$APR = \frac{24 \times \$2,300}{\$10,800 \times 37}$$

$$APR = \frac{\$55,200}{\$399,600} = 13.8\%$$

Here's another example: You're looking at a $1,999 bedroom set for which you pay nothing down and have 2 years to pay. The finance charge is an additional $374. If the payments are monthly, what's the APR? Here's how you figure it out:

$$APR = \frac{2 \times \text{Number of payment periods in one year} \times \text{Finance charge}}{\text{Amount of loan} \times (\text{Total number of payments} + 1)}$$

$$APR = \frac{2 \times 12 \times \$374}{\$1,999 \times (24 + 1)}$$

$$APR = \frac{24 \times \$374}{\$1,999 \times 25}$$

$$APR = \frac{\$8,976}{\$49,975} = 18.0\%$$

Determine the APR for each of the following scenarios:

1. A $20,000 purchase with 5 years of payments at $9\frac{1}{2}\%$ interest
2. A $36,000 purchase for 7 years, with a $2,000 finance charge per year
3. A $15,000 purchase for 2 years, with a $250 finance charge per year

10.3.3 Credit Cards

Chances are, you have at least one credit card. Besides Visa, MasterCard, American Express, and Discover, there are also gasoline credit cards, department and discount store credit cards, and supermarket credit cards. All of them advocate the same message as installment buying: buy now, pay later.

Credit cards definitely have an important use in our society. When you travel, especially if you buy a plane ticket, rent a car, use a hotel, or dine at a restaurant, a credit card is virtually essential. When you pay for a big-ticket item such as furniture, a computer, or a flat-screen TV, it's more convenient to pay by credit card than to carry cash.

Credit cards also provide consumers with thousands of dollars' worth of credit. In your economics courses, you will learn of the "money supply" issues that are fundamental to the health of a country's economy. Credit—the availability to purchase goods and services without cash—is a key point. If you pay off your balance each month, you avoid paying any interest on that money. But if you *don't* pay off your entire balance each month, you can end up paying hundreds—if not thousands—of dollars in interest each year. Indeed, the banks that own those credit cards prefer that you don't pay off everything you owe. Why? Because then they can charge you interest. In fact, earning interest on your purchases is the main reason they issue credit cards in the first place, and the retailer knows that you will purchase more if credit is available to you.

Although credit card interest rates vary widely, they're still usually substantially higher than interest rates charged on mortgages, new car loans, and savings accounts. Many banks charge 15% on credit cards, and the rate can jump another 5% or 6% if you're late with a payment or exceed your credit limit. (Unlike installment loans, most credit cards have variable interest, which, as with variable-rate mortgages, means that the interest rate changes periodically.) For this reason, using your credit card as a way to borrow money isn't a good idea.

Your credit card interest is calculated by multiplying the average daily balance on the card by the monthly (or, sometimes, daily) interest rate. For example, if your average daily balance during June is $1,000 and the yearly interest rate is 18%, you have to first find the monthly interest rate:

$$18\% \div 12 = 1.5\%$$

Then, you multiply that by $1,000 for that month:

$$\$1,000 \times 1.5 = \$15$$

Of course, if your balance is $10,000 or $20,000, that monthly interest charge quickly grows to $150 or $300 per month, respectively. And that payment is only for the interest; it doesn't pay down the credit card balance one bit.

Beware of just paying the monthly minimum payment on your credit card(s). Suppose you have a $2,000 credit card debt at 15%, and the minimum monthly payment is $30. If you make the minimum payment, you may be thinking, "$2,000 divided by 30 payments is about 65 months, which is just over 5 years." Think again: It will take you nearly *12* years to pay off that $2,000 debt. On the other hand, paying $100 per month toward that $2,000 debt pays off the balance in just 2 years.

FOR EXAMPLE

Switching to Low-Interest Credit Cards

With thousands of options for credit cards, some consumers have become savvy credit card shoppers. Suppose you currently have a balance of $10,000 on a credit card that's charging you 14.9%, and you intend to pay it off in 1 year. Upon shopping around, you discover that you qualify for another credit card that's offering you a 1.9% interest rate for 15 months, which is more than the amount of time you need to pay off the loan. By switching to the new card, you stand to save well over $1,000 over the course of the year. It's important to keep in mind two caveats: Low interest rates are usually temporary, so you need to make sure you know what the rate will be after the introductory period ends. Also, the companies offering extremely low rates often don't give you a very large line of credit. So, you might run into trouble if you're planning to transfer a $10,000 balance, but your new low-interest card offers only a $2,000 line of credit. Shop wisely!

SELF-CHECK

- Define **APR**.
- Understand how to calculate the interest paid on installment loans.
- Calculate the monthly interest charged on credit cards.
- Consider the implications of borrowing against a credit card at a high rate of interest.

SUMMARY

Loans and other forms of consumer credit power our national economy, but they cost consumers in terms of the interest paid. Chapter 9 shows how to calculate interest; in this chapter, you began to see how interest adds up, whether in notes, loans, credit card balances, personal loans, or mortgages.

KEY TERMS

Annual percentage rate (APR)	Interest rate paid on an installment loan.
Appreciate	The increased value of a home that occurs as a result of inflation.
Creditworthiness	Having a high credit score due to paying bills on time, not having too many loans at one time, and having a steady source of income.
Declining principal	The steadily decreasing amount you owe on a credit card as you pay it off.
Default	To not pay one's loan obligation.
Discount note	A note in which the interest is deducted from the face value before the loan amount is dispersed.
Equity	The value of a home minus the amount owed on it.
Face value	The total amount borrowed with a note; the principal.
Fixed-rate loan	A loan for which the interest rate does not change over the life of the loan.

Home equity line of credit	A line of credit, issued against the equity in one's home, that's available for the owner to use when needed.
Home equity loan	A loan borrowed against the equity in a home.
Installment buying	Loans in which the consumer receives the item now and pays each month, over a set amount of time, with interest.
Mortgage	A loan collateralized by real estate.
Note	A legal document that requires a consumer to pay back borrowed money in a specified time, with a specified amount of interest. Also called a promissory note.
Personal property loan	A loan made for less-expensive items than real estate, such as a car.
Promissory note	*See* note.
Repossess	To take ownership of personal property or real estate because of nonpayment of a loan against that property.
Reverse mortgage	A situation in which a consumer receives monthly payments from a bank in exchange for the paid-off home belonging to the bank upon the consumer's death.
Unsecured personal loan	A loan given to a borrower because of credit-worthiness, and against which there is no secured item, such as a car or home.
Variable-rate loan	A loan for which the interest rate is tied to the Federal Reserve Board's interest rate decisions and, therefore, changes over the life of the loan. Also called an adjustable-rate loan.

ASSESS YOUR UNDERSTANDING

Go to www.wiley.com/college/slavin to evaluate your knowledge of loans and consumer credit.

Measure your learning by comparing pre-test and post-test results.

Summary Questions

1. A T-bill pays you interest every month. True or False?
2. A variable-rate mortgage
   (a) is tied to the Federal Reserve Board's rates.
   (b) results in higher or lower monthly payments over the life of the loan.
   (c) is also called an adjustable-rate mortgage.
   (d) all of the above.
3. The total interest charged over the life of 15-year loan is lower than that charged for a 30-year loan. True or False?
4. After you establish a home equity line of credit,
   (a) your monthly repayments begin immediately.
   (b) you can choose not to use the money available.
   (c) the payments for your original mortgage go down.
   (d) all of above.
5. Some loans penalize you for paying off your loan early. True or False?
6. Credit card companies charge 6% interest or less on balances. True or False?

Review Questions

1. Unlike other types of loan instruments, a note has both a face value and a purchase price. What is the formula for determining the purchase price?
2. How much more can you expect to pay per month on a 15-year loan than on a 30-year loan?
3. What is the formula for finding APR?
4. If you make the minimum payment of $30 per month on a credit card with a $2,000 balance, will you pay that debt in a couple years or more than a decade?
5. Find the bank discount for a loan of $9,200 with a $9\frac{1}{4}$% interest rate for only 4 months.
6. Wachovia Bank made a loan of $50,000 for 6 months at an 8% discounted rate. How much interest will be paid?

7. What is the APR for a $5,000 loan for a new car to be paid back over 3 years, with an annual finance charge of $1,000.

8. If the finance charge per year is $500 on a $15,000 debt for 2 years, what would be the APR?

Applying This Chapter

1. Christopher takes out a $10,000 bank loan, from which the bank deducts the interest in advance. The interest rate is 8% and the loan is for 1 year.

   (a) How much is the principal (or face value) of this loan?

   (b) What is the effective interest rate paid?

2. Using Table 10-1, determine the monthly payment for a 30-year $168,453 loan at 7%.

3. Cindi purchased living room furniture with "11% financing," nothing down, and 3 years to pay. If she spent $3,000 on the furniture, how much is her APR if she makes monthly payments?

4. The Hughes family purchased a new condo for $1,000,000 at 8% for 30 years. What is the monthly payment?

5. A newlywed couple buys a first home for $350,000 at 7% for 15 years. What is their monthly payment?

6. How much is the APR on a $4,000 loan if you make weekly payments for 1 year and the total finance charge is $250?

7. Bennie bought a motor bike for $7,000. and his monthly finance charge is $200 for 18 months. What is the APR on this loan?

8. The Home Depot purchased $70,000 of plumbing fixtures from its wholesaler. They agreed to payments of $2,000 monthly for 5 years. What is the APR?

9. Elliott purchased a used truck for $9,500. He puts down a $500 down payment and will repay the balance in monthly payments of $365 over the next 3 years. What is the APR of this loan?

10. Lizzie splurged on a spring wardrobe of $2,800, agreeing to pay $200 per month to the Fashion Emporium over the next 18 months. What is the APR?

11. The Sullivans are purchasing a home for $248,000 and have been preapproved for a 30-year fixed-rate loan at 5% interest. If they put down a $30,000 down payment, what will be the monthly payment?

12. Joe's Body Shop needs to buy a rebuilt air compressor for $1,780. Joe's will pay for the compressor with equal monthly payments over 1 year. The total finance charge is $90. What is the APR?

YOU TRY IT

Treasury Bills

Patricia purchased a $50,000, 6-month T-bill that pays 5.5%.

1. What was her purchase price for this bill?
2. What was her effective rate of interest?

Monthly Payments

Using Table 10-1, determine the monthly payment for a $330,000 15-year mortgage at 5.875% interest.

Culinary Grad

A recent graduate of a top-ranked culinary college is purchasing a restaurant listed for $800,000. She will be paying a rate of 9% for 30 years.

1. How much is the total interest?
2. How much could the graduate have saved by using a 15-year term?
3. Calculate the monthly payment for an 8% mortgage over both 15 and 30 years with a $20,000 down payment .

Mary's Coffee Shop

Mary borrowed $9,850 for new chairs and tables for her coffee shop. She borrowed the money for 9 months at a $9\frac{1}{4}$% discounted rate.

1. What is the amount of the discount?
2. How much did Mary repay?

Stocks and Bonds

The Acme Mutual Fund company manages a fund of stocks and bonds. The fund manager purchases $5,000,000 in 6 -month T-bills that pay 4.75%. What is the amount of the discount off the purchase price?

Furnishing a Home

Jane bought a new house and needed to furnish it.

1. She bought a new bedroom set. The price was $1,999. She is making monthly payments of $174.28 for 1 year. What is the APR?
2. Jane also purchased, on credit, carpet for the new house. The carpet was $5,000. She agreed to pay $140 each month for 3 years to her uncle's carpet company. What is the APR?

Pennsylvania Dairy

Joe and Tom are purchasing a dairy farm in Pennsylvania for $3,100,000. Bank A offers them a 9% rate over 30 years. Bank B offers an 11% rate over 15 years. With which bank will they make the lower monthly payment?

Quickie Homes vs. Sturdy Homes

Two builders are selling similar houses for $400,000 each. Both builders are offering 30-year financing. Quickie Homes is offering a 7% rate; Sturdy Homes is offering an 11% rate. How much more will it cost to buy a Sturdy Home than the Quickie Home?

Rising Mortgage Rates

The Murphys have attempted to sell their $200,000 country cottage for 4 years. In that time, mortgage rates have risen from 9% to 12%. How much of a difference would this rate change make in monthly payments on a 15-year mortgage?

Discounting a Note

Jacques makes a note for $23,000 on February 10, to be repaid on August 10 of the same year, with a discount rate of 9%. What is the total discount on the note?

Mortgaging a Dream

The Trout family can afford to pay a monthly mortgage of $1,200. The home of their dreams would have a $185,000 mortgage. They can choose to finance the loan for 15 years at 6% or for 30 years at 7%. Which terms are a better fit for their budget?

11
DEPRECIATION
Loss of Value of Business Property and Equipment

Starting Point

Go to www.wiley.com/college/slavin to assess your knowledge of depreciation.

Determine where you need to concentrate your effort.

What You'll Learn in This Chapter

▲ How to depreciate assets such as equipment and property
▲ The straight-line depreciation method
▲ The usefulness of the units-of-production method
▲ How to define MACRS

After Studying This Chapter, You'll Be Able To

▲ Discuss the relationship between straight-line depreciation and double-declining-balance depreciation
▲ Describe the importance of accelerated depreciation
▲ Calculate the sum-of-years'-digits method
▲ Calculate depreciation, using the double-declining-balance method
▲ Discuss the merits of using a units-of-production method
▲ Understand the purpose of MACRS and of electing not to use it

Goals and Outcomes

▲ Master the terminology, understand the procedures/perspectives, and recognize the tools available for taking depreciation deductions
▲ Identify the main issues that affect which type of depreciation method to use
▲ Understand the implications of MACRS
▲ Use tools and techniques to calculate depreciation
▲ Evaluate depreciation strategies

INTRODUCTION

Machinery, equipment, computer systems, buildings, trucks and cars, and other business assets lose value over time. We call that **depreciation** and consider it an expense (cost) of doing business. (Note that land is not considered depreciable because it does not get used up over time.) As described in this chapter, you have five methods to choose from when deciding how to depreciate your business assets.

11.1 The Straight-Line Method

The **straight-line method** of depreciation is not only the most frequently used method but also the simplest. This method is based on the assumption that the item being depreciated wears out evenly over its useful life.

The **useful life** of property and equipment is an estimate of how long you expect to use it in your business. Although the Internal Revenue Service (IRS) has, for years, supplied estimates for various types of property and equipment (see Section 11.5 for details), if you wreak havoc on your computer through extensive use or because of the business you're in, and you need to have the latest and greatest technology, you may need to replace your computer every year. As long as you do that, no one will expect you to depreciate your computer over 2, 3, or 4 years.

For example, a cash register (that is, a point of sale [POS] terminal) is expected to be used for 10 years and then recycled. Under straight-line depreciation, it would be depreciated by 10% of its purchase price (cost) each year. If it were purchased for $1,500 (called the **basis**), it would depreciate by $150 per year.

Of course, not all business property and equipment gets completely used up and then discarded. Often, it has some scrap value, trade-in value, or **salvage value** (although not cell phones, some older computers, and other technology equipment). Suppose your $1,500 cash register actually has a salvage value of $100. Using the straight-line method of depreciation, how much should that cash register be depreciated each year for 10 years? You use the following equation to figure it out:

$$\text{Yearly depreciation} = \frac{\text{Cost} - \text{Salvage value}}{\text{Estimated useful life, in years}}$$

$$= \frac{\$1,500 - \$100}{10}$$

$$= \frac{\$1,400}{10}$$

$$= \$140$$

Here's another example: An office computer with a basis of $7,000 has an estimated life of 6 years and an estimated salvage value at that time of $120. How much is the annual depreciation? Here is how you figure it out:

FOR EXAMPLE

The 10% Rule

According to the IRS, if you acquire business property that has a useful life of 3 years or more, you can subtract from your salvage value 10% of the basis. If the salvage value is less than 10% of the basis, you can ignore the salvage value when figuring depreciation. (Remember, however, that the IRS changes its rules frequently.)

$$\text{Yearly depreciation} = \frac{\text{Cost} - \text{Salvage value}}{\text{Estimated useful life, in years}}$$

$$= \frac{\$7,000 - \$120}{6}$$

$$= \frac{\$6,880}{6}$$

$$= \$1,147$$

The **book value** of property or equipment is its **original cost** minus its accumulated depreciation. After 4 years, what is the book value of the office computer from the preceding example? Here's how you figure it out:

$$\text{Book value} = \text{Original cost} - \text{Accumulated depreciation}$$

$$= \$7,000 - 4(\$1,147)$$

$$= \$7,000 - \$4,588$$

$$= \$2,413$$

Using the straight-line method, calculate the yearly depreciation for each of the following assets:

1. Cost of new catering van, $42,000; trade-in value, $4,500; life of 5 years
2. Cost of pizza oven (installed), $15,700; salvage value, $500; life of 6 years
3. Cost of new POS terminals, $45,790; scrap value, $2,300; life of 3 years

SELF-CHECK

- Define **useful life, salvage value,** and **book value.**
- Describe the straight-line depreciation method.
- Understand the concept of scrap value.
- Explain how to calculate annual depreciation, using the straight-line depreciation method.

11.2 The Sum-of-Years'-Digits Method

The **sum-of-years'-digits method** is a form of **accelerated depreciation**. It is accelerated because it allows you to depreciate property or equipment more in the first year than in the second, more in the second than in the third, and so on.

The key to the sum-of-years'-digits method is to add up the years of the estimated life of the property or equipment. Suppose the equipment is expected to last 6 years. First, you find the sum of the years: $1 + 2 + 3 + 4 + 5 + 6 = 21$. Then, you depreciate the equipment as follows:

$$\text{First-year depreciation} = \frac{6}{21}(\text{Cost} - \text{Salvage value})$$

$$\text{Second-year depreciation} = \frac{5}{21}(\text{Cost} - \text{Salvage value})$$

$$\text{Third-year depreciation} = \frac{4}{21}(\text{Cost} - \text{Salvage value})$$

$$\text{Fourth-year depreciation} = \frac{3}{21}(\text{Cost} - \text{Salvage value})$$

$$\text{Fifth-year depreciation} = \frac{2}{21}(\text{Cost} - \text{Salvage value})$$

$$\text{Sixth-year depreciation} = \frac{1}{21}(\text{Cost} - \text{Salvage value})$$

For example, suppose a machine is purchased for $100,000 and has an expected life of 4 years, after which it should have a salvage value of $4,000. By how much does it depreciate each year? You figure it out like this:

$$\text{Sum of the years: } 1 + 2 + 3 + 4 = 10$$

$$\text{First-year depreciation} = \frac{4}{10}(\$100,000 - \$4,000) = \$38,400$$

$$\text{Second-year depreciation} = \frac{3}{10}(\$100,000 - \$4,000) = \$28,800$$

$$\text{Third-year depreciation} = \frac{2}{10}(\$100,000 - \$4,000) = \$19,200$$

$$\text{Fourth-year depreciation} = \frac{1}{10}(\$100,000 - \$4,000) = \$9,600$$

Be sure to check your results: Adding up all 4 years should total the original cost minus the salvage value.

Tired of adding up all those numbers? Here's a shortcut you can use when you're adding up a lot of years in the sum-of-years'-digits method:

$$\frac{n(n + 1)}{2}$$

FOR EXAMPLE

The Purpose of Accelerated Depreciation

Why do companies chose to accelerate the depreciation of their assets? First, accelerated depreciation mimics the real world. Using accelerated depreciation better matches the book value to actual resale value (market value). Second, accelerated depreciation gives companies a larger tax deduction in the early years, and in general, companies are looking for the greatest deductions *today*; future deductions will be dealt with then.

---

where n is the estimated useful life of the equipment. Suppose a piece of equipment is going to depreciate over 15 years. Rather than add up all those numbers, you can use the formula as follows:

$$\frac{n(n + 1)}{2} = \frac{15(15 + 1)}{2}$$

$$= \frac{15 \times 16}{2}$$

$$= \frac{15 \times \cancel{16}^{8}}{\cancel{2}_{1}}$$

$$= 120$$

To test your knowledge of the sum-of-years'-digits method, try these examples:

1. A machine that costs \$175,000 is expected to last 18 years and have a salvage value of \$10,000. How much does it depreciate in the first and second years? What is the book value after the first and second years?
2. Calculate the first-year deprecation for a machine by using the sum-of-years'-digits method. The cost of the machine, as installed, was \$68,000, and the machine has a 5-year life and a \$1,200 scrap value.
3. Use the sum-of-years'-digits method to prepare the first-year depreciation for a truck with a basis of \$63,700, a 4-year life, and a \$2,500 trade-in value.

SELF-CHECK

- Explain why accelerated forms of depreciation exist.
- Describe how the sum-of-years'-digits method works.
- Use a shortcut for summing the years in the sum-of-years'-digits method.

11.3 The Double-Declining-Balance Method

The **double-declining-balance method** (sometimes called just the **declining-balance method**) is an accelerated depreciation method that accelerates the depreciation more quickly than does the sum-of-years'-digits method. To use this method, you figure the first year as though you were using the straight-line method, and then you double it. With each additional year, you use that same percentage. When the value becomes lower than the straight-line method's value would have been, you switch to the straight-line method until the property or equipment's value declines to the level of the salvage value. Here's a formula that may help:

$$\text{First-year depreciation} = \text{Cost} \times 2 \times \frac{1}{\text{Useful life, in years}}$$

$$\text{Subsequent-year depreciation} = \text{Book value} \times 2 \times \frac{1}{\text{Useful life, in years}}$$

Say, for example, that you buy a machine for $10,000 that has an expected life of 5 years and a salvage value of $500. You figure the depreciation using the double-declining-balance method this way:

$$\text{First-year depreciation} = \$10,000 \times 2 \times \frac{1}{5} = \$4,000$$

$$\text{Second-year depreciation} = (\$10,000 - \$4,000) \times 2 \times \frac{1}{5} = \$2,400$$

$$\text{Third-year depreciation} = (\$10,000 - \$4,000 - \$2,400) \times 2 \times \frac{1}{5} = \$1,440$$

$$\text{Fourth-year depreciation} = (\$10,000 - \$4,000 - \$2,400 - \$1,440) \times 2 \times \frac{1}{5} = \$864$$

$$\text{Fifth-year depreciation} = (\$10,000 - \$4,000 - \$2,400 - \$1,440 - \$864) \times 2 \times \frac{1}{5}$$

$$= \$518.40$$

Note, however, that as soon as the value drops below the straight-line method value, which is ($10,000 − $500) ÷ 5 = $1,900, most companies switch to the straight-line method, making the depreciation on this machine as follows:

▲ **Year 1:** $4,000 (double-declining-balance method value)
▲ **Year 2:** $2,400 (double-declining-balance method value)
▲ **Year 3:** $1,900 (straight-line method value)
▲ **Year 4:** $1,200 (Cost − First 3 years of depreciation − Salvage value)

Now suppose that an asset is purchased for $25,000, with an expected life of 3 years and a salvage value of $1,000. Using the double-declining-balance method, what are each of the 3 years of depreciation? First, you establish the double-declining-balance depreciation:

$$\text{First-year depreciation} = \$25{,}000 \times 2 \times \frac{1}{3} = \$16{,}667$$

$$\text{Second-year depreciation} = (\$25{,}000 - \$16{,}667) \times 2 \times \frac{1}{3} = \$5{,}555$$

$$\text{Third-year depreciation} = (\$25{,}000 - \$16{,}667 - \$5{,}555) \times 2 \times \frac{1}{3} = \$1{,}852$$

In this case, straight-line value is $8,000 per year ($25,000 cost minus $1,000 salvage value, divided by 3 years of depreciation). You can see that the value drops below the value of the straight-line method in the second year. You therefore compile this answer:

▲ **Year 1:** $16,667 (double-declining-balance method value)
▲ **Year 2:** $7,333 (Cost − First year of depreciation − Salvage value)

To test your knowledge of the double-declining-balance method, try these examples:

1. Prepare a depreciation matrix for the first year, using the following facts and the double-declining balance method: Cost of new machine (installed), $75,000, with a 5-year life and a salvage value or $6,000.
2. Use the double-declining-balance method on the depreciation of the following asset and prepare the first year of its depreciation schedule: Asset cost, $82,000; 5-year life; salvage value, $4,000.
3. Use the double-declining-balance method to calculate the depreciation for the first year in the following scenario: Computer equipment (installed), $98,000; 5-year life, scrap value, $2,100.

FOR EXAMPLE

Section 179

The IRS allows business owners to take a special depreciation deduction called Section 179 (www.irs.gov/publications/p946/index.html). Under this rule, you can deduct the *entire* price of business property or equipment in the year that you buy it instead of depreciating it over its useful life. This is especially helpful for equipment that will soon become obsolescent, such as computers. (Note that this special deduction has a maximum attached to it; there's also talk of this maximum being severely reduced in the future, so don't trust this book for financial advice. Instead, visit www.irs.gov for the lowdown. Chances are, however, that the deduction will reappear in some form, even if this particular one is eliminated.)

- Compare the double-declining-balance method to the straight-line method.
- Use the depreciation method that leads to the greatest depreciation in early years of asset life.
- Calculate real-world examples.

11.4 The Units-of-Production Method

Suppose your Uncle Louie, a traveling salesman, drives 110,000 miles per year in the company car, which is a depreciating business expense. For him, any depreciation method that focuses on time (such as years in service) just doesn't work because after 1 year with that kind of mileage, his car has lost value at a much faster rate than most 1-year-old cars have. In fact, his car has depreciated in 1 year by an amount that may take other cars 5 or 10 years. So, in order for his book value to match the actual value of the car after 1 year, he needs to depreciate in terms of miles (or in some other units of depreciation), using the **units-of-production method.** This method involves the following formulas:

$$\text{Unit depreciation} = \frac{\text{Cost} - \text{Salvage value}}{\text{Useful life, in units produced}}$$

$$\text{Depreciation amount} = \text{Unit depreciation} \times \text{Unit produced}$$

In this case, the unit depreciation is miles driven. So, suppose Louie buys a $25,000 car with a salvage value of $2,500 when it reaches its expected life of 150,000 miles. How much has that car depreciated at the end of 1 year? You figure it out like this:

$$\text{Unit depreciation} = \frac{\text{Cost} - \text{Salvage value}}{\text{Useful life, in units produced}}$$

$$= \frac{\$25,000 - \$2,500}{150,000}$$

$$= \frac{\$22,500}{150,000}$$

$$= \$0.15$$

$$\text{Depreciation amount} = \text{Unit depreciation} \times \text{Unit produced}$$

$$= \$0.15 \times 110,000$$

$$= \$16,500$$

So, the car depreciated by $16,500 during the year that Uncle Louie put 110,000 miles one it.

The units-of-production method is the one to use whenever the expected life is described in terms of actual use (number of pages printed, number of units produced, number of hours of use, and so on) rather than in years. Another situation when you should use the units-of-production method is when the use of equipment is uneven, such as with an ice cream truck, which is driven extensively in the summer but not at all in the winter, or with a snowplow that it used only in winter.

Suppose that Toyota has a stamping machine that can stamp out 200,000 car bodies. It cost $4 million and has no salvage value. You need to figure out how much it has depreciated after stamping out 50,000 car bodies, and you need to determine its book value at that time. Here's how you do it:

$$\text{Unit depreciation} = \frac{\text{Cost} - \text{Salvage value}}{\text{Useful life in units produced}}$$

$$= \frac{\$4,000,000 - \$0}{200,000}$$

$$= \$20$$

$$\text{Depreciation amount} = \text{Unit depreciation} \times \text{Unit produced}$$

$$= \$20 \times 50,000$$

$$= \$1,000,000$$

$$\text{Book value} = \text{Original cost} - \text{Accumulated depreciation}$$

$$= \$4,000,000 - \$1,000,000$$

$$= \$3,000,000$$

You can see that after stamping out 50,000 car bodies, the stamping machine depreciates $1 million and has a book value of $3 million.

FOR EXAMPLE

An Elite Marathon Runner

Running shoes aren't measured in time but in miles—generally 500 miles per pair. Casual runners (people who run 20 miles per week) usually replace their running shoes twice a year, and more serious runners (running 40 to 50 miles per week) may have to buy four or five pairs per year. But consider an elite professional marathon runner who runs 90 miles per week and wears a very lightweight shoe (which is more comfortable than a heavy, stable shoe) that can be used for only 450 miles at a time. This runner needs to replace his shoes every 5 weeks! This professional runner would need to use the units-of-production method to depreciate his business equipment.

Use the units-of-production method to answer the following:

1. A soda bottling plant's new labeling system can label 150 million bottles in its useful life. The machine cost $570,000 and has a salvage value of $5,000. In the first year, it labels 20 million bottles, in the second year, it labels 28 million bottles, and in the next 3 years, it labels the remainder equally. Calculate the first-year depreciation.

SELF-CHECK

- Explain the units-of-production method.
- Describe the types of situations in which you would choose this method.
- Consider the implications of using this method over another method of depreciation.
- Calculate the depreciation on equipment by using the units-of-production method.

11.5 The Modified Accelerated Cost Recovery System (MACRS)

In 1981, the Economic Recovery Tax Act established a depreciation method called the **accelerated cost recovery system (ACRS),** which based depreciation on recovery period instead of useful life. That system is still in use for property and equipment placed into service up until 1986, but given how long ago that was, we don't discuss the ACRS method here. Instead, we discuss the method that replaced ACRS in 1986: the **modified accelerated cost recovery system (MACRS).**

Under MACRS, the IRS categorizes business property and equipment into **classes** and tells you the **property class life** of each class of property or equipment. The property class life is like the useful life, but it is shorter than the actual useful life. In addition, salvage values are always $0 with MACRS (see www.irs.gov/publications/p946/13081f19.html).

Under MACRS, the IRS essentially dictates to you the useful life of your property or equipment, and you then use either the straight-line or double-declining-balance method (using a salvage value of $0) to figure each year's depreciation. If you use another method or if you use a useful life other than the property class life given under MACRS, you need to inform the IRS that you're using a different method for a particular piece of equipment or property. So, for example, the IRS considers computers to have a property class life of 5 years. In many industries, however, a 5-year life is simply too long; they will have purchased two or even three computers in 5 years. For a computer in this situation, you elect to not use MACRS, and you use another useful life that's appropriate for you, letting the IRS know that you're doing so.

FOR EXAMPLE

The Income-Forecast Method

A sixth type of depreciation method is called the **income-forecast method,** which is used to depreciate intellectual property such as motion picture films or videos, sound recordings, copyrights, books, and patents. Under this method, the depreciation each year is the cost of the product, minus the salvage value, multiplied by a fraction. The fraction is derived in this way: The numerator is the current year's net income from the property, and the denominator is the total income the owner of the property expects through the end of the tenth year.

SELF-CHECK

- Describe MACRS.
- Consider the implications of the IRS classes and property class life.

SUMMARY

Depreciation is how businesses account for the declining value of their business property and equipment. The IRS provides a tax deduction for depreciation, and in doing so, it dictates the useful life of depreciable business property and equipment. However, businesses can elect to use other methods of depreciation, as outlined in this chapter.

KEY TERMS

Accelerated depreciation	A form of depreciation that allows you to depreciate assets such as property or equipment more in the first year than in the second, more in the second than in the third, and so on.
Accelerated cost recovery system.(ACRS)	A depreciation method introduced by the IRS in 1981 that is no longer in use except with property and equipment that was placed in service prior to 1986.

Basis	The original cost of a depreciable item.
Book value	The original cost of an asset (property or equipment) minus any accumulated depreciation.
Classes	IRS groupings of depreciable equipment and property.
Depreciation	The allocation of the cost of an asset such as machinery, equipment, a computer system, a building, a truck, or a car over the revenue-producing years of that asset.
Double-declining-balance method	An ultra-accelerated depreciation method that uses a declining book value. Also known as declining-balance method.
Income-forecast method	A method of depreciating intellectual property.
Modified accelerated cost recovery system (MACRS)	A depreciation method used since 1986 in which the IRS categorizes assets (i.e., business property, equipment) into classes and determines the proper class life of each.
Original cost	The cost of an asset, including transportation (delivery) and installation.
Property class life	The IRS version of useful life.
Salvage value	The value of a depreciable item at the end of its useful life. Also known as salvage value, residual value, or trade-in value.
Straight-line method	A depreciation method that assumes an item will be depreciated (expensed) evenly over its useful life.
Sum-of-years'-digits method	An accelerated method of depreciation that sums the useful life and uses that as a multiplier (i.e., denominator of a fraction) to find the annual depreciation.
Units-of-production method	A method of depreciating equipment in terms other than time (often in miles or number of units produced).
Useful life	An estimate of how long you expect to use assets (i.e., equipment, property).

ASSESS YOUR UNDERSTANDING

Go to www.wiley.com/college/slavin to evaluate your knowledge of depreciation. *Determine where you need to concentrate your effort.*

Summary Questions

1. Depreciation refers to the appreciation in value of items over time. True or False?
2. The useful life of property and equipment is
    (a) an estimate of how long it will last.
    (b) an estimate of how much it will be worth in the future.
    (c) an estimate of how long you will use it in your business.
    (d) none of the above.
3. Basis and original cost are synonyms. True or False?
4. Salvage value of equipment refers to
    (a) the price paid for it.
    (b) the value at the end of its useful life.
    (c) the book value.
    (d) all of above.
5. Define **book value**.

Review Questions

1. Without knowing the salvage value of an item, you have difficulty accurately depreciating it. Define **salvage value.**
2. Which is the easiest depreciation method to use?
3. What are the benefits of accelerated depreciation?
4. Why would a company use the units-of-production method?

Applying This Chapter

1. A company purchased a piece of equipment for $80,000. Say that the equipment has an estimated life of 12 years and a salvage value of $3,000.
    (a) How much is the annual depreciation, using the straight-line method?
    (b) How much is the equipment's book value after 2 years?
    (c) How much is the equipment's book value after 8 years?

2. A piece of equipment has a useful life of 8 years. Its original cost is $186,000, and it has a salvage value of $3,000.

   (a) Using the sum-of-years'-digits method, how much does it depreciate in its first year, and what is its book value at the end of the first year?

   (b) Using the sum-of-years'-digits method, how much does it depreciate in its second year, and what is its book value at the end of the second year?

3. A machine is purchased for $75,000 and has a salvage value of $5,000. If its expected life is 7 years, using the double-declining-balance method, by how much does it depreciate in each of the first four years? (Hint: In the fourth year, switch to the straight-line method and take a $10,000 depreciation.)

4. A prominent Long Island, New York, caterer built a huge oven that has an expected life of 9,000 hours and no salvage value. It cost $350,000. How much does the oven depreciate after operating for 2,000 hours, and what is its book value at that time?

Painting Depreciation

A piece of industrial painting equipment cost a startup company $250,000, and it will paint approximately 45,000 units, at which point it will have a salvage value of $1,500. The company produces the following number of units in each of the equipment's first 4 years: 8,000; 10,000; 12,000; and 15,000.

1. Find the first-year depreciation, using the straight-line method.
2. Find the first-year depreciation, using the sum-of-years'-digits method.
3. Find the first-year depreciation, using the double-declining-balance method.
4. Find the first-year depreciation, using the units-of-production method.

UPS, Inc.

UPS, Inc., purchased a large brown truck for $34,000, with an estimated life of 4 years and a trade-in value of $3,000. Use the straight-line depreciation method and determine the book value at the end of the second year.

Advantage Advertising

The Advantage Advertising Company bought a new laser copier for $46,000, with a life of 5 years. The scrap value is $5,600.

1. Calculate the annual depreciation.
2. Calculate the book value at the end of the third year, using the straight-line method.
3. Calculate the first 2 years' depreciation, using the units-of-production method. The copier will produce 350,000 copies over its life. In the first year, it will make 130,000 copies, and in the second year, it will make 180,000.
4. The Advantage Advertising Company switches to using the sum-of-years-digits method. What is the difference in depreciation over the first 2 years compared to using the straight-line method?
5. Determine the first 2 years' depreciation expense, using the double-declining-balance method.

Hilton Hotel

The Hilton hotel located in the Greater Greensboro area bought a new guest van for $36,950, with a life of 5 years. The trade-in value is $1,350. Say that you are the hotel comptroller.

1. Prepare the depreciation, using the sum-of-years'-digits method.
2. Prepare the depreciation, using the double-declining-balance method.

Martelli Sportswear

Phil Martelli, a sportswear company owner, has talked with his accountant to determine the best depreciation method to use for his new computer system. The cost of the system was $67,000, with a scrap value of $2,100 and an estimated life of 3 years. Help the accountant by preparing the depreciation matrix, using the double-declining-balance method.

Bookstore Business

Your local bookstore purchased a new truck for $27,500, with a life of 5 years. The trade-in value is probably $4,500. Prepare the depreciation matrix, using the sum-of-years'-digits method.

Wright Bus Company

The Wright Bus Company purchased a fully loaded customer courtesy van for $45,000. The company planned a life of 5 years and a trade-in value of $6,000. What would be the difference between the book value and the dollar amount received from the van's sale for $7,000 in a private transaction at the end of 4 years? (*Hint:* Use the straight-line method.)

Retail Shelving

One of the largest retailers on the west coast purchased (and had installed) 35,000 linear feet of shelving in a newly opened mall location. The cost was $579,000, with an estimated residual (scrap) value of $7,200 after the 5 years of use.

1. Determine the depreciation, using the double-declining-balance method.
2. Determine the depreciation, using the sum-of-years'-digits method.
3. Determine the depreciation, using the straight-line method.

International Elevator Company

The International Elevator Company brought a small crane for $79,000. The scrap value may be $2,300, with a 3-year life expectancy. Using the double-declining-balance method, calculate the depreciation.

Global Waste Management

Global Waste Management, Inc., recently bought 25 dumpsters (15 cubic yards each) for $3,400 each. The scrap value will be $35 each after 4 years of use. Calculate the yearly depreciation, using the straight-line method. What is the book value after the second year?

Laptop Accounting

An accounting office will use the straight-line method of depreciation on recently acquired laptop computers for its Accounts Payable and Payroll sections. Say that all this equipment costs $74,500 and has a total scrap value of $560 in 3 years.

1. What is the accumulated depreciation after 2 years?
2. What is the book value after 2 years?

Furniture Refinishers

Your small but growing furniture refinishing business purchased a power nail gun for $2,500 and an air compressor for an additional $1,500. The estimated life of this equipment is 4 years. What is the total accumulated depreciation after 3 years of use, with no salvage value? (*Hint:* Use the straight-line method.)

12

FINANCIAL STATEMENTS
The Income Statement and the Balance Sheet

Starting Point

Go to www.wiley.com/college/slavin to assess your knowledge of financial statements.
Determine where you need to concentrate your effort.

What You'll Learn in This Chapter

▲ How to use income statements and balance sheets
▲ How to collect relevant data from these financial statements
▲ How to tabulate dollar amounts from sample financial statements

After Studying This Chapter, You'll Be Able To

▲ Describe the key ratios derived from financial statements
▲ Calculate important financial ratios
▲ Demonstrate company profitability based on financial ratios
▲ Construct comparative financial statements

Goals and Outcomes

▲ Master the terminology related to financial statements
▲ Understand the procedures for completing income statements and balance sheets
▲ Evaluate the profitability of a company when given key financial ratios
▲ Compare two financial statements and determine relative profitability
▲ Predict whether a company is becoming more or less profitable by comparing financial statements
▲ Assess how real-world companies can misrepresent to and thereby fool shareholders and any future investors through dishonest financial statements

INTRODUCTION

Income statements and balance sheets are two of the fundamental accounting tools. An income statement covers a company's finances over a period of time, usually 1 year or 1 quarter (i.e., 3 months). A balance sheet, on the other hand, provides a snapshot of a company's finances on one particular date, perhaps the first day of a year, the first day of a quarter, and so on.

12.1 The Income Statement

An **income statement** (also called a profit and loss statement) tells you—as well as investors in your company—how profitable the company has been over a given period. A company with high sales but even higher expenses is not a profitable company; similarly, a company with low sales but few expenses may be turning a healthy profit.

12.1.1 How an Income Statement Is Set Up

The basic formula used in an income statement is

$$\text{Sales} - \text{Costs} = \text{Net income}$$

For a lemonade stand, finding net income is pretty simple: You add up all the money received; subtract the expenses of lemonade mix, cups, and posters; and arrive at net income. But most companies are far more complex than this, and you have to do some figuring to find out what the **sales** and **costs** amount to. You have to consider the following:

▲ Net sales: The **net sales** is the amount the company sold after all returns, discounts, and other allowances are deducted. To find net sales, you start with **gross sales** (the total amount sold, also called total sales) and subtract returns and allowances. In other words,

$$\text{Net sales} = \text{Gross sales} - \text{Returns and allowances}$$

(Note: Net sales is often referred to as revenue.)

▲ Costs of goods sold: You can figure out the cost of selling products, also called the **cost of goods sold (COGS)**, by starting with the value of the inventory at the beginning of a period (say, the beginning of a quarter, for a quarterly income statement), subtracting the value of the inventory at the end of the period, and adding in any purchases. In other words,

$$\text{Costs of goods sold} = \text{Beginning inventory} - \text{Ending inventory} + \text{Purchases}$$

▲ **Gross profit:** Before you can find net income (or profit), you have to first find **gross profit** (or total profit), which is net sales minus the cost of goods sold. In other words,

$$\text{Gross profit} = \text{Net sales} - \text{Cost of goods sold}$$

▲ **Operating expenses:** Before you can find the net income (or profit), you need to know the **operating expenses,** which are the costs of running the business (e.g., salaries, rent, utilities, equipment, depreciation). In other words,

$$\text{Operating expenses} = \text{Salaries} + \text{Rent} + \text{Utilities} + \text{Equipment} + \text{Depreciation}$$
$$+ \text{Other day-to-day expenses of running the company}$$

▲ **Net income: Net income** (the amount made as profit after all other expenses are subtracted) is gross profit minus the operating expenses. In other words,

$$\text{Net income} = \text{Gross profit} - \text{Operating expenses}$$

12.1.2 Completing an Income Statement

Suppose Company X has $985,400 in gross sales and $9,700 in returns and allowances, as shown in the equation below What are the net sales?

Gross sales	$985,400
Returns and allowances	−9,700
Net sales	**975,700**

As you can see above, net sales for Company X are $975,700. Now you need to find the COGS. Say that beginning inventory on January 1, 2007, is $27,600. Ending inventory on December 3, 2007, is $24,900. Also assume that Company X purchases $390,100 worth of goods during the year.

Beginning inventory, 1/1	$27,600
Ending inventory, 12/31	−24,900
Purchases	+390,100
Cost of goods sold	**392,800**

As you can see above, Company X's COGS is $392,800. Next, you need to find the gross profit, using this formula:

$$\text{Gross profit} = \text{Net sales} - \text{Cost of goods sold}$$

Net sales	$975,700
Cost of goods sold	−392,800
Gross profit	**582,900**

As you can see, Company X's gross profit is $582,900.

As shown in the calculation below, Company X had $107,600 in salaries, $24,000 in rent, $11,200 in utilities, and $6,400 in depreciation on equipment. (Note: The Internal Revenue Service [IRS] can limit deductions for equipment purchases to **depreciation**, by taking the total cost of equipment and dividing it by the number of years that equipment is likely to last. See Chapter 11 for more on depreciation methods.) Company X had no other operating expenses besides these four categories.

Salaries expenses	$107,600
Rent expenses	+24,000
Utilities expenses	+11,200
Depreciation expenses	+6,400
Total operating expenses	**149,200**

As you can see in the calculation above, Company X's total operating expenses are $149,200.

Finally, you can determine Company X's net income by subtracting its operating expenses from gross profit.

Gross profit	$582,900
Operating expenses	−149,200
Net income	**433,700**

As you can see above, net income for Company X for 1 year is $433,700. You have just completed the calculations for your first income statement!

Table 12-1 shows an example of an income statement for Harry's Grocery for the third quarter of 2006. Based on what you've learned so far in this chapter, fill in the blanks in this income statement.

If you calculate the totals in Table 12-1 properly, you come up with net sales of $1,207,400, COGS of $526,300, gross profit of $681,100, operating expenses of $313,100, and net income of $368,000.

12.1.3 Negative Net Income (Loss)

Consider the income statement in Table 12-2 for The Strand Bookstore's first quarter of 2007. Calculate and fill in the necessary data so that you can compute the bookstore's net income for this quarter.

When you fill in Table 12-2, you should come up with net sales of $1,406,400, COGS of $775,300, gross profit of $631,100, operating expenses of 720,200, and net income of −$89,100. Is the net income value a mistake? How can you get a negative number for net income? The only way that net income can be negative is when a company has a loss for the period.

Table 12-1: Harry's Grocery Income Statement, July 1, 2006, to September 30, 2006

Revenue:	
Gross sales	$1,231,600
Returns and allowances	24,200
Net sales	‒‒‒‒‒‒‒‒
Cost of Goods Sold:	
Beginning inventory, 7/1	174,700
Ending inventory, 9/30	186,500
Purchases	538,100
Cost of goods sold	‒‒‒‒‒‒‒‒
Gross profit	‒‒‒‒‒‒‒‒
Operating Expenses:	
Salaries	185,200
Advertising	63,800
Rent	36,000
Utilities	15,200
Depreciation	12,900
Operating expenses	‒‒‒‒‒‒‒‒
Net income	‒‒‒‒‒‒‒‒

Companies can stay in business while losing money because they have loans that cover their purchases and operating expenses. In fact, many new companies expect to lose money—or at least break even (i.e., have a net income of $0)—during their first 1 or 2 years in business. However, if a company loses money for 2 or more years, it will likely end up going out of business.

12.1.4 Finding the Percentage of Net Sales

To make an income statement even more useful, business owners often determine what percentage of net sales was spent on advertising or salaries or what percentage of net sales ended up as returns and allowances. If, after looking at the following two examples, you're unsure how to compute the percentage of net sales for an income statement, review Chapter 3. (Hint: Use Net sales as the denominator of a fraction, with each other item as the numerator.)

Table 12-2: The Strand Bookstore Income Statement, January 1, 2007, to March 31, 2007

Revenue:	
Gross sales	$1,486,200
Returns and allowances	79,800
Net sales	_____
Cost of Goods Sold:	
Beginning inventory, 1/1	153,600
Ending inventory, 3/31	160,200
Purchases	781,900
Cost of goods sold	_____
Gross profit	_____
Operating Expenses:	
Salaries	378,400
Advertising	197,800
Rent	84,000
Utilities	31,300
Depreciation	28,700
Operating expenses	_____
Net income (loss)	(_____)

Table 12-3 shows an example of an income statement that includes percentage of net sales. You simply divide each item by the net sales (not gross sales) to find the percentage of net sales.

To test your understanding of percentage of net sales, try filling the percentage of net sales values in Table 12-4 (Note: By convention, negative numbers are placed in parentheses, so (89,000) means −$89,000.) Check your answers against those shown in Table 12-5.

12.1.5 The Operating Ratio

Business owners usually have a good idea of how well their companies are doing. But sometimes, they'd like to have some hard numbers to back up

Table 12-3: Harry's Grocery Income Statement, July 1, 2006, to September 30, 2006

		Percentage of Net Sales
Revenue:		
Gross sales	$1,231,600	102.0%
Returns and allowances	24,200	2.0
Net sales	1,207,400	100.0
Cost of Goods Sold:		
Beginning inventory, 7/1	174,700	14.5
Ending inventory, 9/30	186,500	15.4
Purchases	538,100	44.6
Cost of goods sold	526,300	43.6
Gross profit	**681,100**	**56.4**
Operating Expenses:		
Salaries	185,200	15.3
Advertising	63,800	5.3
Rent	36,000	3.0
Utilities	15,200	1.3
Depreciation	12,900	1.1
Operating expenses	313,100	25.9
Net income	**368,000**	**30.5**

their seat-of-the-pants estimates. They generally use three measures—operating ratio, gross profit margin ratio (described in Section 12.1.6), and profit margin on net sales (described in Section 12.1.7)—to see just how profitable business is.

A business's **operating ratio** tells whether the firm is making or losing money:

▲ An operating ratio of less than 1 means the company is turning a profit.
▲ An operating ratio of 1 means the company is breaking even.
▲ An operating ratio of more than 1 means the company is losing money.

Table 12-4: The Strand Bookstore Income Statement, January 1, 2007, to March 31, 2007

		Percentage of Net Sales
Revenue:		
Gross sales	$1,486,200	_____%
Returns and allowances	79,800	_____
Net sales	1,406,400	_____
Cost of Goods Sold:		
Beginning inventory, 1/1	153,600	_____
Ending inventory, 3/31	160,200	_____
Purchases	781,900	_____
Cost of goods sold	775,300	_____
Gross profit	**631,100**	_____
Operating Expenses:		
Salaries	378,400	_____
Advertising	197,800	_____
Rent	84,000	_____
Utilities	31,300	_____
Depreciation	28,700	_____
Operating expenses	720,200	_____
Net income	**(89,000)**	_____

To find the operating ratio, you use the following formula:

$$\text{Operating ratio} = \frac{\text{Cost of goods sold} + \text{Operating expenses}}{\text{Net sales}}$$

Try finding the operating ratio of a company that has net sales of $500,000, operating expenses of $100,000, and COGS of $300,000. Here's how you figure it out:

$$\text{Operating ratio} = \frac{\text{Cost of goods sold} + \text{Operating expenses}}{\text{Net sales}}$$

$$= \frac{\$300,000 + \$100,000}{\$500,000} = \frac{\$400,000}{\$500,000} = \frac{4}{5} = 0.8$$

Table 12-5: The Strand Bookstore Income Statement, January 1, 2007, to March 31, 2007 (Answers)

		Percentage of Net Sales
Revenue:		
Gross sales	$1,486,200	105.7%
Returns and allowances	79,800	5.7
Net sales	1,406,400	100.0
Cost of Goods Sold:		
Beginning inventory, 1/1	153,600	10.9
Ending inventory, 3/31	160,200	11.4
Purchases	781,900	55.6
Cost of goods sold	775,300	55.1
Gross profit	**631,100**	**44.9**
Operating Expenses:		
Salaries	378,400	26.9
Advertising	197,800	14.1
Rent	84,000	6.0
Utilities	31,300	2.2
Depreciation	28,700	2.0
Operating expenses	720,200	51.2
Net income	**(89,000)**	**(6.3)**

Now use the values in Table 12-3 and the following formula to find the operating ratio for Harry's Grocery:

$$\text{Operating ratio} = \frac{\text{Cost of goods sold} + \text{Operating expenses}}{\text{Net sales}}$$

$$= \frac{\$526,300 + \$313,100}{\$1,207,400} = \frac{\$839,400}{\$1,207,400} = 0.695 = 0.7$$

You might notice a potential shortcut if you've already figured the percentage of net sales. If you use the percentage of net sales for COGS (43.6%) and for operating expenses (25.9%), all you need to do is add them:

$$43.6 + 25.9 = 69.5$$

Then you convert that number from a percentage to a decimal:

$$69.5\% = 0.695$$

Finally, you round 0.695 to 0.7.

Now try to find the operating ratio for The Strand Bookstore (refer to Table 12-5):

$$\text{Operating ratio} = \frac{\text{Cost of goods sold} + \text{Operating expenses}}{\text{Net sales}}$$

$$= \frac{\$775,300 + \$720,200}{\$1,406,400} = \frac{\$1,495,500}{\$1,406,400} = 1.06 = 1.1$$

or

$$\text{Cost of goods sold (55.1\%)} + \text{Operating expense (51.2\%)} = 106.3\% = 1.1$$

Therefore, the operating ratio of The Strand Bookstore is 1.1. What does this mean? It means the numerator is greater than the denominator, which means that the total of the COGS and the operating expense is greater than net sales, which ultimately means the store is losing money, at least for this particular quarter.

12.1.6 Gross Profit Margin Ratio

Another quick measure business owners use is **gross profit margin ratio,** which highlights how much of a profit the business is making on the goods it is buying and selling, regardless of its operating expenses. The ratio is between −1 and +1:

▲ A negative gross profit margin ratio means the company has spent more on goods than it has sold.

▲ A positive gross profit margin ratio close to 0 means the company is selling only a little more than it's buying.

▲ A gross profit margin ratio close to +1 means the company is selling far more than it's buying.

Note that numbers close to +1 do not always indicate smooth sailing for the company. Numbers at or near +1 may mean that the company isn't buying enough inventory to sustain the level at which it's selling. A store that's going out of business and selling its entire inventory, for example, would have a number close to +1, but that's a temporary phenomenon that can't be matched in future quarters. In the same way, a company manufacturing a product that has low material costs but high labor costs, such as hand-knitted scarves, would have a gross profit margin ratio very close to +1 but may actually be losing money because of the high cost of wages. (This third measure is discussed in Section 12.1.7.)

To find a company's gross profit margin ratio for a particular quarter or year, you use the following formula:

$$\text{Gross profit margin ratio} = \frac{\text{Net sales} - \text{Cost of goods sold}}{\text{Net sales}}$$

or

$$\text{Gross profit margin ratio} = \frac{\text{Gross profit}}{\text{Net sales}}$$

If a company has net sales of \$400,000 and a COGS of \$300,000, what is its gross profit margin ratio? You figure it out as follows:

$$\text{Gross profit margin ratio} = \frac{\text{Net sales} - \text{Cost of goods sold}}{\text{Net sales}}$$

$$= \frac{\$400,000 - \$300,000}{\$400,000} = \frac{\$100,000}{\$400,000} = \frac{1}{4} = 0.25$$

So, the gross profit margin ratio for this company during this quarter or year is 0.25.

If you've already figured a company's percentage of net sales, you can take an easy shortcut to finding the gross profit margin ratio because the percentage of net sales of the gross profit already gives you the gross profit divided by net sales. You simply take the percentage of net sales of gross profit and change it from a percentage into a decimal by dividing it by 100. For example, for Harry's Grocery, you know that the gross profit is 56.4% of net sales. Change that to a decimal, and you get a gross profit margin ratio of 0.564, which you can round to 0.57.

Can you figure the gross profit margin ratio for The Strand Bookstore? The percentage of net sales of The Strand's gross profit is 44.9%. Change that to a decimal, and you have 0.449, which you can round to 0.45.

12.1.7 Profit Margin on Net Sales

The last of the three quick measures business owners use is the **profit margin on net sales** (or return on sales), which compares net income to net sales. Because net income takes into account all of a company's costs of doing business (returns, COGS, salaries, advertising, rent, and the like), this measure quickly shows how much profit a company is making.

A company's profit margin on net sales is always between −1 and +1:

▲ If the costs of buying, making, and/or selling products is more than the amount sold, the profit margin on net sales is negative.

▲ If costs are very close to sales, the profit margin on net sales is close to 0.

▲ If the company is controlling its costs while also selling a lot of products, the profit margin on net sales is close to 1.

To find a company's profit margin on net sales, you use the following formula:

$$\text{Profit margin on net sales} = \frac{\text{Net income}}{\text{Net sales}}$$

If a company has net sales of $400,000 and a net income of $62,000, what is its profit margin on net sales? You figure it out like this:

$$\text{Profit margin on net sales} = \frac{\text{Net income}}{\text{Net sales}}$$

$$= \frac{\$62,000}{\$400,000} = 0.155 = 0.12$$

The profit margin on net sales for this company during this quarter or year is 0.12, which is pretty close to 0. The company is not losing money, but it is also not making much of a profit.

As with gross profit margin ratio, if you've already figured a company's percentage of net sales, you have an easy shortcut to finding the profit margin on net sales because the percentage of net income to net sales is already figured for you. You simply change the percentage of net sales of net income from a percentage to a decimal by dividing it by 100. For example, for Harry's Grocery, you know that the net income is 30.5% of net sales. Change that to a decimal, and you get a gross profit margin ratio of 0.305, which you can round to 0.31.

Can you figure the profit margin on net sales for The Strand Bookstore? The percentage of net sales of The Strand's gross profit is −6.3%. Change that to a decimal, and you have −0.063, which you can round to −0.06. As you already knew, The Strand is losing money this quarter, but because that number is still very close to 0, you now know the bookstore is close to breaking even this quarter. (With the advent of Amazon, Barnes & Noble, and Borders, independent bookstores are having a tough time making a profit, so most just try to cover their expenses and hope to stay in business.)

12.1.8 Comparative Income Statements

When a business owner asks him- or herself, "How am I doing?" what does he or she mean? How is he or she doing in comparison to what? Generally, the business owner has an answer, such as compared to last year, compared to last quarter, compared to companies that sell or make similar products, compared to companies that are of similar size, or compared to companies that are in the same neighborhood. To answer these questions, business owners use a **comparative income statement,** which, just as it sounds, compares two income statements and calculates the differences.

Let's return to the Harry's Grocery example. Table 12-6 shows the store's income statements for the third quarters of 2006 and 2007. You want to know whether the store is doing better or worse in 2007 than it was in 2006. See whether you can fill in the two right-hand columns of Table 12-6; double-check your work against the values shown in Table 12-7. In general, would you say that Harry's Grocery did better or worse in the third quarter of 2007 than it did in the third quarter of 2006?

Clearly, Harry's Grocery did much better in 2007 than it did in 2006. In fact, virtually everything went up. And even though returns, purchases, salaries, advertising, and depreciation went up (which is not always a good thing), sales

Table 12-6: Harry's Grocery Comparative Income Statement, July 1 to September 30, 2006, and 2007

	2006	2007	Increase Amount	Percentage
Revenue:				
Gross sales	$1,231,600	$1,387,200	_____	_____%
Returns and allowances	24,200	32,400	_____	_____
Net sales	1,207,400	1,354,800	_____	_____
Cost of Goods Sold:				
Beginning inventory, 7/1	174,700	196,100	_____	_____
Ending inventory, 9/30	186,500	199,200	_____	_____
Purchases	538,100	601,700	_____	_____
Cost of goods sold	526,300	598,600	_____	_____
Gross profit	681,100	756,200	_____	_____
Operating Expenses:				
Salaries	185,200	214,600	_____	_____
Advertising	63,800	88,500	_____	_____
Rent	36,000	36,000	_____	_____
Utilities	15,200	16,800	_____	_____
Depreciation	12,900	12,900	_____	_____
Operating expenses	313,100	368,800	_____	_____
Net income	**368,000**	**387,400**	_____	_____

Table 12-7: Harry's Grocery Comparative Income Statement, July 1 to September 30, 2006, and 2007 (Answers)

	2006	2007	Increase Amount	Percentage
Revenue:				
Gross sales	$1,231,600	$1,387,200	155,600	12.6%
Returns and allowances	24,200	32,400	8,200	33.9
Net sales	1,207,400	1,354,800	147,400	12.2
Cost of Goods Sold:				
Beginning inventory, 7/1	174,700	196,100	21,400	12.2
Ending inventory, 9/30	186,500	199,200	12,700	6.8
Purchases	538,100	601,700	63,600	11.8
Cost of goods sold	526,300	598,600	72,300	13.7
Gross profit	**681,100**	**756,200**	**75,100**	**11.0**
Operating Expenses:				
Salaries	185,200	214,600	29,400	15.9
Advertising	63,800	88,500	24,700	38.7
Rent	36,000	36,000	0	0.0
Utilities	15,200	16,800	1,600	10.5
Depreciation	12,900	12,900	0	0.0
Operating expenses	313,100	368,800	55,700	17.8
Net income	**368,000**	**387,400**	**19,400**	**5.3**

increased enough to offset these higher costs. Note that some of the higher costs—such as salaries and purchases—are anticipated along with increased sales.

Because The Strand Bookstore is struggling to make a profit, the owner wants to do a comparative analysis against the income statement of a bookstore with similar sales in another city. Although this information is not readily available to the general public, The Strand is a member of the Independent Booksellers Association, and through this organization, the owners were able to get an income statement for a similar store called Books, Etc. (see Table 12-8). Calculate the differences in sales, costs, and profit for the two bookstores and compare your answers to those in Table 12-9.

FOR EXAMPLE

Cooking the Books

When companies **cook the books** (that is, fudge the numbers on income statements and other financial documents), they're almost always *overreporting* income and *underreporting* expenses. (A small business operator may have a different motive, though: to lower taxes.) Essentially, companies cook the books to make themselves appear to be more profitable than they are. Why would they do this? To get more people to invest in (i.e., give money to) the company. Companies need funds from investors to build and expand their businesses; people like to invest in profitable companies because they feel confident that they'll see a return on their investments. Cooking the books encourages people to invest their money without telling them that the investment may not be such a good risk.

Energy giant Enron cooked its books in a number of ways, one of which was by classifying projected earnings as current revenue. This is the lemonade-stand equivalent of mom asking you how much you made today, and instead of telling her that you made $2, you say that you made $10 because you feel confident that you'll make $8 tomorrow, based on some tweaks you're making to the posters that market your stand. When you make only $3 tomorrow, mom thinks you have $13 in your pocket, when, in fact, you have only $5. If she wants you to pay her back for the $10 in startup costs she lent you, you could be in trouble.

Telecommunications leader WorldCom classified operating expenses as long-term capital investments. The company, in fact, hid its expenses to the point that its losses turned into profits. In lemonade-stand terminology, this is like classifying your lemons, sugar, and cups as "investments" instead of as everyday operating expenses. If you spent $3 on these items and made only $2 by selling lemonade, by classifying those expenses as investments, you can report that your income was $2, plus you have $3 in investments, resulting in a profit of $5. The problem is, that $3 wasn't invested; it was spent on supplies, so the stand actually had a loss of $1 ($2 − $3).

Electronic component manufacturer Tyco was even more creative than the other two companies. It used a technique called *spring-loading,* in which it *underreported* the earnings of a company it was about to purchase so that, a few months later, after the merger was complete, Tyco executives appeared to be business geniuses when the purchased company reported stellar profits. This is like acquiring Jimmy's lemonade stand one block over and telling everyone that Jimmy's stand was making 50 cents a day, when, in fact, it made $4 per day. A week later, when your stand is making $5 per day, you look pretty impressive because you were able to take Jimmy's "failing" stand and make a much better profit than he ever did. Tyco executives also participated in an unusual program of *loan forgiveness,* which is a fancy way of saying that executives used corporate money to pay for private expenses, called these expenses "loans," and then applied for these "loans" to be "forgiven" (i.e., paid off in full). And they never reported these "loans," forgiven or otherwise, to investors.

Table 12-8: The Strand Bookstore and Books, Etc., Comparative Income Statement, January 1, 2007, to March 31, 2007

	The Strand	Books, Etc.	Difference	Percentage
Revenue:				
Gross sales	$1,486,200	$1,477,200	_____	_____%
Returns and allowances	79,800	66,400	_____	_____
Net sales	1,406,400	1,410,800	_____	_____
Cost of Goods Sold:				
Beginning inventory, 7/1	153,600	155,100	_____	_____
Ending inventory, 9/30	160,200	159,200	_____	_____
Purchases	781,900	801,700	_____	_____
Cost of goods sold	775,300	797,600	_____	_____
Gross profit	631,100	613,200	_____	_____
Operating Expenses:				
Salaries	378,400	254,600	_____	_____
Advertising	197,800	108,500	_____	_____
Rent	84,000	90,000	_____	_____
Utilities	31,300	35,800	_____	_____
Depreciation	28,700	31,900	_____	_____
Operating expenses	720,200	520,800	_____	_____
Net income	(89,000)	92,400	_____	_____

Table 12-9: The Strand Bookstore and Books, Etc., Comparative Income Statement, January 1, 2007, to March 31, 2007 (Answers)

	The Strand	Books, Etc.	Difference	Percentage
Revenue:				
Gross sales	$1,486,200	$1,477,200	(9,000)	−0.61%
Returns and allowances	79,800	66,400	(13,400)	−20.18
Net sales	1,406,400	1,410,800	4,400	0.31
Cost of Goods Sold:				
Beginning inventory, 7/1	153,600	155,100	1,500	0.98
Ending inventory, 9/30	160,200	159,200	(1,000)	−0.63
Purchases	781,900	801,700	19,800	2.53

Table 12-9: *Continued*

	The Strand	Books, Etc.	Difference	Percentage
Cost of goods sold	775,300	797,600	22,300	26.35
Gross profit	**631,100**	**613,200**	**(18,900)**	**−2.92**
Operating Expenses:				
Salaries	378,400	254,600	(123,800)	−48.63
Advertising	197,800	108,500	(89,300)	−82.30
Rent	84,000	90,000	6,000	7.14
Utilities	31,300	35,800	4,500	14.28
Depreciation	28,700	31,900	3,200	11.15
Operating expenses	720,200	520,800	(199,400)	−38.29
Net income	**(89,000)**	**92,400**	**181,400**	**196.32**

SELF-CHECK

- Describe the main components of an income statement.
- Construct a basic income statement.
- Find the percentage of net sales for each item on an income statement.
- Determine a company's profitability by using the operating ratio.
- Establish the profit on goods sold by finding the gross profit margin ratio.
- Compare net income to net sales by using the profit margin on net sales.
- Compare two income statements for evaluation between periods or companies.

12.2 The Balance Sheet

A **balance sheet** is a financial statement that illustrates how much a business is worth as of a certain date. It has three basic components:

▲ **Assets: Assets** include what the company owns and what it is owed by others. Typical assets include cash, **accounts receivable** (accounts [customers] that have been billed and are due to a company), merchandise inventory, buildings, and equipment.

▲ **Liabilities: Liabilities** are everything the company owes. Typical liabilities include taxes owed, accounts payable (items purchased but not yet paid for), and notes (or loans) payable.

▲ **Owner's equity: Owner's equity** tells how much a business is actually worth. It is simply

$$\text{Assets} - \text{Liabilities}$$

12.2.1 How a Balance Sheet Is Set Up

A balance sheet is set up according to the following formula:

$$\text{Assets} - \text{Liabilities} = \text{Owner's equity}$$

A useful way to turn this formula around is to say that Assets = Liabilities + Owner's equity. Remember: It's called a balance sheet because the two sides are balanced (assets on one side; liabilities and owner's equity on the other).

Assets are divided into three categories:

▲ **Current assets: Current assets** are cash and other assets anticipated to be converted to cash within a year.

▲ **Fixed assets: Fixed assets** are those that will be kept and used for more than a year. (For the purposes of illustration in this chapter, we consider only buildings and equipment to be fixed assets.)

▲ **Intangible assets: Intangible assets** are copyrights, patents, and other intellectual property.

Liabilities are divided into two categories:

▲ **Current liabilities: Current liabilities** are those that are due and payable within 1 year.

▲ **Long-term liabilities: Long-term liabilities** are due in more than 1 year.

After you subtract liabilities from assets, owner's equity can be either a positive number or a negative one:

▲ A positive number means the owner of the business (an individual, a partnership, or investors) has a stake, or value, in the company; that is, what the company has of value is worth more than what the company owes.

▲ A negative number means what the company has of value is worth less than what the company owes.

Table 12-10 shows an example of a balance sheet. It shows the financial condition of ABC Plumbing Supply as of September 30, 2006.

Table 12-10: ABC Plumbing Supply Balance Sheet, September 30, 2006	
Assets	
Current assets:	
Cash	$7,500
Accounts receivable	12,300
Merchandise inventory	14,600
Total current assets	34,400
Plant and equipment:	
Building	121,000
Equipment	7,200
Total plant and equipment	128,200
Total assets	162,600
Liabilities	
Current liabilities:	
Accounts payable	9,700
Notes payable	10,000
Wages payable	2,400
Total current liabilities	22,100
Total liabilities	22,100
Owner's equity	140,500
Total liabilities and owner's equity	162,600

Notice in Table 12-10 that current assets ($34,400) and plant and equipment ($128,200) add up to total assets of $162,600. There are no long-term liabilities, so current liabilities ($22,100) are identical to total liabilities ($22,100). Finally, total liabilities ($22,100) and owner's equity ($140,500) add up to total assets ($162,600).

12.2.2 Percentage of Total Assets

In this section, we look at each asset, liability, and component of owner's equity as a percentage of total assets. Table 12-11 shows an example of a balance sheet with a percentage distribution of all the items on the balance sheet. (If you don't recall how to calculate percentage distributions, turn to Chapter 3.)

Table 12-11: ABC Plumbing Supply Balance Sheet, September 30, 2006

Assets

Current Assets:

Cash	$7,500	4.6%
Accounts receivable	12,300	7.6
Merchandise inventory	14,600	9.0
Total current assets	34,400	21.2

Plant and Equipment:

Building	121,000	74.4
Equipment	7,200	4.4
Total plant and equipment	128,200	78.8
Total assets	162,600	100.0

Liabilities

Current Liabilities:

Accounts payable	9,700	6.0
Notes payable	10,000	6.2
Wages payable	2,400	1.5
Total current liabilities	22,100	13.6
Total liabilities	22,100	13.6
Owner's equity	140,500	86.4
Total liabilities and owner's equity	162,600	100.0

Note: In Table 12-11, 21.2% is the total current assets ($34,400) as a percentage of the total assets ($162,600).

Now it's your turn. Table 12-12 gives you a chance to work out the percentage distribution for a balance sheet. Check your answers against those shown in Table 12-13.

12.2.3 The Current Ratio

When you're running a business, there are always bills that need to be paid. And to pay those bills, you need cash. Your current liabilities are everything you owe

Table 12-12: UltraNet Web Design Balance Sheet, March 31, 2007

Assets

Current Assets:

Cash	$4,000	_____%
Accounts receivable	17,500	_____
Merchandise inventory	26,400	_____
Total current assets	47,900	_____

Plant and Equipment:

Building	195,000	_____
Equipment	24,900	_____
Total plant and equipment	219,900	_____
Total assets	267,800	_____

Liabilities

Current Liabilities:

Accounts payable	17,000	_____
Notes payable	4,000	_____
Wages payable	2,600	_____
Total current liabilities	23,600	_____
Total liabilities	23,600	_____
Owner's equity	244,200	_____
Total liabilities and owner's equity	267,800	_____

that must be paid off within 1 year. And your current assets are the sum of your cash and anything else you own—or are owed—that can be turned into cash within 1 year.

The **current ratio** is the ratio of your current assets to your current liabilities:

$$\text{Current ratio} = \frac{\text{Current assets}}{\text{Current liabilities}}$$

The larger the current ratio, the better the financial condition of the company. A ratio of at least 2:1 (that is, a result of 2.0 or higher from the current ratio equation) is considered desirable.

Table 12-13: UltraNet Web Design Balance Sheet, March 31, 2007 (Answers)

Assets

Current Assets:

Cash	$4,000	1.5%
Accounts receivable	17,500	6.5
Merchandise inventory	26,400	9.9
Total current assets	47,900	17.9

Plant and Equipment:

Building	195,000	72.8
Equipment	24,900	9.3
Total plant and equipment	219,900	82.1
Total assets	267,800	100.0

Liabilities

Current Liabilities:

Accounts payable	17,000	6.3
Notes payable	4,000	1.5
Wages payable	2,600	1.0
Total current liabilities	23,600	8.8
Total liabilities	23,600	8.8
Owner's equity	244,200	91.1
Total liabilities and owner's equity	267,800	100.0

For practice, look back at Table 12-11 and figure out the current ratio for ABC Plumbing Supply:

$$\text{Current ratio} = \frac{\text{Current assets}}{\text{Current liabilities}} = \frac{\$34,400}{22,100} = 1.6$$

Also find the current ratio for UltraNet Web Design (refer to Table 12-13). Note that UltraNet is in better financial shape than ABC:

$$\text{Current ratio} = \frac{\text{Current assets}}{\text{Current liabilities}} = \frac{\$47,900}{23,600} = 2.0$$

12.2.4 The Acid Test Ratio

The formula for the **acid test ratio** is similar to that for the current ratio, but liquid assets are substituted for current assets. Liquid assets are cash and anything that can be converted into cash. For most businesses, that would be **accounts receivable.** The formula for the acid ratio test is as follows:

$$\text{Acid test ratio} = \frac{\text{Liquid assets}}{\text{Current liabilities}}$$

An acid ratio test of at least 1:1 (that is, a result of 1.0 or greater from the acid test ratio equation) is considered desirable.

How much would the acid ratio test be for a firm that had $20,000 in cash, $25,000 in accounts receivable, and $40,000 in current liabilities? You figure it out like this:

$$\text{Acid test ratio} = \frac{\text{Liquid assets}}{\text{Current liabilities}} = \frac{\$45,000}{40,000} = \frac{11}{8} = 1.375 = 1.4$$

This company has a desirable acid ratio test.

Here's one more example to try: Find the acid test ratio of a firm that has $55,000 in current liabilities, $12,000 in cash, and $17,000 in accounts receivable. Figure it out like this:

$$\text{Acid test ratio} = \frac{\text{Liquid assets}}{\text{Current liabilities}} = \frac{\$29,000}{55,000} = 0.5$$

This company does not have a desirable acid ratio test.

12.2.5 Comparative Balance Sheets

As with income statements, you can do a comparative analysis of two balance sheets—comparing different quarters or years of the same company or comparing two different companies against one another. Because a balance sheet gives you a snapshot of a company's financial condition at a certain point in time, by doing a comparative analysis of two balance sheets, you can see how a company's financial condition has changed over time.

Table 12-14 is a comparative analysis of two balance sheets for Oceanside Spa. Four columns of figures are shown: The two left-hand columns show the company's balance sheets for 2006 and 2007. The next column to the right shows the amount of increase or decrease in each item between these years. The final column shows the percentage increase.

First, look at cash in Table 12-14. Cash increased from $7,500 in 2006 to $9,000 in 2007, so the amount of increase is $1,500. Accounts receivable fell from $19,100 in 2006 to $18,200 in 2007, so the decrease was $900. Was the

Table 12-14: Oceanside Spa Comparative Balance Sheet, July 1, 2006, and 2007

	2007	2006	Increase Amount	Percentage
Assets				
Current Assets:				
Cash	$9,000	$7,500	$1,500	20.0%
Accounts receivable	18,200	19,100	(900)	−4.7
Merchandise inventory	26,900	22,800	4,100	18.0
Total current assets	54,100	49,400	4,700	9.5
Plant and Equipment:				
Building	77,000	79,000	(2,000)	−2.5
Equipment	12,500	14,000	(1,500)	−10.7
Total plant and equipment	89,500	93,000	(3,500)	−3.8
Total assets	143,600	142,400	1,200	−0.8
Liabilities				
Current Liabilities:				
Accounts payable	16,400	18,700	(2,300)	−12.3
Notes payable	10,000	7,500	2,500	33.3
Wages payable	3,200	4,800	(1,600)	−33.3
Total current liabilities	29,600	31,000	(1,400)	−4.5
Total liabilities	29,600	31,000	(1,400)	−4.5
Owner's equity				
Total liabilities and owner's equity	114,000	111,400	2,600	2.3

financial condition of Oceanside Spa better in 2007 than in 2006? To find out, you calculate the current ratios and acid test ratios:

$$2006 : \text{Current ratio} = \frac{\text{Current assets}}{\text{Current liabilities}} = \frac{\$49,400}{31,000} = 1.6$$

$$2007 : \text{Current ratio} = \frac{\text{Current assets}}{\text{Current liabilities}} = \frac{\$54,100}{29,600} = 1.8$$

$$2006 : \text{Acid test ratio} = \frac{\text{Liquid assets}}{\text{Current liabilities}} = \frac{\$26,000}{31,000} = 0.8$$

$$2007 : \text{Acid test ratio} = \frac{\text{Liquid assets}}{\text{Current liabilities}} = \frac{\$27,200}{29,600} = 0.9$$

Based on this information, what can you say about the financial condition of Oceanside Spa in 2006 and 2007? According to the current ratio, there was some improvement between 2006 and 2007 because the current ratio went from 1.6 to 1.8. But a ratio of less than 2 is still not good. Similarly, the acid test ratio rose from 0.8 in 2006 to 0.9 in 2007. Given that an acid ratio test of 1 or higher is desirable, in 2007, Oceanside Spa still just missed the mark.

Now do your own comparative balance sheets by completing Table 12-15. Check your answers against in Table 12-16 and then we'll do a little analysis of how this company is doing.

Table 12-15: Sasha's Pet Supplies Comparative Balance Sheet, December 31, 2006, and 2007

	2007	2006	Increase Amount	Percentage
Assets				
Current Assets:				
Cash	$46,400	$41,800	_____	_____%
Accounts receivable	73,600	70,200	_____	_____
Merchandise inventory	29,100	32,700	_____	_____
Total current assets	149,100	144,700	_____	_____
Plant and Equipment:				
Building	36,500	37,000	_____	_____
Equipment	4,200	4,500	_____	_____
Total plant and equipment	40,700	41,500	_____	_____
Total assets	189,800	186,200	_____	_____
Liabilities				
Current Liabilities:				
Accounts payable	15,100	16,800	_____	_____
Notes payable	5,000	7,000	_____	_____
Wages payable	2,200	1,400	_____	_____
Total current liabilities	22,300	25,200	_____	_____
Total liabilities	22,300	25,200	_____	_____
Owner's Equity				
Total liabilities and owner's equity	167,500	161,000	_____	_____

Table 12-16: Sasha's Pet Supplies Comparative Balance Sheet, December 31, 2006, and 2007 (Answers)

	2006	2007	Increase Amount	Percentage
Assets				
Current Assets:				
Cash	$46,400	$41,800	$4,600	11.0%
Accounts receivable	73,600	70,200	3,400	4.8
Merchandise inventory	29,100	32,700	(3,600)	(11.0)
Total current assets	149,100	144,700	4,400	3.0
Plant and Equipment:				
Building	36,500	37,000	(500)	(1.4)
Equipment	4,200	4,500	(300)	(6.7)
Total plant and equipment	40,700	41,500	(800)	(1.9)
Total assets	189,800	186,200	3,600	1.9
Liabilities				
Current Liabilities:				
Accounts payable	15,100	16,800	(1,700)	(10.1)
Notes payable	5,000	7,000	(2,000)	(28.6)
Wages payable	2,200	1,400	800	57.1
Total current liabilities	22,300	25,200	(2,900)	(11.5)
Total liabilities	22,300	25,200	(2,900)	(11.5)
Owner's Equity				
Total liabilities and owner's equity	167,500	161,000	6,500	4.0

So how is Sasha's Pet Supplies doing? To find out, you calculate the current ratios and the acid test ratios:

$$2006 : \text{Current ratio} = \frac{\text{Current assets}}{\text{Current liabilities}} = \frac{\$144,700}{25,200} = 5.7$$

$$2007 : \text{Current ratio} = \frac{\text{Current assets}}{\text{Current liabilities}} = \frac{\$149,100}{22,300} = 6.7$$

$$2006 : \text{Acid test ratio} = \frac{\text{Liquid assets}}{\text{Current liabilities}} = \frac{\$112,000}{25,200} = 4.4$$

$$2007 : \text{Acid test ratio} = \frac{\text{Liquid assets}}{\text{Current liabilities}} = \frac{\$120,000}{22,300} = 5.4$$

FOR EXAMPLE

Footnotes Point to Balance-Sheet Truths

A balance sheet is a balance sheet is a balance sheet, right? Not so fast. By deftly employing the use of a very small footnote, a balance sheet can quickly look much better than it should. Suppose a company has a great deal of debt, but much of that debt exists for something in particular, such as closing several stores but still having to pay the leases on that land and those buildings. If you're the K-Mart Corporation in 2000 and you want to keep investors happy, you simply don't include those lease obligations under liabilities; instead, you list your other liabilities, show a healthy debt structure, and then add a footnote saying, in effect, "$943 million in additional debt falls under the category of lease obligations, and we don't think these should count as liabilities." This type of shenanigan is called an *off-balance-sheet arrangement* or *off-balance-sheet accounting*. Little wonder that K-Mart had to file for bankruptcy less than 2 years later, although the company has more recently begun to emerge from bankruptcy and pay its debts and other obligations. Check www.fasb.org for information regarding reports to owners. Also, you should check the SEC regulations at www.sec.gov/info/smallbus.html.

Was the company's financial condition desirable in both years? How desirable? Did the financial condition of the company improve or deteriorate between 2006 and 2007?

Judging from the current ratios in 2006 and 2007, the company is in excellent financial condition (the numbers are well over 2). In addition, the current ratio rose from 5.7 in 2006 to 6.7 in 2007, so an already good financial condition improved. In addition, an acid test ratio of 1 or more is desirable, so Sasha's is in very good financial shape, and it is even improving.

SELF-CHECK

- Describe the main components of a balance sheet.
- Set up a basic balance sheet.
- Find a company's percentage of total assets.
- Determine the ratio of a company's current assets to current liabilities.
- Make conclusions about a company's ability to pay bills, using the acid test ratio.
- Compare two balance sheets.

SUMMARY

Income statements and balance sheets are powerful accounting tools that help managers and investors gauge the health of a business. An income statement shows sales and expense data for a company over a specific period of time: a year, a quarter, a month, and so on. A balance sheet gives a snapshot of a company's financial picture on a given day. From these two financial documents, you can calculate percentages, margins, and ratios that tell at a glance how healthy and profitable a company is.

KEY TERMS

Accounts receivable	Accounts (customers) that have been billed and are due to a company.
Acid test ratio	The ratio of liquid assets to current liabilities. The larger the acid test ratio, the better the financial condition of the company; a ratio of 1.0 or greater is considered desirable.
Assets	What a company owns and how much it is owed by others.
Balance sheet	A financial statement that shows how much a company is worth as of a certain date.
Comparative income statement	Two income statements compared side-by-side.
Cook the books	To make illegal changes to the numbers on financial statements in order to deceive shareholders, the government, or the investing public.
Cost of goods sold (COGS)	The amount spent on procuring goods for sale.
Costs	Money spent to run a company.
Current assets	Cash or other assets that can be converted to cash within 1 year.
Current liabilities	Liabilities, or debts, that are owed to a company within 1 year.
Current ratio	The ratio of current assets to current liabilities. The larger the current ratio, the better the financial condition of the company; a ratio of at least 2:1 is considered desirable.

Depreciation	The allocation of the cost of an asset such as machinery, equipment, a computer system, a building, a truck, or a car over the revenue-producing years of that asset.
Fixed assets	Assets that a company plans to keep and use for more than a year.
Gross profit	The amount a company earned after cost of goods sold is subtracted from net sales. Also known as *total profit*.
Gross profit margin ratio	A ratio that determines how much of a profit a company is making on the goods it's buying and selling, regardless of operating expenses.
Gross sales	Total sales, including cash sales and credit sales.
Income statement	A statement that shows how much revenue is coming to a company and the cost outflows during a certain period of time. Also known as a *profit and loss (or P and L) statement*.
Intangible assets	Copyrights, patents, and other intellectual property that belong to a company.
Liabilities	Everything a company owes to others; debts.
Long-term liabilities	Liabilities, or debts, that are due in more than 1 year.
Net income	The amount a company makes as a profit after all operating expenses are subtracted from the gross profit. Also known as *profit*.
Net sales	The amount a company sells after all returns, discounts, and other allowances are deducted. Also known as *revenue*.
Operating expenses	The cost associated with running a company (salaries, rent, utilities, equipment, etc.).
Operating ratio	A ratio that can be quickly calculated to determine whether a company is making or losing money. An operating ratio of less than 1 means the company is turning a profit.
Owner's equity	How much a company is worth on a given date. Also known as *net worth*.
Profit margin on net sales	A ratio that compares net income to net sales and shows how much profit a company is making; the closer this ratio is to 1, the better. Also known as *return on sales*.
Sales	The amount of money resulting from customers buying a company's goods or services.

ASSESS YOUR UNDERSTANDING

Go to www.wiley.com/college/slavin to assess your knowledge of financial statements.

Measure your learning by comparing pre-test and post-test results.

Summary Questions

1. Cost of goods sold = Beginning inventory − Ending inventory. True or False?

2. Gross profit and total profit are the same. True or false?

3. An operating ratio of more than 1 means a company is turning a profit. True or False?

4. A gross profit margin ratio near +1 is always good news for a company. True of False?

5. Profit margin on net sales is always between −1 and +1. True or False?

6. Assets are everything a company owes to others. True or False?

7. Long-term liabilities are not due for at least 1 year. True or False?

8. The larger the current ratio, the better the financial condition of a company. True or False?

9. An acid test ratio of 0.5 is considered desirable. True or False?

Review Questions

1. Raleigh Motors had a beginning inventory of $400,000 on January 1 and an ending inventory of $420,000 on December 31. If its purchases of cars to sell were $1 million, how much was its COGS during the year?

2. The Phoenix Corporation had net sales of $2 million, its COGS was $1.6 million, and its operating expenses were $500,000. How much were its gross profit and its net income?

3. The George Washington Hotel had net sales of $4 million, gross profit of $2.1 million, and the following expenses: salaries and wages, $550,000; utilities, $230,000; advertising, $75,000; and depreciation, $45,000. How much was its net income?

4. The Sixth Street Garage had a net income of $35,000. If its operating expenses were $380,000, how much was its gross profit?

5. The Fleetwood Martini Bar had net sales of $970,000, COGS of $320,000, and operating expenses of $280,000. How much were its

   (a) operating ratio?

   (b) gross profit margin?

   (c) profit margin on net sales?

6. In 2006, the operating expenses of MP3 Players to Go was $175,000, and the gross profit was $240,000. In 2007, operating expenses rose to $200,000, and the gross profit rose to $290,000. By what percentage did net income change from 1996 to 1997?

7. ColorWorks Paint Store has these assets: cash, $15,000; accounts receivable, $20,000; merchandise inventory, $5,000; building, $45,000; equipment, $10,000. It has these liabilities: wages payable, $3,000; accounts payable, $5,000; taxes payable, $1,000; and notes payable 1 one year, $10,000. Find the following:

   (a) total assets

   (b) total liabilities

   (c) owner's equity

   (d) cash as a percentage of total assets

   (e) accounts payable as a percentage of total assets

8. Ace Taxi has these assets: cash, $13,300; accounts receivable, $4,500; building, $32,000; and equipment, $78,200. It has these liabilities: wages payable, $500; accounts payable, $2,400; and notes payable, $3,000.

   (a) What is the current ratio?

   (b) What is the acid test ratio?

   (c) Are the company's current ratio and acid test ratio desirable?

9. Downtown Grill & Brewery has a current ratio of 2.5. If its current assets are $50,000, how much are its current liabilities?

10. Cranford Gourmet Grocery has total liabilities of $35,000, and its owner's equity is $15,000. If its cash is 20% of its total assets, how much cash does it have?

11. Plank, Plank, and Coniff, a law firm, has owner's equity of $75,000. If its only assets are $15,000 in cash and $80,000 in accounts receivable, how much are its total liabilities as a percentage of its assets?

Applying This Chapter

1. Teresa's Pie Shoppe has the income statement shown in Table 12-17. After you calculate various ratios, what is your opinion of the financial condition of this company?

Table 12-17: Teresa's Pie Shoppe Income Statement, January 1, 2007, to December 31, 2007

Revenue:

Gross sales	$71,200
Returns and allowances	235
Net sales	_____

Cost of Goods Sold:

Beginning inventory, 1/1	210
Ending inventory, 12/31	330
Purchases	8,100
Cost of goods sold	_____
Gross profit	_____

Operating Expenses:

Salaries	24,200
Advertising	400
Rent	12,000
Utilities	2,800
Depreciation	1,900
Operating expenses	_____
Net income	_____

2. At the end of 2007, Teresa's Pie Shop has the balance sheet shown in Table 12-18. After you calculate various ratios, what is your opinion of the financial condition of this company?

3. The following accounts are for the Cummings Import Company, dated last October:

Accounts receivable	$57,500
Accounts payable	$23,000
Notes receivable	$31,000
Long-term mortgage payable	$250,000
Merchandise inventory	$34,000
Sales tax payable	$8,900
Cash in bank	$51,900

Table 12-18: Teresa's Pie Shoppe Balance Sheet, December 31, 2007

Assets

Current Assets:

Cash	$8,500
Accounts receivable	300
Merchandise inventory	330
Total current assets	

Plant and Equipment:

Building	0
Equipment	18,200
Total plant and equipment	
Total assets	

Liabilities

Current Liabilities:

Accounts payable	2,150
Notes payable	0
Wages payable	615
Total current liabilities	
Total liabilities	

Owner's equity

Total liabilities and owner's equity	

Cash on hand	$4,100

(a) What is the company's acid test ratio?

(b) What is the company's current ratio?

4. Use the financial statement information here and calculate the profit margin on net sales:

Cash	$45,000
Net sales	$678,900
Net income	$56,000
Accounts payable	$5,600
Total assets	$450,090
Total liabilities	$569,310

Teresa's Pie Shoppe—Income Statement

Teresa's Pie Shoppe has the comparative income statement shown in Table 12-19. First, flesh out the income statement. Then calculate the differences between the 2 years as well as the percentage differences.

Table 12-19: Teresa's Pie Shoppe Comparative Income Statement, January 1, 2006, to January 31, 2006, and January 1, 2007, to December 31, 2007

	2006	2007	Difference	Percentage
Revenue:				
Gross sales	$64,700	$71,200	_____	_____%
Returns and allowances	175	235	_____	_____
Net sales	_____	_____	_____	_____
Cost of Goods Sold:				
Beginning inventory, 1/1	542	210	_____	_____
Ending inventory, 12/31	210	330	_____	_____
Purchases	5,400	8,100	_____	_____
Cost of goods sold	_____	_____	_____	_____
Gross profit	_____	_____	_____	_____
Operating expenses:				
Salaries	22,700	24,200	_____	_____
Advertising	540	400	_____	_____
Rent	12,000	12,000	_____	_____
Utilities	2,540	2,800	_____	_____
Depreciation	1,800	1,900	_____	_____
Operating expenses	_____	_____	_____	_____
Net income	_____	_____	_____	_____

Teresa's Pie Shoppe—Balance Sheet

Teresa's Pie Shoppe has the comparative balance sheet shown in Table 12-20. Flesh out the balance sheet and then calculate the increase amount between the 2 years and the percentage differences.

Table 12-20: Teresa's Pie Shoppe Comparative Balance Sheet, December 31, 2006, and 2007

	2006	2007	Increase Amount	Percentage
Assets				
Current Assets:				
Cash	$8,250	$8,500	_____	_____ %
Accounts receivable	157	300	_____	_____
Merchandise inventory	210	330	_____	_____
Total current assets	_____	_____	_____	_____
Plant and Equipment:				
Building	0	0	_____	_____
Equipment	16,500	18,200	_____	_____
Total plant and equipment	_____	_____	_____	_____
Total assets	_____	_____	_____	_____
Liabilities				
Current liabilities:				
Accounts payable	2,080	2,150	_____	_____
Notes payable	0	0	_____	_____
Wages payable	600	615	_____	_____
Total current liabilities	_____	_____	_____	_____
Total liabilities	_____	_____	_____	_____
Owner's equity				
Total liabilities and owner's equity	_____	_____	_____	_____

Gladstone Cement Company

The following data is from the Gladstone Cement Company, located in southern Alabama:

Cash	$45,000
Accounts receivable	$76,000
Stone inventory	$78,000
Accounts payable	$43,000
Long-term loan payable	$100,000

1. What is the company's acid test ratio?
2. What is the company's current ratio?

Profit Margin on Net Sales

Using the following financial statement information from the Heinz Foodservice Company, calculate the profit margin on net sales:

Total Assets	$789,900,955
Net Income	$45,070,500
Net Sales	$136,008,900
Total liabilities	$567,000

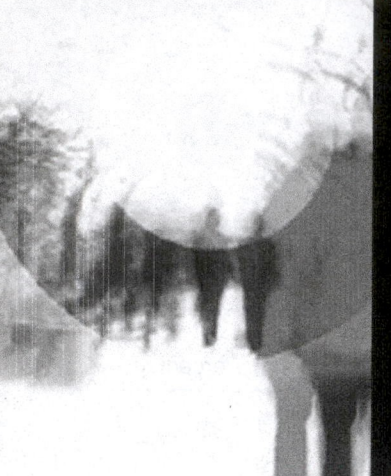

13

BUSINESS STATISTICS
Calculating the Mean, Median, Mode, and Range

Starting Point

Go to www.wiley.com/college/slavin to assess your knowledge of the basics of business statistics.
Determine where you need to concentrate your effort.

What You'll Learn in This Chapter

▲ How to tabulate data in a frequency distribution
▲ How to select the most appropriate chart or graph to display your data
▲ How to describe the mean, median, mode, and range of data

After Studying This Chapter, You'll Be Able To

▲ Illustrate the results of a survey by grouping data into a frequency distribution
▲ Construct a bar graph, line graph, or pie chart
▲ Calculate the mean and weighted average from a distribution
▲ Determine the median, mode, and range of a given data set

Goals and Outcomes

▲ Master the terminology and recognize the tools of business statistics
▲ Survey people, chart the results, and graph the data in a meaningful way
▲ Evaluate which statistical measure sums data most accurately
▲ Apply chapter ideas and techniques to problems related to the material
▲ Evaluate decision strategies used in the real world

INTRODUCTION

Before data can be graphed, it has to put it into a manageable format, and using a frequency distribution is the way to do that. You can then make raw data visually appealing by creating a bar graph, line graph, or pie chart. Finally, you can calculate the mean (average), median (middle number), mode (most frequently appearing number), and range (highest to lowest number) of your data.

13.1 Frequency Distribution

Have you ever gotten a call from someone doing market research? Or received a questionnaire in the mail? The market researcher might want to know what toothpaste you use, which breakfast cereals you have tried during the past year, or which TV programs you watch. Market research firms and their corporate clients are constantly gathering data that provides them with a pretty accurate picture of our likes and dislikes and our consumption patterns. These data are tabulated and analyzed to help companies advertise and market their goods and services.

One of the most powerful statistical tools is a **frequency distribution**, which organizes raw data into a more manageable format. For example, say that Joshua, Jessica, and Jasmine decided to do a survey of their office to determine what drinks to serve at the next meeting. The following are the responses to the question in their survey (What's your favorite cold beverage?):

Soda, iced tea, lemonade, water, iced tea, soda, lemonade, orange juice, soda, iced tea, water, soda, iced tea, grape juice, lemonade, soda, water, lemonade, limeade, water, lemonade, iced tea, soda, grape juice, soda, iced tea, lemonade, water, lemonade, soda, soda, lemonade, water, lemonade

Table 13-1 shows this data organized into a frequency distribution.

Table 13-1: Favorite Cold Beverage Frequency Distribution

Beverage	Tally	Frequency
Soda	11111 1111	9
Lemonade	11111 1111	9
Iced tea	11111 1	6
Water	11111 1	6
Grape juice	11	2
Orange juice	1	1
Limeade	1	1

FOR EXAMPLE

A Real-Life "Jam" Session

Besides tabulating surveys, how can businesses use frequency distributions? One of the most effective uses of a frequency distribution is in quality control. Here's an example: Suppose Smucker's needs to fill jars with 8 ounces of raspberry jam. If it fills less than 8 ounces, it's cheating the customer because the label specifies 8 ounces of jam. But if it fills more than 8 ounces, it's giving jam away for free. By taking samples of the weight measurements of filled jars, Smucker's can determine whether it's underfilling, overfilling, or right on target. It doesn't need to weigh every jar; it just needs to remove a sample out of every case—or every 100 cases—weigh it, and record that weight. At the end of the shift or day, that information can then be tabulated in a frequency distribution (by hand or by using statistical software that sums up the information automatically) and communicated back to the line supervisor and jar fillers on the line.

This information helps the three coworkers decide which beverages to serve. Certainly, soda would be a good choice, although Joshua, Jessica, and Jasmine would need to conduct another survey to determine which types of soda their coworkers like best. Bottled water would also likely be a good choice because it would sell moderately well and keep for the next day.

SELF-CHECK

- Explain the purpose of a frequency distribution.
- Organize raw data into a frequency distribution.
- Explain how a frequency distribution can help a company make better business decisions.

13.2 Basic Graphing Techniques

When you have data organized into frequency distributions, you can organize those data into graphs and charts. The whole idea behind graphs and charts is to take raw data, combine them in a meaningful way, and then draw a picture of this information. The following sections describe how to compile data into bar graphs, line graphs, and pie charts.

13.2.1 Bar Graphs

You've often seen bar graphs in newspapers and newsmagazines and on the Internet. **Bar graphs** are used to present data so that the observer can get the picture in just a couple of seconds. As an example, the results of Joshua's, Jessica's, and Jasmine's survey in the preceding section have been placed into a bar graph in Figure 13-1.

This happens to be a *vertical bar graph,* which means the bars run up and down (vertically). The same data could also be used to draw a *horizontal bar graph,* a graph in which the bars run side-to-side (horizontally), as shown in Figure 13-2.

13.2.2 Line Graphs

Line graphs, graphs in which points are plotted and then connected by lines, tend to show trends better than bar graphs do. Generally, if you have more than 8 or 10 results, using a line graph is the most appropriate way to display the data. Table 13-2 lists the quarterly sales figures, in millions of dollars, of the Inland Empire Bancorp, a financial company started by three college roommates

Figure 13-1

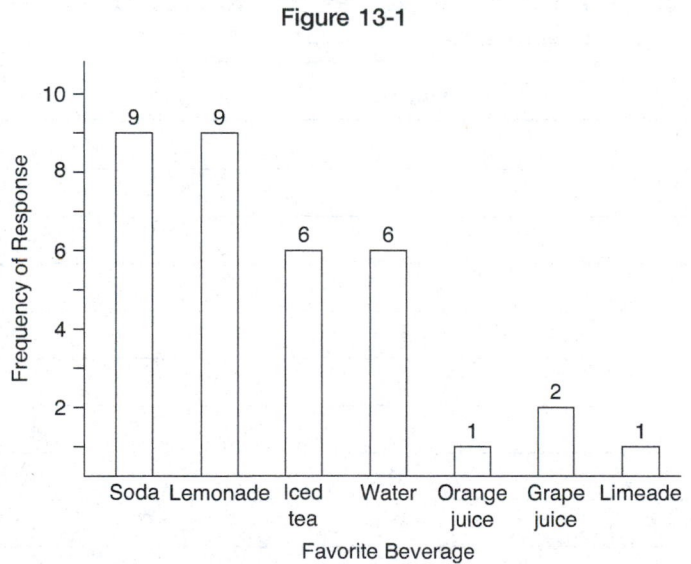

A vertical bar graph of favorite beverages.

Figure 13-2

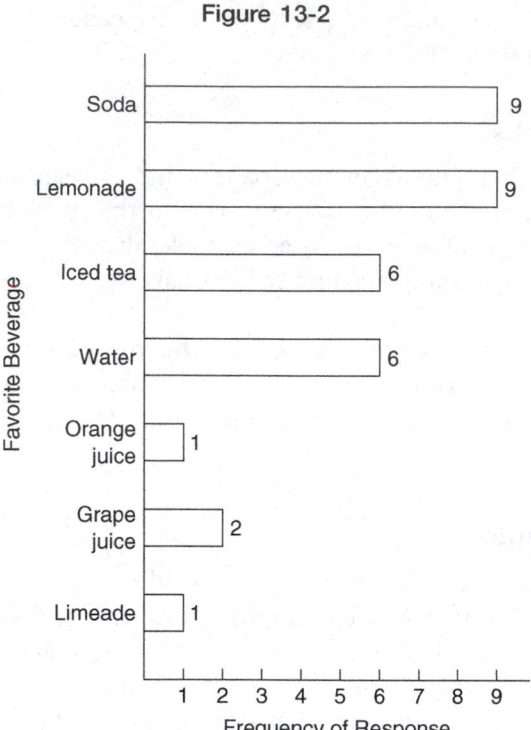

A horizontal bar graph of favorite beverages.

Table 13-2: Quarterly Sales Figures (in Millions of Dollars) for Inland Empire Bancorp

Year	Quarter	Sales
2002	I	106
2002	II	113
2002	III	118
2002	IV	121
2003	I	123
2003	II	138
2003	III	145
2003	IV	151
2004	I	163
2004	II	174
2004	III	180

Table 13-2: *Continued*

Year	Quarter	Sales
2004	IV	196
2005	I	201
2005	II	216
2005	III	234
2005	IV	256
2006	I	289
2006	II	302
2006	III	316
2006	IV	331

who built the company from scratch. Figure 13-3 shows a line graph for the company's annual corporate sales. (Note: *Annual sales* is simply the total of quarterly sales for the four quarters each year.)

13.2.3 Pie Charts

Pie charts, also called circle graphs, are circular charts used to compare parts of a total to the total. The circle represents the total amount of data, and the

Figure 13-3

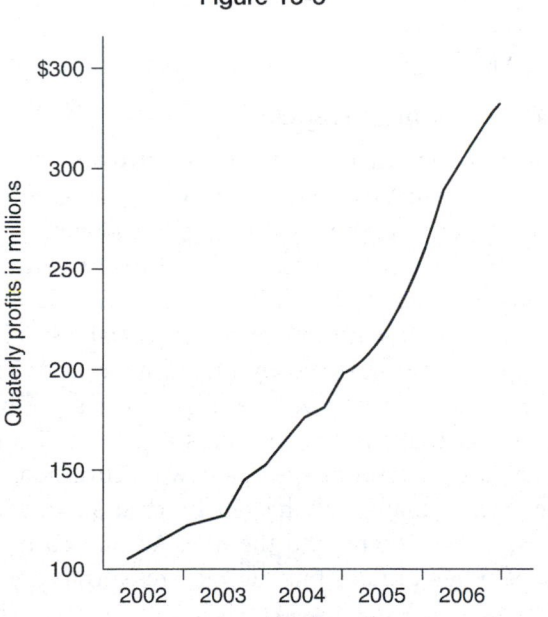

Inland Empire Bancorp's Annual Corporate Sales.

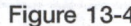

Figure 13-4

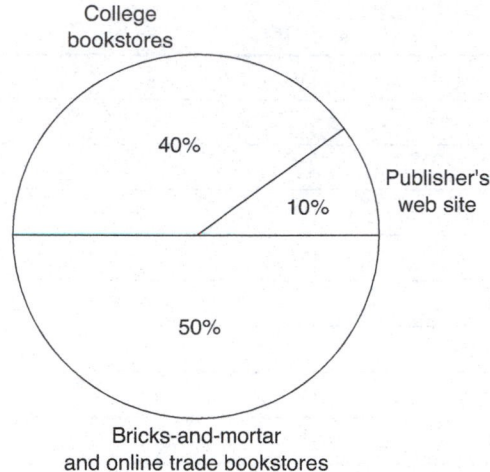

Pie chart illustrating publisher sales.

sectors, or slices, represent the parts. Suppose, for example, that a publisher sells 10% of its books through its website, 40% through college bookstores, and 50% through brick-and-mortar and Internet-based trade bookstores. If you were to draw a pie chart using these data, the circle would represent 100% of the publisher's sales, and three sectors would need to be drawn to represent 10%, 40%, and 50% of the circle, as shown in Figure 13-4.

FOR EXAMPLE

Where to Find Charts and Graphs

A *business plan* is a tool that helps banks, investors, and others decide whether a new (or expanded) business seems like a good place to loan or invest their money. Entrepreneurs thinking of starting a business spend countless hours writing up business plans, stressing over each word. But time-pressed banking executives and investors tend to look only at the pictures, so charts and graphs are critical to any business plan. Graphs in a business plan might show projected profits over the next 5 years and/or the projected cash flow for the first year, and pie charts might show the percentage of the market that the new business intends to capture and/or how expenses can be categorized. In the same way, corporate reports (usually issued quarterly and annually) rely heavily on charts and graphs to illustrate profits, expenses, market share, and the like. Annual corporate reports may total hundreds of pages of text, but the pictures attract the most attention.

SELF-CHECK

- Identify the three main types of graphs.
- Using raw data, select the most appropriate type of graph.
- Sketch a graph, using data from a frequency distribution or other table.

13.3 Basic Statistical Measures

When you think of statistics, do you visualize column after column of numbers, complex formulas, and graphs that could pass for abstract art? In this section, you'll find out how easily you can calculate the four main statistical measures: the mean, the median, the mode, and the range.

13.3.1 The Mean

The **mean** is an average of a series of numbers. Suppose you received scores of 90, 65, and 80 on three exams. To find your mean, you add all the numbers together to get 235 and divide by 3 (the total number of exams you took). The mean is 78.3, which means you have a C or C+ average over those three exams.

Here's another example: The Lewis family had a grand opening for their gift shop on a Wednesday and had the following sales during the first week: Wednesday, $895.32; Thursday, $808.74; Friday, $796.15; and Saturday, $743.91. How much were their mean sales for the first 4 days? If you add all 4 days' sales numbers together, you get $3,244.12. Divide by 4, and you get mean sales of $811.03.

In a **weighted average,** some numbers, when added up to find an average, are worth more than other numbers. The most common type of weighted average is a grade point average (GPA). As you know, virtually every college, when computing GPAs, calls A's 4, B's 3, C's 2, D's 1, and F's 0. (Some also use numbers in between, such as 3.5 for a B+.) If you get all C's during one semester, your GPA for that semester is 2.0. If you get all A's, your GPA is a perfect 4.0.

But in figuring your GPA, you must also consider the number of credits you receive for each course. Some courses are worth 4 credits, many are 3 credits, and some are even 2, 1, or [1/2] credit; a few courses with labs may even be 5 credits. Now suppose you got the following grades last semester:

Course	Credits	Grade
Intro to Accounting	4	D
Macroeconomics	3	C
Oral Communications	2	A
Intro to Psychology	3	B
Marketing	3	B

You want to figure out your weighted average—in this case, your GPA. To do this, you need to multiply the credits by the grade (4 for an A, and so on), add up these numbers, and then divide by the total number of credits (15). Here's how you do it:

Course	Credits	Grade	Formula
Intro to Accounting	4	D	$4 \times 1 = 4$
Macroeconomics	3	C	$3 \times 2 = 6$
Oral Communications	2	A	$2 \times 4 = 8$
Intro to Psychology	3	B	$3 \times 3 = 9$
Marketing	3	B	$3 \times 3 = 9$
Total	15		36

Now, when you divide 36 by 15, you find that your GPA for last semester was 2.4, which is a C average. That D in accounting really brought down your GPA!

13.3.2 The Median

The median of a highway is the strip that runs down the middle of the highway, dividing the traffic going one way from the traffic going the other way. If you have five children in a family, the median child is the one born third. If you line up children according to their height, the median child is the one standing smack in the middle. If you arrange a group of numbers in order of size, the median is the middle number. In other words, the **median** is the middle number.

For example, suppose you are given the following numbers and asked to find the median: 84, 37, 96, 115, 22, 9, 53. The median is *not* 115. Rather, you have to first put the list in order, either from largest to smallest or from smallest to largest, like this: 9, 22, 37, 53, 84, 96, 115. The median is the middle number: 53.

When you have an even number of terms, you find the median by doing some averaging. Suppose you have the following numbers: 14, 22, 34, 38, 59, 71.

The median is the halfway point, which is halfway between the third number (34) and the fourth number (38). If you average the two (add them and divide by 2), you get 36. So, the median is 36.

Finding the median can be very useful when the data have very large values on either end. If you take only the mean, any number that is significantly larger than the others raises the mean, perhaps making it seem higher than it is. In those cases, the median gives you a better idea of where the halfway point really is. Take, for example, the following five numbers: 2, 3, 4, 5, 27. Now suppose these represent the ages of people attending a puppet show. If you take the average, you get 8.2, which could make you believe that the average attendee is about 8 years old. But if you take the median, 4, you see that the one adult greatly skews the average age of the children in attendance.

13.3.3 The Mode

The **mode** is the most frequent value in set of numbers. For example, identify the mode in the following set: 17, 31, 14, 29, 17, 28, 15, 63. The mode is 17 because that number occurs twice, and each of the others occurs only once.

Likewise, find the mode for the following data: 4, 19, 13, 29, 19, 17, 31, 34, 13, 39, 19, 12. The mode is 19 because it occurs three times, whereas 13 occurs only twice.

In a **bimodal distribution**, which two different numbers are modes. For example, pick out the two modes here: 2, 9, 15, 2, 19, 7, 9, 6. In this bimodal distribution, 2 and 9 are both modes.

See what you can do with this distribution: 16, 8, 9, 12, 17, 13, 0, 12, 4, 5, 11, 26, 17, 10, 4, 15, 8, 23, 4, 29, 36, 17, 3, 8, 0, 33. It takes a bit of work,

FOR EXAMPLE

Mean Versus Median Income

Ever wonder why average U.S. income is reported as median income instead of mean or average income? Because of the multimillionaires and billionaires! Suppose 100 million working Americans make between $10,000 and $60,000 per year, and the average wage is $25,000. But add in 100 people who make $1 billion dollars each, and suddenly, the average shoots up to $26,000 per year. If what you really want to know is how much the average American has to live on, including the income of billionaires distorts that picture. But, by using the median income, you can take those 100 billionaires out of the picture (and also knock out 100 people living below the poverty line) and have a better picture of what the typical American makes each year.

huh? (Hint: To help you more easily find modes, put each list of numbers in order, from smallest to largest or largest to smallest.) The three modes are 4, 8, and 17; we call this a **trimodal distribution** because it has three modes. A distribution can have far more than three modes, too.

Note in some distributions there is no mode because no value occurs more than once.

Like the median, the mode isn't affected by extreme values. However, when there is no number that occurs more than once, or if every number is the same, the mode is a useless measure.

13.3.4 The Range

The range of a distribution of numbers is the difference between the highest and lowest values. For example, find the range of this array of numbers: 14, 16, 17, 23, 45, 119, 186, 209. You find the range this way: $209 - 14 = 195$. So, the range of numbers is 195.

What if the numbers aren't in order? You put them in order first. Here's an example: 19, 36, 94, 37, 53, 12, 115, 29, 16, 5, 80. When you put them in order, you find that 5 is the smallest number, and 115 is the largest, so the range is $115 - 5 = 110$. And really, you don't need to put the numbers in order to find the range, as long as you're adept at picking out the smallest and largest values.

Note that if a distribution of numbers contains negatives, they are the smallest numbers. Here's an example: 50, −5, 0, 17, 39, 116, 12, −19, 46, 2. The smallest number is −19, and the largest is 116, so the range is $116 - (-19) = 135$.

SELF-CHECK

- Define the terms **mean, median, mode,** and **range.**
- Explain how to calculate a GPA.
- Discuss the benefits and drawbacks of using mean, median, and mode.

SUMMARY

To successfully run a business, you must know how to organize your data, display it in a visually appealing way, and sum up that data with key statistical measures. The most important tool for organizing data is the frequency distribution, and the three most common tools for displaying data are bar graphs, line graphs, and pie charts. Finally, the four most basic statistical measures—mean, median, mode, and range—help you begin to draw conclusions about data.

KEY TERMS

Bar graph	A chart that uses vertical or horizontal bars to depict a frequency distribution.
Bimodal distribution	A distribution that has two modes.
Frequency distribution	A table that shows the number of times each variable occurs.
Line graph	A comparison of a variable made over time by a single line, rising and falling.
Mean	The average of two or more numbers. Also known as the average.
Median	The middle number in a list of numbers that begins with the lowest and ends with the highest.
Mode	The most frequent value in a set of numbers.
Pie chart	A circular chart with sectors or slices that are in proportion to the percentage share of each sector. Also known as a circle graph.
Range	The difference between the highest and lowest values in a list of numbers.
Trimodal distribution	A distribution that has three modes.
Weighted average	An average in which some of the numbers that will be added up to find an average are worth more than others.

ASSESS YOUR UNDERSTANDING

Go to www.wiley.com/college/slavin to evaluate your knowledge of the basics of business statistics.

Measure your learning by comparing pre-test and post-test results.

Summary Questions

1. A frequency distribution:
   (a) draws a vertical bar graph.
   (b) shows trends better than bar graphs.
   (c) organizes data into a pie chart.
   (d) organizes information into a manageable format.

2. A bar graph is most effective when displaying percentages of a whole. True or False?

3. A line graph is drawn by:
   (a) placing points on a graph and connecting the points.
   (b) putting data into horizontal rows.
   (c) putting data into vertical columns.
   (d) none of the above.

4. A pie chart is also known as a circle graph. True or False?

5. The mean is the middle number in a distribution. True or False?

6. A weighted average is:
   (a) the number that occurs most often in a distribution.
   (b) an average in which some numbers are worth more than others.
   (c) the difference between the lowest and highest numbers in a distribution.
   (d) the same as the mean.

7. Not every distribution has a mode. True or False?

8. Define **bimodal distribution.**

Review Questions

1. The Ricco Development Corporation is interested in building off-campus housing in Madison for students attending the University of Wisconsin. The corporation does a survey of students, asking them how much they would pay for a 20 × 30 studio apartment. The results of the survey are as follows:

   $450, $400, $500, $450, $500, $450, $400, $550, $500, $350, $500,
   $450, $400, $550, $600, $450, $550, $350, $450, $400, $550, $500,

$400, $450, $600, $450, $550, $500, $450, $450, $400, $550, $500, $600, $450, $550, $400, $500, $450, $450

Arrange the results using $50 intervals, from $350 to $600.

2. Forty people, selected at random, who attended an Atlanta Falcons game, were asked how far they had traveled to reach the stadium, in miles. Responses to the question resulted in the following answers:

4, 12, 9, 72, 55, 6, 21, 10, 46, 35, 7, 19, 68, 24, 11, 17, 43, 28, 14, 2, 15, 88, 7, 26, 9, 4, 1, 54, 116, 20, 5, 79, 38, 3, 1, 80, 23, 4, 2, 4

Arrange these data in a frequency distribution, using intervals of less than 10 miles, 10 to 19 miles, 20 to 29 miles, 30 to 39 miles, 40 to 49 miles, and 50 miles or more.

3. Jared and Nina Adams run a market research firm based in Springfield, Massachusetts. Their firm was hired by an entrepreneur who was interested in opening a beading shop in downtown Springfield. Respondents were asked, "If a bead shop were opened in downtown Springfield, how many times a month would you frequent the shop?" Using the following data, draw up a frequency distribution, using intervals of 0, 1, 2, 3, 4, and more than 4 times per month:

1, 0, 1, 0, 0, 4, 1, 0, 3, 6, 1, 0, 0, 4, 0, 2, 5, 0, 0, 0, 4, 2, 1, 1, 0, 8, 3, 0, 0, 3, 0, 1, 0, 0, 2, 4, 0, 0, 4, 0, 1, 1, 4, 0, 4, 0, 3, 2, 0, 0, 0, 1, 0, 0, 3, 1, 0, 10, 2, 0, 1, 1, 0, 4, 0, 6, 0, 3, 0, 4, 0, 1, 0, 0, 8, 1, 2, 0, 4, 1, 4, 0, 0, 0, 0, 5, 0, 1, 1, 4, 0, 10, 6, 0, 0, 3, 1, 4, 2, 1, 4, 0, 2, 0, 1, 1, 4, 4, 0, 2, 1, 2

4. Draw a vertical bar graph, using the data from Review Question 1.

5. Draw a horizontal bar graph, using the data from Review Question 3.

6. The *Lynchburg Historical Directory* provides tourists and native Virginians with a wealth of information about Amherst, Bedford, Campbell, and Appomattox counties. The annual number of copies of the directory sold over a 20-year period are shown in the following table:

Year	Copies Sold
1985	413
1986	422
1987	463
1988	496
1989	492
1990	503
1991	520

Year	Copies Sold
1992	526
1993	531
1994	520
1995	538
1996	541
1997	560
1998	566
1999	573
2000	582
2001	604
2002	615
2003	604
2004	622

Use this information to draw a line graph in the chart provided in Figure 13-5, showing sales from 1985 to 2004.

Figure 13-5

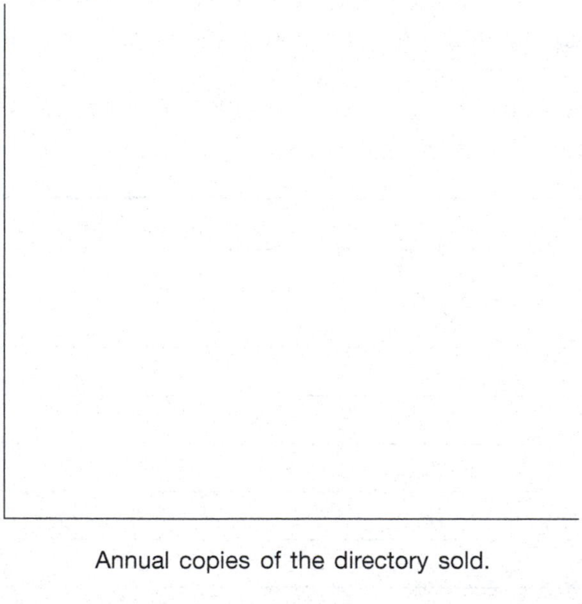

Annual copies of the directory sold.

Figure 13-6

Percentage distribution of cases handled
by the Sandy Hampton Detective Agency.

7. The Sandy Hampton Detective Agency handled 40 cases last year.
Of these cases, 12 involved missing persons, 18 involved matrimonial
disputes, 6 involved business disputes, and 4 involved murders.
Calculate the percentage distribution and then draw a pie chart to show
this percentage distribution in the space provided in Figure 13-6.

8. The Brooks Cleaning Service had a profit of $8,304.17 in the first quar-
ter, a profit of $25,850.02 in the second quarter, a loss of $5,930.75 in
the third quarter, and a profit of $12,835.18 in the fourth quarter. How
much were its average quarterly profits?

9. In Alpha Company, 8 recruits were 17 years old, 12 were 18 years old, 7
were 19 years old, 4 were 20 years old, 2 were 21 years old, and 1 was
22 years old, as shown in this table:

Age	Number of Recruits	Total Year of Age
17	8	136
18	12	216
19	7	133
20	4	80
21	2	42
22	1	22
Total	34	629

What is the weighted average of the recruits' ages?

10. For the following set of data, find the median, mode (or modes), and range: 10, 17, 0, 4, 12, 17, 9, 4, 10, 5, 0, 10, 4, 17, 20, 3, 12, 14, 6, 23, 4, 15, 9.

Applying This Chapter

1. The people attending a retirement workshop were asked to estimate their incomes to the nearest thousand dollars. The following responses were obtained:

    62, 23, 78, 18, 142, 97, 46, 25, 88, 15, 34, 75, 195, 72, 28, 45, 60, 54, 33, 90, 29, 41, 68, 80, 105, 75, 215, 42, 17, 36, 82, 65

    Using the responses given, arrange this data in a frequency distribution using the intervals less than \$20,000, \$20,000–\$39,999, \$40,000–\$59,999, \$60,000–\$79,999, \$80,000–\$99,999, \$100,000 and above.

2. Of the people who came into Susie's Boutique yesterday, 48 made no purchase, 29 spent less than \$10, 23 spent between \$10 and \$25, 14 spent more than \$25 but less than \$100, and 4 spent more than \$100.

    (a) Find the percentage distribution of customers by how much they spent.

    (b) Draw a graph or chart showing this percentage distribution.

3. Find the mean, median, mode, and range for the following set of numbers: 15, 8, 26, −4, 15, 3, 0, 23, 10, −15, 35.

Michigan State English Class

Students at Michigan State University were surveyed about their preferences for a new English class to be offered the following fall semester. The possible choices were Celtic mythology, young adult literature, fantasy and science fiction, James Joyce, and literary women. The results were as follows:

Celtic mythology, fantasy and sci fi, James Joyce, fantasy and sci fi, young adult literature, fantasy and sci fi, literary women, young adult literature, Celtic mythology, fantasy and sci fi, fantasy and sci fi, James Joyce, literary women, literary women, fantasy and sci fi, Celtic mythology, fantasy and sci fi, young adult literature, Celtic mythology, fantasy and sci fi, Celtic mythology.

1. Using the responses given, arrange these data into a frequency distribution.
2. Find the class that can be considered the mode. Place the results in an appropriate graph.
3. Determine which two new classes the English Department should offer.

GLOSSARY

1099 An IRS form that clients send to report self-employment income for the year.

Accelerated cost recovery system (ACRS) A depreciation method introduced by the IRS in 1981 that is no longer in use except with property and equipment that was placed in service prior to 1986.

Accelerated depreciation A form of depreciation that allows you to depreciate assets such as property or equipment more in the first year than in the second, more in the second than in the third, and so on.

Accounts receivable Accounts (customers) that have been billed and are due to a company.

Acid test ratio The ratio of liquid assets to current liabilities. The larger the acid test ratio, the better the financial condition of the company; a ratio of 1.0 or greater is considered desirable.

Annual percentage rate (APR) Interest rate paid on an installment loan.

Appreciate The increased value of a home that occurs as a result of inflation.

Assessed value The estimated price (value) of real estate's worth in today's market.

Assets What a company owns and how much it is owed by others.

Auto insurance Insurance for a vehicle.

Balance sheet A financial statement that shows how much a company is worth as of a certain date.

Bank service charge A fee that a financial institution charges for a service, such as covering a bounced check or printing checks.

Bar graph   A chart that uses vertical or horizontal bars to depict a frequency distribution.

Base   The beginning whole amount on which the rate operates.

Basis   The original cost of a depreciable item.

Beneficiary   The person a policyholder designates to receive the value of a life insurance policy.

Bimodal distribution   A distribution that has two modes.

Book value   The original cost of an asset (property or equipment) minus any accumulated depreciation.

Bounced check   A check for which funds are unavailable in the account.

Cap   An upper limit a policy will pay for each occurrence or over the policyholder's lifetime. For example, most vehicle insurance is subject to a $100,000/$300,000 cap.

Cash value   Money in a life insurance account that the policyholder can withdraw or borrow against.

Certificates of deposit (CDs)   A savings account that locks in money for a predetermined amount of time, usually from 30 days to 5 years.

Chain discounts   Two or more trade discounts that are applied in a series, often offered to large retail chains because they buy in volume.

Check   To substitute the solution into a problem to confirm that the correct answer has been determined.

Checkbook register   A system for keeping track of checkbook transactions that is useful in maintaining an accurate balance.

Claim   Paperwork filed if damage is done to property, vehicle, or person insured by a policy.

Classes   IRS groupings of depreciable equipment and property.

Collision   The portion of auto insurance that covers accidents that occur on the road.

Commission   Income that is based on a percentage of the goods or services sold.

Common denominator   A number divisible by both denominators in a multiplication problem.

Comparative income statement   Two income statements compared side-by-side.

Compound interest   Interest that is calculated periodically and then added to the principal.

Compound interest tables   Tables that help you calculate compound interest.

Comprehensive   The portion of auto insurance that covers off-road claims. Often referred to as "act of God" coverage.

Cook the books   To make illegal changes to the numbers on financial statements in order to deceive shareholders, the government, or the investing public.

Cost   The amount a store pays to purchase an item.

Cost of goods sold (COGS)   The amount spent on procuring goods for sale.

Costs   Money spent to run a company.

Counting number   A whole number other than zero.

Creditworthiness   Having a high credit score due to paying bills on time, not having too many loans at one time, and having a steady source of income.

Current assets   Cash or other assets that can be converted to cash within 1 year.

Current liabilities   Liabilities, or debts, that are owed to a company within 1 year.

Current ratio   The ratio of current assets to current liabilities. The larger the current ratio, the better the financial condition of the company; a ratio of at least 2:1 is considered desirable.

Debit card   A card that looks like a credit card but operates like a paper check.

Decimal point   A period located between units and tenths.

Declining principal   The steadily decreasing amount you owe on a credit card as you pay it off.

Deductible   An amount that a policyholder pays out before the insurance company begins paying for losses.

Default   To not pay one's loan obligation.

Denominator   The bottom number in a fraction.

Deposit   Money that is put into an account to increase its balance.

Depreciation   The allocation of the cost of an asset such as machinery, equipment, a computer system, a building, a truck, or a car over the revenue-producing years of that asset.

Direct deposit   A feature offered by employers that electronically deposits a person's pay into his or her account on payday.

Disability insurance   Insurance that covers employees against debilitating illnesses or accidents.

Discount note   A note in which the interest is deducted from the face value before the loan amount is dispersed.

Double-declining-balance method   An ultra-accelerated depreciation method that uses a declining book value. Also known as declining-balance method.

EFT   Stands for electronic funds transfer; provides for electronic collections and payments.

End-of-month discount   A cash discount offered when customers pay within a set number of days (usually 10) from the end of the month in which the invoice is sent (dated).

EOM   End of month.

Equity   The value of a home minus the amount owed on it.

Excess liability   *See* umbrella policy.

Exclusion   Categories of claims that cannot be made against a policy.

Extended warranty   A low-cost insurance policy that prolongs the standard warranty on appliances and electronics.

Face value   The total amount borrowed with a note; the principal.

FIFO   Stands for first in, first out. An inventory evaluation method that is based on the assumption that (1) the oldest inventory is sold first, and (2) the current inventory is what was acquired most recently.

Fixed assets   Assets that a company plans to keep and use for more than a year.

Fixed-rate loan   A loan for which the interest rate does not change over the life of the loan.

Fraction   A portion of a whole number, expressed as one number over the other. Also known as a *proper fraction*.

Frequency distribution   A table that shows the number of times each variable occurs.

Future value   How much $1 invested or borrowed today is worth in the future.

Gap   The difference in the amount of an insurance claim and the cap on the policy.

Gross pay   Total wages earned, before deductions.

Gross profit   The amount a company earned after cost of goods sold is subtracted from net sales. Also known as *total profit*.

Gross profit margin ratio   A ratio that determines how much of a profit a company is making on the goods it's buying and selling, regardless of operating expenses.

Gross sales   Total sales, including cash sales and credit sales.

Home equity line of credit   A line of credit, issued against the equity in one's home, that's available for the owner to use when needed.

Home equity loan   A loan borrowed against the equity in a home.

Homeowner's insurance   Insurance for a building, usually a home.

Identity theft   A crime in which criminals access personal financial accounts and use those accounts for their own gain.

Improper fraction   A fraction with a numerator that's larger than the denominator.

Income statement   A statement that shows how much revenue is coming to a company and the cost outflows during a certain period of time. Also known as a *profit and loss (or P and L) statement*.

Income-forecast method   A method of depreciating intellectual property.

Inflation   The general upward price movement of goods and services in an economy.

Installment buying   Loans in which the consumer receives the item now and pays each month, over a set amount of time, with interest.

Intangible assets   Copyrights, patents, and other intellectual property that belong to a company.

Integer   A positive or negative whole number.

Interest   An amount paid in order to borrow money or received for lending money.

Interest rate   A percent charged for lending or borrowing money.

Inventory turnover   The number of times a company's inventory turns over in a year.

Invert   To flip a fraction so that the denominator is the numerator and the numerator is the denominator.

Level-term   Term life insurance that has leveled premiums, which stay the same for a set period—usually 20 or 30 years.

Liabilities   Everything a company owes to others; debts.

Life insurance   Insurance that pays beneficiaries when a person dies.

LIFO   Stands for "last in, first out." An inventory method that is based on the assumption that (1) the newest inventory is sold first, and (2) the current inventory was acquired earliest. Therefore, the cost of the ending inventory is based on the cost of the oldest stock.

Line graph   A comparison of a variable made over time by a single line, rising and falling.

List price   The suggested retail price offered to the customer. The list price is the same as the retail price or sticker price.

Long-term liabilities   Liabilities, or debts, that are due in more than 1 year.

Loss leader   An item that is heavily marked down in order to draw customers to a store.

Lowest common denominator   The smallest possible number divisible by both the denominators in an addition or subtraction problem.

Luxury tax   Tax on luxury items that is meant to be paid by the wealthy.

Malpractice insurance   Insurance that protects against lawsuits arising from mistakes a company or person makes.

Markdown   The percentage of the original selling price by which a discounted selling price is reduced.

Markup   The selling price of an item minus its cost. Markup can be measured in percentage or in dollars.

Maturity date   Predetermined date for withdrawal of money on a CD.

Maturity value   The money you get when a loan matures; it is equal to Interest + Principal.

Mean   The average of two or more numbers. Also known as the average.

Median   The middle number in a list of numbers that begins with the lowest and ends with the highest.

Medical insurance   Insurance that covers the costs of illness and injury.

Medicare   The tax that funds the Medicare program.

Mill   1/1000 of a dollar (e.g., 43.10 mills is 4.31%). Mills are used in real estate tax determination.

Mixed fraction   A fraction that mixes a whole number and a fraction.

Mode   The most frequent value in a set of numbers.

Modified accelerated cost recovery system (MACRS)   A depreciation method used since 1986 in which the IRS categorizes assets (i.e., business property, equipment) into classes and determines the proper class life of each.

Money market account   A higher-earning account that allows limited check writing and requires a high minimum balance.

Mortgage   A loan collateralized by real estate.

Multiple markdowns   Additional markdowns, in addition to the original markdown.

Natural number   A positive integer or zero. Also known as a *whole number*.

Negative number   A number less than zero.

Net income   The amount a company makes as a profit after all operating expenses are subtracted from the gross profit. Also known as *profit*.

Net sales   The amount a company sells after all returns, discounts, and other allowances are deducted. Also known as *revenue*.

Note   A legal document that requires a consumer to pay back borrowed money in a specified time, with a specified amount of interest. Also called a promissory note.

NSF   Insufficient funds in an account to cover transactions. Stand for nonsufficient funds.

Numerator   The top number in a fraction.

Online bank   A bank that has no (or few) brick-and-mortar locations.

Online banking   Conducting banking business using a computer instead of at a brick-and-mortar banking location.

Online bill paying   Transferring funds from a bank account to the account of the companies that are owed money.

Operating expenses   The cost associated with running a company (salaries, rent, utilities, equipment, etc.).

Operating ratio   A ratio that can be quickly calculated to determine whether a company is making or losing money. An operating ratio of less than 1 means the company is turning a profit.

Ordinary dating method discount   A cash discount offered if customers pay within a set number of days from the date of the invoice.

Original cost   The cost of an asset, including transportation (delivery) and installation.

Outstanding checks   Checks written on an account but not shown on a bank statement.

Overdraft protection   A feature offered by banks in which a savings account, secondary checking account, or credit card is debited the amount of the check written if the balance in the primary checking account is not high enough to cover the check.

Owner's equity   How much a company is worth on a given date. Also known as *net worth*.

Passbook account   Another name for a savings account.

Passbook   A booklet in which all deposits and withdrawals for an account are recorded.

Percentage change   The amount by which a percentage (an amount) increases or decreases.

Percentage distribution   The percentage (part) of the total in each class or category.

Percentage   The part of the base that is determined by the rate.

Personal property loan   A loan made for less-expensive items than real estate, such as a car.

Pie chart   A circular chart with sectors or slices that are in proportion to the percentage share of each sector. Also known as a circle graph.

Piecework   Income that is based on the number of pieces produced.

Policy   Insurance coverage relating to a specific person, vehicle, home, office, and so on.

Positive number   A number greater than zero.

Premium   The amount paid to put an insurance policy in force.

Present value   How much $1 received at some date in the future is worth today. It is the amount needed to be invested today at a given compounded rate in order to accumulate to a certain future value.

Principal   The amount of money originally deposited, borrowed, or loaned; represented by p.

Profit margin on net sales   A ratio that compares net income to net sales and shows how much profit a company is making; the closer this ratio is to 1, the better. Also known as *return on sales*.

Promissory note   *See* note.

Proper fraction   A portion of a whole number, expressed as one number over another. Also known as a *fraction*.

Property class life   The IRS version of useful life.

Property tax   A tax on real estate.

Quantity discounts   Discounts offered by suppliers (sellers) for ordering large quantities of goods.

Range   The difference between the highest and lowest values in a list of numbers.

Rate   A number that is followed by a percent sign, which expresses how the base and percentage are related to each other.

Receipt-of-goods discount   A cash discount offered when customers pay within a set number of days from the day they receive the items. The discount period starts the day the goods are received, not from when they are ordered.

Reconciliation   Matching a checkbook register with a monthly banking statement. Also called bank reconciliation.

Renter's insurance   Insurance on the contents of a home or an office but not the building itself.

Repossess   To take ownership of personal property or real estate because of nonpayment of a loan against that property.

Retail price   The price customers pay for goods. *See also* list price.

Reverse mortgage   A situation in which a consumer receives monthly payments from a bank in exchange for the paid-off home belonging to the bank upon the consumer's death.

ROG   Receipt of goods.

Sales tax   Tax on retail purchases.

Sales   The amount of money resulting from customers buying a company's goods or services.

Salvage value   The value of a depreciable item at the end of its useful life. Also known as salvage value, residual value, or trade-in value.

Selling price   The amount a store charges customers to buy an item, which is typically the cost of that item or service plus a profit margin.

Simple interest formula   A formula for determining simple interest; Interest = Principal $\times$ Rate $\times$ Time.

Simple interest   Money paid for the use of principal; represented by I.

Simplified fraction   A fraction that cannot be reduced any further.

Social Security   The tax that funds the Social Security program. Also known as *FICA (Federal Insurance Contributions Act)*.

Straight-line method   A depreciation method that assumes an item will be depreciated (expensed) evenly over its useful life.

Sum-of-years'-digits method   An accelerated method of depreciation that sums the useful life and uses that as a multiplier (i.e., denominator of a fraction) to find the annual depreciation.

Term life   Basic life insurance that covers a person for a particular term, usually 1 year.

Time   The length of an investment or a loan, usually expressed in years or months; represented by t.

Toll   A tax on some roads, interstates, and highways.

Tourism tax   A tax on hotels and restaurants.

Travel insurance   Insurance that protects the policyholder if he or she becomes ill or is otherwise unable to travel. Also known as trip-interruption insurance.

Trimodal distribution   A distribution that has three modes.

Trip-interruption insurance   *See* travel insurance.

Umbrella policy   Insurance that provides additional coverage, up to $5 million. Also known as excess liability.

Units-of-production method   A method of depreciating equipment in terms other than time (often in miles or number of units produced).

Unsecured personal loan   A loan given to a borrower because of creditworthiness, and against which there is no secured item, such as a car or home.

Use tax   A tax on the use of items you own.

Useful life   An estimate of how long you expect to use assets (i.e., equipment, property).

Variable-rate loan   A loan for which the interest rate is tied to the Federal Reserve Board's interest rate decisions and, therefore, changes over the life of the loan. Also called an adjustable-rate loan.

W-2   An IRS form that employers send to report employee income and taxes withheld for the year.

W-4   An IRS form that an employer uses to determine federal withholding for an employer.

W-9   A form used to gather information to prepare a 1099 form.

Wages   Income earned from an employer.

Weighted average   An average in which some of the numbers that will be added up to find an average are worth more than others.

Weighted average inventory evaluation   A method of calculating the value of identical items in an inventory that may have been purchased at different prices over the course of time.

Whole life   Traditional life insurance, plus a cash value account. Also called straight life.

Whole number   A positive integer or zero. Also known as a *natural number*.

Withdrawal   A transaction that reduces the balance of an account.

Withholding tax   Tax withheld from income to cover a person's income tax liability. Also known as *federal income tax (FIT)* and *federal withholding tax (FWT)*.

YTD   The amount made or paid since January 1 of the current year. Stands for *year-to-date*.

INDEX